LSAT®
Logic Games Workbook
Fourth Edition

Other Kaplan Books on Law School Admissions

Kaplan LSAT Premier Live Online

Kaplan LSAT Strategies, Practice, and Review

Kaplan LSAT Advanced

Kaplan LSAT Direct

Kaplan LSAT Logic Games in a Box

Kaplan LSAT Writing Workbook

First Year Law Student

Get into Law School: A Strategic Approach

LSAT®
Logic Games
Workbook

Fourth Edition

The Staff of Kaplan Test Prep and Admissions

PUBLISHING

New York

Published by Kaplan Publishing, a division of Kaplan, Inc.
1 Liberty Plaza, 24th Floor
New York, NY 10006

Printed in the United States of America

10 9 8 7 6 5 4 3 2 1

ISBN-13: 978-1-60714-690-2

Table of Contents

How to Use This Book

Welcome to Kaplan's LSAT Logic Games Workbook. You have purchased the most comprehensive book on the market that focuses exclusively on the Logic Games section of the LSAT. Kaplan has prepared students to take standardized tests for over 60 years. Our team of researchers and editors knows more about preparing for the LSAT than anyone else, and you'll find their accumulated knowledge here.

This book is designed to benefit those who hope to significantly increase their LSAT scores by improving Logic Games performance. You may have already taken the LSAT, or at least one or more simulated LSATs, and you may be comfortable with your skills in Logical Reasoning and Reading Comprehension, but need to boost your Logic Game speed or accuracy in order to get into the school of your choice.

If you want a book that covers the entire LSAT, we recommend Kaplan's *LSAT Premier Live Online* or *LSAT Strategies, Practice, and Review*. If you're confident in all test sections, but want to get additional practice with the hardest questions in the hope of earning a perfect score, try Kaplan's *LSAT Advanced*.

PART ONE: GETTING STARTED

In Part One of this book, you'll find background information on the different sections of the test, what they cover, and how the test is scored. The first step to a higher score is to be sure you know exactly what you can expect. Next comes a brief introduction to the different types of Logic Games, the question types, how to recognize them, and the Kaplan Method for handling them, along with some basic strategies and principles. If you have already used one of Kaplan's LSAT programs, this material will be familiar; we repeat it here for ease of reference.

PART TWO: GAMES AND STRATEGIES

Once you have the big picture, it's time to focus on the specifics of the different types of Logic Games—that's Part Two. We dedicate a chapter to each, examining its variations, how to set up your scratchwork, the question types you'll encounter on each, and exactly how to approach them. Everything is demonstrated using real LSAT sample games and questions.

PART THREE: PRACTICE LOGIC GAMES SECTIONS

When you are comfortable with the Kaplan Method and the many strategies offered for handling different game and question types, you'll want to try them out with more questions. The two practice test sections contained in Part Three are followed by detailed explanations. As you work through these, look for patterns—question types or game types that you tend to find easy or difficult, or tend to score well or badly on. Note your areas of strength, but focus the bulk of your study time on your areas of weakness. With sufficient practice, you'll be ready for anything that could appear on test day.

PART ONE

Logic Games Overview

Chapter 1: **Getting Started**

- The LSAT
- Logic Games
- Logic Game Types and Skills
- Question Types

The LSAT is unlike any other test, and Logic Games is the LSAT section test takers find the least familiar. Most tests you've encountered required you to know a certain body of facts, formulas, theorems, or other acquired knowledge. The LSAT Logic Games test data management and analytical thinking skills—all you'll be asked to do is think, thoroughly, quickly, and strategically.

You already have these skills, but you probably haven't acquired the know-how to use them to your best advantage in the rarified atmosphere of a standardized skills-based test.

That's where test preparation comes in. You can't study for a skills-based test, but you can and must prepare for it. Every strategy and method you'll learn and practice in this Workbook is designed to improve your timing, build your confidence, and save your energy on test day. Kaplan's LSAT program will teach you to tailor your existing deductive and analytical skills to the idiosyncratic tasks required by the LSAT.

THE LSAT

The LSAT consists of five multiple-choice sections: two Logical Reasoning sections, one Logic Games section, one Reading Comprehension section, and one unscored "experimental" section that will look exactly like one of the other multiple-choice sections. At the end of the test, there will be a Writing Sample section in which you'll have to write a short essay. Here's how the sections break down.

Section	Number of Questions	Minutes
Logical Reasoning	24–26	35
Logical Reasoning	24–26	35
Logic Games	22–24	35
Reading Comprehension	26–28	35
"Experimental"	22–28	35
Writing Sample	n/a	35

The five multiple-choice sections can appear in any order; the Writing Sample comes last. There's a 10 or 15 minute break between the third and fourth sections of the test.

For the most up-to-date information about the test, request the *LSAT/LSDAS Registration & Information Book* from LSAC by visiting www.LSAC.org or calling (215) 968-1001. You must register in advance, and the earlier you register, the better your chances of getting your first or second choice test center.

How the LSAT is Scored

Logic Games accounts for just under 25 percent of your total LSAT score. You'll receive only one score for the test, ranging between 120 and 180. Here's how that score is calculated:

There are roughly 100 scored multiple-choice questions on each exam:

- About 50 from the two Logical Reasoning sections
- About 23 from the Logic Games section
- About 27 from the Reading Comprehension section

Your **raw score**, the number of questions that you answer correctly, will be plugged into a scoring formula (different for each test, to accommodate differences in difficulty level) to yield the **scaled score**—the one that will fall somewhere in that 120–180 range—which is reported to the schools.

Because the test is graded on a largely preset curve, the scaled score will always correspond to a certain percentile, which will also be given on your score report. A score of 160, for instance, corresponds roughly to the 80th percentile, meaning that 80 percent of test takers scored at or below your level.

All scored questions are worth the same amount—one raw point—and there's no penalty for guessing. That means that you should always fill in an answer for every question, whether you get to that question or not!

LOGIC GAMES

There are 22–24 questions in the Logic Games (a.k.a. Analytical Reasoning) section, based on four games with 5–7 questions each. They require an ability to reason clearly and deductively from a given set of rules or restrictions, all under tight time restrictions. Games are highly susceptible to systematic technique and the proper use of scratch work.

The section tests your command of detail, your formal deductive abilities, your understanding of how rules limit and order behavior, and your ability to cope with many pieces of data simultaneously to solve problems.

Here's a sample:

<u>Directions:</u> Each group of questions in this section is based on a set of conditions. In answering some of the questions, it may be useful to draw a rough diagram. Choose the response that most accurately and completely answers each question and blacken the corresponding space on your answer sheet.

<u>Questions 1–2</u>

Exactly six guideposts, numbered 1 through 6, mark a mountain trail. Each guidepost pictures a different one of six animals—fox, grizzly, hare, lynx, moose, or porcupine. The following conditions must apply:

The grizzly is pictured on either guidepost 3 or guidepost 4.

The moose guidepost is numbered lower than the hare guidepost.

The lynx guidepost is numbered lower than the moose guidepost, but higher than the fox guidepost.

1. Which of the following animals CANNOT be the one pictured on guidepost 3?

    (A) fox
    (B) grizzly
    (C) lynx
    (D) moose
    (E) porcupine

2. If guidepost 5 does not picture the moose, then which of the following must be true?

    (A) The lynx is pictured on guidepost 2.
    (B) The moose is pictured on guidepost 3.
    (C) The grizzly is pictured on guidepost 4.
    (D) The porcupine is pictured on guidepost 5.
    (E) The hare is pictured on guidepost 6.

The correct answer choice for both questions is (A). This game and the questions will be further explained in Chapter 4.

On the LSAT, you'll be answering roughly 125 multiple-choice questions (100 of which are scored) over the course of three intense hours. On average, that's just a little over a minute per question, not counting the time required to read passages and set up games. Clearly, you have to move fast. But don't get careless. Taking control means increasing the speed only to the extent you can do so without sacrificing accuracy!

Because Logic Games is, for many students, the most time-sensitive section of the test, it's also the section in which you can improve your timing the most.

LOGIC GAME TYPES AND SKILLS

Although Logic Games can contain a wide variety of situations and scenarios, there are four common types:

- Sequencing
  - Strict
  - Loose
- Grouping
  - Selection
  - Distribution
- Matching
- Hybrids

Certain skills are required again and again, with variations on the following being the most common:

Sequencing

Logic Games requiring **sequencing** skills—putting entities in order—have long been a test makers' favorite. There are two types: **strict** sequencing and **loose** sequencing, each covered in its own chapter. In a typical sequencing game, you may be asked to arrange the cast of characters numerically from left to right, from top to bottom, in days of the week, in a circle, and so on. The sequence may be a matter of degree—say, ranking the eight smartest test takers from one to eight. Or it may be based on time, such as one that involves the order of shows broadcast on a radio station. Occasionally there are two or even three orderings to keep track of in a single game.

Grouping

Distribution and **selection** are the two main types of grouping games, each covered in its own chapter. In a pure **grouping** game, unlike sequencing, there's no call for putting the entities in order. Instead, you'll select a smaller group from the initial group or distribute the entities into more than one subgroup. You're not concerned with what order the entities are in, but rather who's in, who's out, and who can and cannot be with whom in various subgroups.

Matching

As the name implies, **matching** games ask you to match up two or more sets of entities. A game may involve three animals, each assigned a name, a color, and a particular size. It's no wonder test takers get bogged down in these types—there's a lot to keep track of. Some feel that these games bombard them with information. They don't know where to start. Organization is especially crucial. A table or grid can be helpful, depending on the game.

Distinguish each characteristic by using CAPS for one category, lowercase for another—and any other variants that work for you. Remember that thinking must always precede writing. A visual representation of a mental thought process can be invaluable; scribbling thoughtlessly for the sake of getting something down on the page is useless, even detrimental.

Hybrid and Other Games

Many games are hybrids, requiring you to combine sequencing, grouping, or matching skills. In hybrid games, consider how you can combine the sketches. Keep in mind that it's not necessary to attach a strict name to every game you encounter. It really doesn't matter if you categorize a game as a sequencing game with a grouping element or as a grouping game with a sequencing element, as long as you're comfortable with both sets of skills.

Very rarely, other formats appear on a test. We'll discuss some of these in Part Two.

QUESTION TYPES

Within each game, only a few distinct question types will occur:

Acceptability Questions

If the question asks which choice would be "acceptable," one answer choice will satisfy all the rules; each wrong choice will violate at least one rule. These questions can be answered quickly and efficiently by simply applying each rule to the choices.

Could vs. Must Questions

When the question asks you a general question about what must, can, or cannot happen, focus on the nature of the right and wrong answer choices:

If the question reads	The right answer will be
Which one of the following statements could be true?	A statement that could or even must be true, and the four wrong choices will be statements that definitely cannot be true (that is, statements that must be false).
Which one of the following statements CANNOT be true?	A statement that cannot be true (must be false), and the four wrong choices will be statements that either must be true or merely could be true.
Which one of the following statements must be true?	A statement that must be true, and the four wrong choices will be statements that either must be false or merely could be false.
Each of the following statements could be true EXCEPT	A statement that cannot be true, and the four wrong choices will be statements that either must be true or merely could be true.
Each of the following statements must be true EXCEPT	A statement that either must be false or merely could be false, and the four wrong choices will be statements that must be true.
Which one of the following statements could be false?	A statement that could be false or even must be false, and the four wrong choices will be statements that must be true.
Which one of the following statements must be false?	A statement that cannot be true, and the four wrong choices will be statements that either must be true or merely could be true.

New "If" Questions

When the question adds a new "if" condition, treat the "if" as a new rule that applies only to that question, draw a new sketch if necessary, and then focus on the nature of the right and wrong answer choices.

Complete and Accurate List Questions

When the question asks you for a full list of possible outcomes, answer the other questions first; their sketches will help you narrow down the answer choices. Then, use the remaining answer choices to decide what possibilities you have to test.

Numbers Questions

When a question asks you for the minimum or maximum number of entities that can be selected, the earliest or latest position in which an entity can be placed, or the number of possible outcomes for a given scenario, answer the other questions first; again, their sketches can help you narrow down the answer choices.

Changed Rule Questions

If the last question of a game changes one of the original conditions (instead of merely adding a new one), you may have to start over from the beginning and reconstruct a brand new sketch. Definitely save these questions for last.

Now that you know the basics and what you can expect, learn (or refresh your memory of) some basic principles that apply to all Logic Games and the Kaplan Method for handling them before moving on to Part Two.

Chapter 2:
Kaplan's Method and Strategies

- Kaplan's 5-Step Method
- Six Basic Logic Games Principles
- Two Essential Formal Logic Principles

Now that you have some Logic Games background, you're ready to marshal that knowledge into a systematic approach to games. Trial and error with the answer choices should be your last resort, not your first.

If you have already used Kaplan's LSAT Premier or Comprehensive Programs some of this material will be familiar; we summarize it here for those who have not—and for ease of reference.

KAPLAN'S 5-STEP METHOD FOR LOGIC GAMES

Step 1: Overview

Carefully read the game's introduction and rules to establish the Situation, the Entities involved, the Action, and the number Limitations governing the game ("SEAL"). Make a mental picture of the situation, and let it guide you as you create a sketch or other scratch work, to help you keep track of the rules and handle new information.

Step 2: Sketch

Developing good scratch work will speed your performance on Logic Games. A master sketch that encapsulates the game's information in an easy-to-follow form will help to solidify in your mind the action of the game, the rules, and whatever deductions you make, and will provide a quick reference.

Keep scratch work simple—you get no points for elaborate, painstakingly drawn diagrams, and the less time you spend drawing the more time you'll have for thinking and answering questions and the less cluttered your sketch will be.

Step 3: Rules

Not all rules are equal. Focus most on the concrete ones and the ones that involve the greatest number of the entities or otherwise have the greatest impact on the action. These are also the rules to turn to first whenever you're stuck on a question and don't know how to set off the chain of deduction. As you think through the meaning and implications of each rule you can:

- Build it directly into your sketch whenever possible.
- Jot down the rule in shorthand if it cannot be built into your sketch.

Step 4: Deduction

Look for common elements among the rules; that's what will lead you to make deductions. Based on what you already know, what else *must* be true? Treat these deductions as additional rules, good for the whole game. Be on the lookout for "blocs"—entities that must be in fixed relationships to each other—and "floaters"—entities not covered by any of the rules that can go in any open position.

Step 5: Questions

Skipping difficult questions is *strategic* (see chapter 3). Get the points you're sure of before spending time on others that may be less certain. Read the question stems carefully, taking special notice of words such as *must, could, cannot, not* and *except*. Use new "ifs" to set off a new chain of deduction in a new sketch.

Don't worry about recalling all of this now, as long as you get the general idea. You'll be reviewing each step in every chapter of Part Two, with special focus on its application to each game type.

SIX BASIC LOGIC GAMES PRINCIPLES

For many students, Logic Games is the most time-sensitive section of the test. If you could spend hours methodically trying out every choice, you'd probably get everything right. On the LSAT, it's all about efficiency. And that brings you to the first, and somewhat paradoxical, Logic Games principle:

Slow Down To Go Faster

Spending a little extra time thinking through the stimulus, the action of the game, and the rules, and creating a solid setup, help you to recognize key issues and make important deductions that will save you time. Games are structured so that in order to answer the questions quickly and correctly you need to search out relevant pieces of information that combine to form valid new deductions (inferences). You can do this once, up front, or you can piece together the same basic deductions for each question. That is the basis of the first four steps of Kaplan's Method.

Learn to Spot "Limited Options"

If a game breaks down into only two or three possible results, work out those results and you'll fly through the questions. Limited options can appear in any game type, wherever you see one entity or a bloc of entities that are restricted to one of two locations, or where arithmetic limitations force only two distinct possibilities. In these cases, it often makes sense to draw two master sketches, one reflecting each option, and then see if the other rules fill in all or most of the blanks. New "if" questions may mean only one option can apply. You'll see examples in each chapter and practice test section.

No "Best" Choice

The answers in Logic Games—like answers to math questions—are objectively correct or incorrect. So when you find an answer that's definitely right, have the confidence to circle it and move on, without checking the others. This is one way to improve your timing on the section.

Don't second-guess yourself; just because an answer comes easily (when you know how to approach it) doesn't mean it's wrong.

Know What a Rule Means, Not Just What It Says

The LSAT measures critical thinking, and virtually every sentence in a Logic Game has to be filtered through some sort of analytical process to be of any use. So it's not enough just to copy a rule off the page (or shorthand it); it's imperative that you *understand* the rule thoroughly and think through any implications it might have. And don't limit this to the indented rules; statements in the stimulus are very often rules that warrant the same consideration.

Set Off New Chains of Deduction

When a question stem offers a **hypothetical**—an *if-clause* offering information pertaining only to that question—use it to set off a new chain of deductions. Only if you're entirely stuck should you resort to trial and error. Instead, incorporate the new piece of information into your view of the game, creating a new sketch if it helps. Apply the rules and any previous deductions to the new information in order to set off a new chain of deductions. Then follow through until you've taken the new information as far as it can go, just as you took the game and rules as far as you could before moving on to the questions.

Know the Question Types

You must have a solid command of the limited number of Logic Games question stems that were introduced in the first chapter and are reviewed throughout this Workbook: acceptability, new "if," complete and accurate list, "could" vs. "must," numbers, and changed rule questions. When you take a few seconds to think through what kind of statements would be the right and wrong answers to a particular question, your work becomes more efficient.

TWO ESSENTIAL FORMAL LOGIC PRINCIPLES

Two principles of formal logic are tested frequently in Logic Games, so it's best to get a solid handle on them before you start. Look at an example:

> Ian will go to the movies only when his wife is out of town. He'll go to a matinee alone, but will see a movie at night only if accompanied by Ezra and Mabel.

This scenario is made up of a couple of formal logic statements, each fraught with its own implications.

The Contrapositive

The **contrapositive** of any *if/then* statement is formed by reversing and negating the terms. The general model goes like this:

> Original: If X, then Y.
> Contrapositive: If not Y, then not X.

For any *if/then* statement, the contrapositive will be equally valid. Now apply the contrapositive to the following statement:

> Ian will go to the movies only when his wife is out of town.

You can translate this into an if/then statement without changing its original meaning:

> If Ian goes to the movies, then his wife must be out of town.

If that statement is true, what statement must also be true? Its contrapositive:

> If Ian's wife is not out of town, then Ian does not go to the movies.

Warning 1: Wrong answers often result from either forgetting to switch around the terms before negating them, switching them without negating them, or negating only one of the terms. If Ian doesn't go to the movies, you can't infer anything about whether his wife is in or out of town. If Ian's wife is out of town, you can't tell whether Ian goes to the movies or not.

Warning 2: If one part of a formal logic statement contains a compound phrase, both parts of the phrase must be taken into account:

> Ian will see a movie at night only if accompanied by Ezra and Mabel.

If/then Translation: If Ian sees a movie at night, then he's accompanied by Ezra and Mabel.

Contrapositive: If Ian is not with Ezra *and* Mabel, then he does not see a movie at night.

Correct Interpretation: If either Ezra or Mabel is missing, then Ian doesn't see a night movie.

Warning 3: If one part of a formal logic statement is *already* negative, the same rules that apply to math apply to forming the contrapositive: negating a negative yields a positive. If the sun is shining, then Samantha does not wear green. What is the contrapositive?

Contrapositive:_____

You should have written something along the lines of: If Samantha is wearing green (if she's not *not* wearing green), then the sun is not shining.

Necessary versus Sufficient Conditions

For success in formal logic, it's crucial that you distinguish clearly between necessary and sufficient conditions. Consider these two statements:

- If I yell loudly at my cat Adrian, he will run away.
- The TV will work only if it is plugged in.

My yelling loudly is a **sufficient** condition for Adrian to run away. It's all I need to do to get the cat to run; it's sufficient. But it's **not necessary**. My cat might run if I throw water at him, even if I don't yell loudly.

The TV's being plugged in, on the other hand, is a **necessary** condition for it to work. My TV won't work without it. But it's **not sufficient**. Other conditions must apply for the TV to work (for example, the electricity to the house must be on).

Recognizing these distinctions is vital to knowing what kinds of deductions you can and can't make. A sufficient condition is essentially an *if/then* statement, which means that the contrapositive can be used.

- If I yell loudly at my cat Adrian, he will run away.

If that statement is true, which one of the following must also be true?

• If I don't yell loudly at my cat Adrian, he will not run away.	valid ❏	not valid ❏
• If my cat Adrian has run away, then I yelled loudly at him.	valid ❏	not valid ❏
• If my cat Adrian has not run away, then I did not yell loudly at him.	valid ❏	not valid ❏

The third statement, the contrapositive, is the only one of the three that's valid based on the original. My yelling loudly is sufficient to make Adrian run away, but it's not necessary; it's not the only possible thing that will make him run. He might run if I squirt him with a water gun, so the first two statements are not valid.

Necessary conditions, on the other hand, are usually signaled by the words *only if* (or similar words or phrases like *only when)*:

- The TV will work only if it is plugged in.

If that statement is true, which of the following statements must also be true?

- If my TV is plugged in, it will work.   valid ☐   not valid ☐
- If my TV is not working, then it must not be plugged in.   valid ☐   not valid ☐
- If my TV is working, then it must be plugged in.   valid ☐   not valid ☐
- If my TV is not plugged in, then it won't work.   valid ☐   not valid ☐

The original statement means that being plugged in is *necessary* for the TV to work, but it is not *sufficient*. So, if the TV is working, it *must* be plugged in. Similarly, if the TV is not plugged in, then it certainly won't work. However, plugging the TV in is not a guarantee that the TV will work. Maybe the picture tube is broken. Therefore, the first two statements are *not* valid based on the original statement, while the last two statements are.

You'll have a chance to see these major Logic Games principles in action when you review the explanations to the games in the following chapters and in the practice Logic Games sections at the back of this book.

Chapter 3: **Take Control of the Test**

Don't forget to practice general testing strategies while you focus on Logic Games. If you took a test in college and got a quarter of the questions wrong, you'd probably receive a pretty low grade. But on the LSAT, you can get a quarter of the questions wrong and still score higher than the 80th percentile. So don't let one bad game or passage ruin an entire section, and don't let what you consider a below-par performance on one section ruin your performance on the rest of the test.

If you feel you've done poorly on a section, it could be the experimental section. And even if it's not, chances are it's just a difficult section—a factor that will already be figured into the scoring curve. Remain calm; do your best on each section and, once a section is over, forget about it and move on. Losing a few extra points won't do you in, but losing your head will.

TEST EXPERTISE

It's one thing to answer a Logic Games question correctly, and quite another to answer 24 of them correctly in 35 minutes. Time pressure affects virtually every test taker.

On most tests you take in school, you wouldn't dream of not making at least an attempt at every one of the questions. If a question seems particularly difficult, you spend significantly more time on it, since you'll probably earn more points for correctly answering a hard question.

Not so on the LSAT. Every LSAT question, no matter how hard, is worth a single point. And since there are so many questions to do in so little time, it's foolish to spend three minutes getting a point for a hard question and then not have time to get a couple of quick points from two easy questions later in the section.

Given this combination—limited time and all questions being equal in weight—you have to develop a way of handling the test sections to make sure you get as many points as you can, as quickly and easily as you can. The following are the test strategies that will help you do that.

Answer Questions in the Order That's Best for You

Recognize and deal first with the questions, games, and passages that are easier and more familiar to you. Temporarily skip those that promise to be difficult and time consuming—come back to them at the end, and if you run out of time, you're much better off not getting to questions you may have had difficulty with, rather than missing easier ones. (Since there's no wrong-answer penalty, always fill in an answer to every question on the test, whether you get to it or not.)

Remember, LSAT questions, games, and passages are not necessarily presented in order of difficulty; in fact, the test makers scatter easy and difficult questions throughout the section, in effect rewarding those who get to the end. If you find sequencing games particularly easy, seek out the sequencing game on the Logic Games section and, if you find one, do it first.

Know That There Will Be Difficult Questions

It's imperative that you remain calm and composed while working through a section. Don't be rattled by one hard logic game or reading passage. Expect to find at least one difficult passage or game on every section; you won't be the only one to have trouble with it. The test is curved to take the tough material into account. Understand that part of the test maker's goal is to reward those who keep their composure.

Grid In Answers Efficiently

You not only have to pick the right answers, you also have to mark those right answers on the answer grid in an efficient and accurate way. It sounds simple, but it's extremely important: Don't make mistakes filling out your answer grid! When time is short, it's easy to get confused going back and forth between your test book and your grid. Here are a few methods for avoiding mistakes:

1. **Always Circle Answers You Choose:** Circle the correct answers in your test booklet, but don't transfer the answers to the grid right away. That wastes too much time, especially if you're doing a lot of skipping around. Circling your answers in the test book will also make it easier to check your grid against your book.

2. **Grid About Five Answers at Once:** Transfer your answers at the end of each Logic Game. You won't keep breaking your concentration, so you'll save time and improve accuracy.

3. **Always Circle Questions You Skip:** Put a big circle in your test book around the number of any question you skip (or circle the whole question). When you go back, it will be easy to locate them. And if you accidentally skip a box on the grid, you can more easily check your grid against your book to see where you went wrong.

4. **Save Time at the End for a Final Grid Check:** Take time at the end of every section to check your grid. Make sure you've got an oval filled in for each question in the section. Remember, a blank grid has no chance of earning a point.

LOGIC GAMES SECTION MANAGEMENT

Managing the Section

First, and most important, preview the section. Literally flip through the pages, having a glance at each game in order to decide which games look the easiest and most familiar to you. Previewing is not foolproof; a game that looks fairly straightforward at first glance could easily turn out to be daunting. But practice and familiarity will improve your ability to choose wisely.

The goal is to tackle the games in order of difficulty, from easiest to hardest. But if you achieve nothing more than saving the hardest game for last, the strategy is a winner.

The best way to know which games may be difficult is to be familiar with the game types, and to have a sense of which types you're strongest in.

A game that doesn't look familiar at all could be an oddball game—a good candidate to postpone. But don't be scared off by games with a lot of rules; sometimes this works to your advantage. The more rules they give you, the more definite and concrete the game is, and the easier it will be to answer the questions. Games with few rules often turn out to be tough because they're inherently ambiguous.

Pacing

Four games in 35 minutes means roughly 8.5 minutes per game with a minute reserved to preview the section. Remember, this is an average—games that are harder or have more questions should take a little more time than others.

The last thing you want is to have time called on a section before you've gotten to half the questions. It's essential, therefore, that you pace yourself. Of course, some questions can be answered more quickly than others. But you should have a sense of the average time you have to do each question, so you know when you're exceeding the limit and should start to move faster.

Keeping track of time is also important for guessing. It pays to leave time at the end to guess on any questions you couldn't answer. For instance, let's say you never get a chance to do the last logic game in the section. If you leave the grids for those questions blank, you'll get no points for that entire game. If, on the other hand, you give yourself a little time at the end to fill in a guess for each of those questions, you'll have a very good chance of getting lucky on one or two questions.

Once you've mastered Kaplan's Method and strategies, build gradually to the point where you're ready to take full-length sections. First attempt one game in 8–9 minutes. Next, try two games in 16–18 minutes. When you're ready to move on, try three games in 24–27 minutes, until finally you can reliably handle a full four-game section in 35 minutes.

Finally, remember the way the test makers test efficiency. They're crafty—they'll sometimes throw an intentionally time-consuming question at the end of a game, possibly one involving a rule change that requires you to backtrack and set the game up all over again. When this happens, they may not be testing who's smart enough to get the right answer, but rather who's clever enough to skip the troublesome question in order to devote precious time to the next game, with a possible payoff of six or seven new points.

PART TWO

Game Types and Strategies

Chapter 4: **Strict Sequencing Games**

As you saw in Chapter 1, there are two types of sequencing games. The first type, the subject of this chapter, is the **strict** sequencing game, in which the placement of entities is very strictly defined. You may be told, for example, that "A is third," or that "X and Y are adjacent," and so on. These are definite, concrete pieces of information, and the game centers around placing as many entities into definite spots as possible.

GAME 1: THE METHOD

Game 1 offers a good example of a typical strict sequencing game. Follow along, focusing on how Kaplan's 5-Step Method is applied. This will start your development of the organized, systematic approach that is the key to Logic Games success.

> Questions 1–6
>
> Exactly six guideposts, numbered 1 through 6, mark a mountain trail. Each guidepost pictures a different one of six animals—fox, grizzly, hare, lynx, moose, or porcupine. The following conditions must apply:
>
> > The grizzly is pictured on either guidepost 3 or guidepost 4.
> >
> > The moose guidepost is numbered lower than the hare guidepost.
> >
> > The lynx guidepost is numbered lower than the moose guidepost, but higher than the fox guidepost.

Step 1: Overview

Read the game's introduction and rules carefully to establish SEAL (situation, entities, action, and limitations).

Situation: Guideposts on a trail.

Entities: Six animals.

Action: Determine the order, or sequence, in which the animals appear on the guideposts.

Limitations: Each guidepost pictures a different animal, so there are six guideposts and six animals, all of which will be used.

Step 2: Sketch

Remember the first general principle of Logic Games: slow down to go fast. Let your overview guide you to create a sketch or other helpful scratch work. The sketch for this game is quite simple: six slots, arranged horizontally. The slots should be numbered 1 through 6, from left to right. Also, list the six animals by initial.

Step 3: Rules

Know what each rule means, not just what it says, and remember that what a rule doesn't say can be as important as what it says. The following is a list of the key issues in sequencing games, each followed by one or more corresponding rule formats.

Typical Sequencing Game Issues

Issue	Wording of Rule
Which entities are concretely placed in the ordering?	X is third.
Which entities are forbidden from a specific position in the ordering?	Y is not fourth.
Which entities are next to, adjacent to, or immediately preceding or following one another?	X and Y are consecutive. X is next to Y. No event comes between X and Y. X and Y are consecutive in the ordering.
Which entities cannot be next to, adjacent to, or immediately preceding or following one another?	X does not immediately precede or follow Z. X is not immediately before or after Z. At least one event comes between X and Z. X and Z are not consecutive in the sequence.
How far apart in the ordering are two particular entities?	Exactly two events come between X and Q.
What is the relative position of two entities in the ordering?	Q comes before T in the sequence. T comes after Q in the sequence.

The first rule stipulates that the grizzly must be third or fourth. Make a note of this next to your sketch. The second rule provides a relative relationship, with the moose being placed before the hare. Using ellipses (…), draw the relationship next to the sketch. The final rule gives us a larger relationship, with the lynx being placed before the moose and after the fox. Also draw this relationship next to the sketch.

Step 4: Deductions

With the moose mentioned in two rules, you can combine information to form one complete diagram of relationships. The last rule provides the relative order of fox, then lynx, then moose. Adding in what is given in the second rule, we can add hare to the end of the string to create a relationship between all four animals. So, the final sketch will look like so:

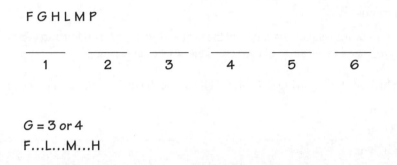

$G = 3$ or 4

$F...L...M...H$

While none of this information can be placed directly into the sketch, knowing the relationship among four out of the six entities will be extremely helpful in answering the questions effectively. Also, it's good to note that the porcupine is a floater—it's never mentioned in any rule and is not directly restricted from any position.

Step 5: Questions

When you've taken the scenario and rules as far as you can, you can move onto the questions. Before test day, be sure you have a solid command of the limited number of question types that will appear in the Logic Games section. Think through what kind of statements would be the right and wrong answers to a particular question, and your work becomes more efficient.

Acceptability Questions

1. Which of the following could be an accurate list of the animals pictured on the guideposts, listed in order from guidepost 1 to guidepost 6?

   (A) fox, lynx, grizzly, porcupine, moose, hare

   (B) fox, lynx, moose, hare, grizzly, porcupine

   (C) fox, moose, grizzly, lynx, hare, porcupine

   (D) lynx, fox, moose, grizzly, hare, porcupine

   (E) porcupine, fox, hare, grizzly, lynx, moose

This is an acceptability question. All that is asked is which choice doesn't violate any of the rules. This type of question is the only exception to the general prohibition against looking back at the original rules. Use the rules as a checklist. Apply each individual condition to each choice and eliminate any that violates that condition. The first rule tells us that the grizzly must be third or fourth. Choice (B) violates that rule by placing the grizzly fifth, and is therefore eliminated. Choice (E) places the moose after the hare, violating the second rule, so that choice is eliminated. Choice (C) places the lynx after the moose and choice (D) places the lynx before the fox. Both of these choices violate that last rule. Only (A) is an acceptable assignment of animals to guideposts, and is therefore correct.

Could vs. Must Questions

For these questions, start by focusing on the nature of the right and wrong choices. Refer to the chart at the end of Chapter 1 whenever you need to refresh your memory of the limited set of possibilities.

2. Which of the following animals CANNOT be the one pictured on guidepost 3?

   (A) fox
   (B) grizzly
   (C) lynx
   (D) moose
   (E) porcupine

This is where the combination of the last two rules comes in handy. The fox has to come before the lynx, the moose and the hare. So it seems that the highest guidepost it could be pictured on is guidepost 3. However, that would make the lynx fourth, the moose fifth and the hare sixth. That would fill up both guidepost 3 and guidepost 4, leaving no space for the grizzly. Therefore, the fox cannot be on guidepost 3, making (A) the correct choice.

3. Which of the following animals could be pictured on any of the six guideposts?

   (A) fox
   (B) hare
   (C) lynx
   (D) moose
   (E) porcupine

Once again, this was considered before going to the questions. The porcupine is the only animal unaffected by the rules. In addition, the fox, hare, lynx, and moose are all restricted to the general order dictated by the last two rules. Therefore, only the porcupine (the floater) could be on any of the six guideposts, making choice (E) correct.

New "If" Questions

When the question adds a new "if" condition (a hypothetical), treat it as a new rule and draw a new sketch if necessary.

4. If guidepost 5 does not picture the moose, then which of the following must be true?

   (A) The lynx is pictured on guidepost 2.
   (B) The moose is pictured on guidepost 3.
   (C) The grizzly is pictured on guidepost 4.
   (D) The porcupine is pictured on guidepost 5.
   (E) The hare is pictured on guidepost 6.

Since the moose cannot be on guidepost 5, it's important to consider which guidepost it *can* be on. It's on a lower number than the hare, so it can't be on guidepost 6. Also, it's on a higher number than the lynx and fox, so it can't be on guideposts 1 or 2. Therefore, it must be on either guidepost 3 or guidepost 4—just like the grizzly. That means the grizzly and the moose will be third and fourth, in either order. Then, the lynx and fox must take up the first two positions, with the fox on the first guidepost and the lynx on the second:

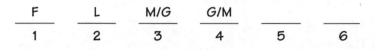

F	L	M/G	G/M	___	___
1	2	3	4	5	6

Since the lynx must be on guidepost 2, (A) is the correct choice.

5. If the moose guidepost is numbered exactly one higher than the lynx guidepost, then which of the following could be true?

(A) Guidepost 5 pictures the hare.

(B) Guidepost 4 pictures the moose.

(C) Guidepost 4 pictures the porcupine.

(D) Guidepost 3 pictures the lynx.

(E) Guidepost 3 pictures the porcupine.

The condition for this question puts the moose immediately after the lynx. Since this bloc must be placed after the fox and before the hare, it is limited to positions 2–3, 3–4, and 4–5. However, it cannot be in 3–4 because that would leave no space for the grizzly. So, we only need to draw out the sketches for the other two possibilities.

If the lynx-moose pair was in 2–3, that would force the fox to be on guidepost 1 and the grizzly to be on guidepost 4. If the lynx-moose pair was in 4–5, that would force the grizzly to be on guidepost 3 and the hare to be on guidepost 6.

F	L	M	G	___	___
1	2	3	4	5	6

or

___	___	G	L	M	H
1	2	3	4	5	6

Only choice (A) is possible (in the first sketch), and is therefore the correct answer.

Minimum/Maximum Questions

In sequencing games, minimum/maximum questions typically ask for the earliest or latest position in which a particular entity could be placed. In other games, you may be asked to determine the number of entities that could be placed in a particular group or that could be selected from a larger group.

6. If the moose is pictured on guidepost 3, then which of the following is the lowest numbered guidepost that could picture the porcupine?

    (A) Guidepost 1
    (B) Guidepost 2
    (C) Guidepost 4
    (D) Guidepost 5
    (E) Guidepost 6

Normally, the porcupine could be on any guidepost. However, this minimum/maximum question comes with an additional "if" condition. The moose must be on guidepost 3. Since the moose must come after the fox and the lynx, those animals must be on guideposts 1 and 2, respectively. Furthermore, the grizzly now must appear on guidepost 4. That leaves only guidepost 5 and guidepost 6 for both the porcupine and the hare. And since their order doesn't matter, the lowest guidepost that can picture the porcupine is guidepost 5, making (D) the correct choice.

Complete and Accurate List Questions

This particular game did not feature this question type. However, it's important to understand how to approach such a question when it does occur in other games. These questions ask for a complete and accurate listing of entities that meet a given requirement. For example, in this game, you may have been asked: "Which of the following is a complete and accurate list of the animals any of which could be pictured on guidepost 1?" As described in the question, the correct answer must be complete (i.e., include every possible animal that could appear on guidepost 1) and accurate (i.e., not include any animal that cannot appear on guidepost 1).

By the combined relationship of the last two rules, the lynx, moose, and hare all must be on higher numbered guideposts than the fox. So those animals cannot be in the correct choice. Furthermore, the grizzly can only be on guidepost 3 or guidepost 4, so the grizzly cannot be in the correct choice, either. That leaves us with the fox and the porcupine, either of which could appear on guidepost 1. Therefore, the correct choice has to read "fox, porcupine." Any choice that omits one of these animals is incomplete, and any answer that includes one of the other animals is inaccurate.

GAME 2: PRACTICE

Game 1 provided a good review of Kaplan's 5-Step Method and of the question types you'll encounter. Applying Kaplan's Method, try the next game on your own, using the extra space provided for your scratch work. Don't worry too much about your timing—yet.

<u>Questions 1–5</u>

During a period of seven consecutive days—from day 1 through day 7—seven investors—Fennelly, Gupta, Hall, Jones, Knight, López, and Moss—will each view a building site exactly once. Each day exactly one investor will view the site. The investors must view the site in accordance with the following conditions:

Fennelly views the site on day 3 or else day 5.

López views the site on neither day 4 nor day 6.

If Jones views the site on day 1, Hall views the site on day 2.

If Knight views the site on day 4, López views the site on day 5.

Gupta views the site on the day after the day on which Hall views the site.

1. Which of the following could be the order in which the investors view the site, from day 1 through day 7?

    (A) Hall, Gupta, Fennelly, Moss, Knight, López, Jones

    (B) Hall, Gupta, López, Fennelly, Moss, Knight, Jones

    (C) López, Gupta, Hall, Moss, Fennelly, Jones, Knight

    (D) López, Jones, Fennelly, Knight, Hall, Gupta, Moss

    (E) López, Jones, Knight, Moss, Fennelly, Hall, Gupta

2. If Jones views the site on day 1, which one of the following investors must view the site on day 4?

    (A) Fennelly
    (B) Gupta
    (C) Knight
    (D) López
    (E) Moss

3. If Knight views the site on day 4 and Moss views the site on some day after the day on which Jones views the site, which one of the following must be true?

    (A) Jones views the site on day 1.
    (B) Jones views the site on day 2.
    (C) Jones views the site on day 6.
    (D) Moss views the site on day 2.
    (E) Moss views the site on day 6.

4. If Hall views the site on day 2, which one of the following is a complete and accurate list of investors any one of whom could be the investor who views the site on day 4?

    (A) Knight
    (B) Moss
    (C) Jones, Moss
    (D) Knight, Moss
    (E) Jones, Knight, Moss

5. If Hall views the site on the day after the day Knight views the site, and if Fennelly views the site on the day after the day López views the site, then Jones must view the site on day

    (A) 1.
    (B) 2.
    (C) 3.
    (D) 4.
    (E) 5.

6. If the day on which Gupta views the site and the day on which López views the site both come at some time before the day on which Fennelly views the site, which one of the following is an investor who could view the site on day 3?

    (A) Fennelly
    (B) Gupta
    (C) Jones
    (D) Knight
    (E) Moss

Use this space for scratch work

Game 2 Answers and Explanations

Were you able to finish in the time you allowed? Keep in mind that your goal is to average under 9 minutes per game on Test Day. But working methodically should come before focusing on your speed.

Step 1: Overview

Situation: A building site.

Entities: Seven investors.

Action: Determine the order, or sequence, in which the investors visit the building site.

Limitations: Seven investors, seven days; one different investor each day.

Step 2: Sketch

As is typical for sequencing games, draw seven slots representing the seven viewings, plus a list of entities.

Step 3: Rules

The first rule gives two options for Fennelly—day 3 or day 5. Make a note of this to the side of the sketch.

The second rule dictates that Lopez cannot be on day 4 or day 6. Write "No L" under spots 4 and 6.

The third rule is conditional: if Jones is on day 1, Hall is on day 2. Write this rule in shorthand next to the sketch and also write its contrapositive (if Hall is not on day 2, then Jones is not on day 1).

The fourth rule is also conditional, so be sure to shorthand both the original rule (if Knight is on day 4, Lopez is on day 5) and its contrapositive (if Lopez is not on day 5, Knight is not on day 4).

The last rule creates a bloc of entities, with Hall immediately before Gupta. Note this, as with all the other rules, beside your sketch.

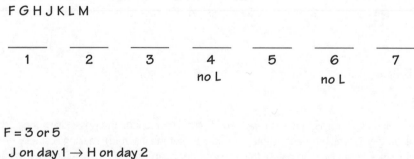

F G H J K L M

1	2	3	4	5	6	7
			no L		no L	

F = 3 or 5
J on day 1 → H on day 2
H not on day 2 → J not on day 1
K on day 4 → L on day 5
L not on day 5 → K not on day 4
HG

KAPLAN

Step 4: Deductions

There aren't really any deductions to make. There aren't major blocs of entities and two of the rules are conditionals (the *if/then* rules). Since conditionals only focus on specific situations, they don't offer much in the way of figuring out anything that *must* be true at all times. Too many *if/then* rules will usually lead to few, if any, deductions. The only certainty is the "HG" bloc, which can go anywhere. Now go on to the questions.

Step 5: Questions

1. E

The question set begins with the typical acceptability question, so we can use the Kaplan strategy of using the rules to eliminate choices. Rule 1 is violated by (B), which has Fennelly fourth. Rule 2 eliminates (A), which has Lopez sixth. Rule 3 isn't triggered by any of the choices. Rule 4 eliminates (D), which has Knight fourth without Lopez fifth. Finally, (C) gets Rule 5 backwards. Only (E) remains.

2. E

This "if" question tells us that Jones is on 1. According to the third rule, that means that Hall is on 2, which places Gupta on 3 to satisfy the last rule. That eliminates (B). Since Gupta is on 3, Fennelly must be on 5 (based on the first rule). That eliminates (A). L is never fourth, so that eliminates (D). And, since Fennelly is on day 5, that means Lopez can't be on day 5. According to the contrapositive of the fourth rule, that means Knight can't be on day 4, which eliminates (C). So Moss is the only one that can go fourth, choice (E).

3. C

This "if" question comes with two new conditions. First, Knight is on day 4, which means that Lopez is on day 5 according to rule four. With Lopez on day 5, Fennelly must be on day 3 (rule one). Second, Moss has to be some time after Jones (J…M). Besides Jones and Moss, we also have the "HG" bloc. HG can go in 1–2 (putting J and M into 6 and 7, respectively) or HG can go into 6–7 (putting J and M into 1 and 2, respectively). However, if J and M were first and second, that would violate rule three, which tells us that whenever J is first, H must be second. So we can't place the HG pair in 6–7; they have to be in 1–2, making J and M sixth and seventh, respectively:

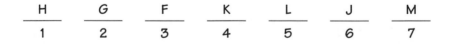

H	G	F	K	L	J	M
1	2	3	4	5	6	7

Only (C) must be true.

4. C

Here's a complete and accurate list question, with an "if" condition to limit the possibilities. According to the "if" condition, Hall is on day 2, which means Gupta is on day 3 (per the last rule), making Fennelly on day 5 (per rule one). Once again, since Fennelly is on day 5, that means Lopez can't be on day 5. According to the contrapositive of the fourth rule, that means Knight can't be on day 4. Therefore, Knight will not be on the list of investors who can be on day 4, eliminating (A), (D), and (E). The two remaining choices have M in common, so there's no need to test M.

We *know* M must be a part of the correct choice. We only have to check to see whether J can be fourth in this question. And yes, we can place J fourth. One such acceptable arrangement is LHGJFMK. So (C) is correct.

5.   D

Once again, there are two conditions to this "if" question. First, if Hall is immediately after Knight, that creates a larger bloc of KHG. Second, If Fennelly is immediately after Lopez, Fennelly cannot be fifth, since that would place Lopez fourth, which would violate rule two. So Fennelly must be third and Lopez must be second. Since Lopez is on day 2, that means Lopez isn't on day 5, which means (based on rule four) that Knight can't be on day 4. The bloc KHG must therefore be on days 5, 6, and 7

____	L	F	____	K	H	G
1	2	3	4	5	6	7

Since Hall can no longer be on day 2, that triggers the contrapositive of rule 3, meaning that Jones can't be on day 1, leaving only day 4 for Jones. That's choice (D).

6.   B

A final "if" question. If Gupta (and therefore Hall) and Lopez are both before Fennelly, Fennelly couldn't be third. So Fennelly must be fifth. So, Lopez must view the site on one of the first four days. Lopez can't be on day 4, so that leaves just the first three days. Lopez could be on day 3, but Lopez is not a choice. If Lopez was on day 2, then the Gupta-Hall pair would be on days 3–4, meaning Gupta could be on day 3, making (B) a possible choice. To ensure this is correct, the only other possible day for Lopez is day 1. In that case, the Gupta-Hall pair would have to be on days 2–3 or 3–4. Either way, day 3 would feature either Gupta or Hall. However, like Lopez, Hall is not a choice. In any case, none of the other investors can take up day 3, so Gupta is the only possible investor in the choices for day 3.

GAME 3: PACING

Now try another test-like game on your own. Allow yourself no more than 11 minutes—less if you're up to it. Never push your pacing at the expense of learning and internalizing the methods and strategies. But developing a sense of timing and keeping up your sense of urgency about moving through each game expeditiously (rather than allowing yourself the luxury of unlimited time to solve it) is as much a part of winning Logic Games as getting the right answers.

On Test Day, you'll have to average about 8.75 minutes per game. If one game takes you 10 minutes, you'll have to do another in about 7 minutes to make up the difference. Less time than that for a Logic Game is unrealistic, so you have to get very sensitive to that 8.75 minute average, varying it only slightly for the harder games.

Questions 1–7

Jill, Kurt, Larisa, Manny, and Olga are the clerks in a supermarket. The supermarket has exactly nine parallel aisles, numbered consecutively 1 through 9 from one end of the store to the other. Each aisle is stocked by exactly one clerk and no clerk stocks more than two aisles. Stocking assignments must meet the following conditions:

> Olga stocks exactly one aisle.
>
> Kurt stocks aisle 2.
>
> Manny does not stock aisle 1.
>
> Jill does not stock consecutive aisles.
>
> Kurt stocks the only aisle between the two aisles Manny stocks.
>
> Exactly one of Larisa's aisles is an end aisle.
>
> Olga's aisle is a number higher than either of Kurt's aisles, and lower than at least one of Larisa's.

1. Which of the following clerks could stock consecutive aisles?

    (A) Jill
    (B) Kurt
    (C) Larisa
    (D) Manny
    (E) Olga

2. Which one of the following is a pair of clerks, neither of whom could stock aisle 5?

    (A) Jill and Manny
    (B) Kurt and Olga
    (C) Larisa and Manny
    (D) Kurt and Manny
    (E) Larisa and Olga

3. Which one of the following is a complete and accurate list of clerks, any one of whom could stock aisle 3?

    (A) Jill, Kurt, Larisa
    (B) Jill, Larisa, Manny
    (C) Jill, Larisa, Olga
    (D) Jill, Kurt, Larisa, Manny
    (E) Jill, Kurt, Larisa, Olga

4. Which one of the following is a complete and accurate list of aisles, any one of which could be one of the aisles Manny stocks.

    (A) 1, 3, 4, 5
    (B) 3, 5, 7, 9
    (C) 3, 4, 5, 6
    (D) 3, 4, 5, 6, 7
    (E) 3, 5, 7

5. If Larisa's aisles are separate by the maximum number of aisles that could separate her aisles, which of the following could be true?

    (A) Jill stocks aisle 6.
    (B) Manny stocks aisle 7.
    (C) Both of Jill's aisles are numbered lower than Olga's.
    (D) Jill stocks only even-numbered aisles.
    (E) Only one clerk stocks a higher numbered aisle than Olga does.

6. If Jill stocks aisle 3, then which one of the following CANNOT be true?

    (A) Jill stocks aisle 9.
    (B) Kurt stocks aisle 6.
    (C) Larisa stocks aisle 4.
    (D) Manny stocks aisle 4.
    (E) Olga stocks aisle 6.

7. Suppose that, rather than just one, Larisa stocks both end aisles; all other conditions remaining in effect, which one of the following CANNOT be true?

    (A) Jill stocks aisle 3.
    (B) Olga stocks aisle 6.
    (C) Olga stocks the only aisle between the aisles that Jill stocks.
    (D) Kurt stocks only even-numbered aisles.
    (E) One of Larisa's aisles is immediately next to Olga's.

Use this space for scratch work

Game 3 Answers and Explanations

Step 1: Overview

Situation: Supermarket.

Entities: Five clerks.

Action: Assigning the aisles to the clerks; they're in a straight-line sequence.

Limitations: Critical here: Nine aisles to be stocked and five clerks to stock them. Since every clerk must stock at least one aisle and no one stocks more than two aisles, it has to be the case that four clerks stock two aisles each, and one clerk stocks one.

Step 2: Sketch

Until you know which clerk stocks only one aisle, simply draw nine slots left to right for the nine aisles and list the five entities.

Step 3: Rules

Right away, the first rule gives us a crucial piece of information. Olga is the one clerk that stocks exactly one aisle. That means all of the other clerks will stock exactly two aisles. So, add an extra J, K, L, and M to the entity list so that you have nine entities total to enter into the nine slots.

The second rule tells us Kurt stocks aisle 2, so place one of the K's in the second position.

The third rule tells us that Manny can't stock aisle 1, so jot down "No M" under the first slot.

The fourth rule means that we'll never see "JJ" anywhere in the sequence.

The fifth rule gives us a solid bloc of three consecutive aisles that we *will* see: "MKM."

The sixth rule is very specific. Larisa will stock aisle 1 or aisle 9, but *not both*. Make sure to note this when you jot the rule down.

The final rule provides a lot of information. The one aisle Olga stocks will be after both of Kurt's aisles and before at least one of Larisa's. The final sequence for this rule is

K…K…O…L.

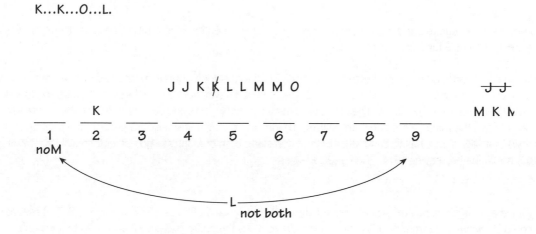

Step 4: Deductions

Because Manny cannot stock aisle 1, the MKM bloc cannot be in aisles 1–3. Therefore, that bloc comes after the K in aisle 2. Combining this information with the last rule, we get a long string of sequencing:

K…MKM…O…L

That string lays the order for six of the nine aisles. And, since that first K is already established in aisle 2, that leaves only seven aisles for the last five entities in the string. Most important is the MKM bloc, which is limited to 3-4-5, 4-5-6, or 5-6-7. No matter what, that bloc must overlap aisle 5. That means that only Manny or Kurt can ever stock that aisle. This is information that is very helpful to notice ahead of time because it can often save a lot of time when answering the questions.

Step 5: Questions

1. C

Rule 4 directly prohibits Jill from stocking consecutive aisles, so that quickly eliminates (A). The MKM bloc keeps Manny's aisles separate and also separates Kurt's aisles (seen in the sequencing string made during deductions). That eliminates (B) and (D). Finally, Olga stocks only one aisle, so that eliminates (E). Larisa is all that's left, making (C) the correct choice.

2. E

Based on our deductions, we already determined that the MKM block must overlap aisle 5, so Manny and Kurt are the only clerks who could stock aisle 5. Once you eliminate any choice that includes Manny or Kurt, you're left with the correct choice: (E). A little extra time spent analyzing the game before answering the questions can save you lots of time on test day.

3. B

With Complete and Accurate List questions, look for entities that are mentioned in multiple choices. These entities will offer the greatest chance for quick elimination.

Jill and Larisa are mentioned in every choice, so you don't need to test them. Kurt is mentioned in three of the choices, but the sequencing string from the deductions reveals that Kurt can never stock aisle 3 because Kurt's second aisle must be between two aisles by Manny. Therefore, we can eliminate (A), (D), and (E) immediately. We've already considered the fact the Manny could be third, making (B) look like the right answer. Sure enough, the sequencing string shows that Olga's aisle has to come after both of Kurt's and both of Manny's—no earlier than aisle 6. Therefore, choice (C) is eliminated, leaving (B) as the correct answer.

4. D

Once again, the deductions pay off. As determined, the MKM block could be in 3-4-5, 4-5-6 or 5-6-7. That means Manny could stock any aisle from 3 to 7. Only answer (D) contains the entire list without adding forbidden aisles.

5. A

Remember the important aspect of rule 6: Larisa cannot stock both end aisles. So, to separate Larisa by as many aisles as possible, you could place Larisa in aisles 1 and 8 or aisles 2 and 9. However, since Kurt is already in aisle 2, you must use aisles 1 and 8 for Larisa. Before aisle 8, you still need the MKM bloc and O. Therefore, only Jill is left to stock aisle 9. Jill's other aisle will be somewhere among the MKM bloc and O in aisles 3 through 7.

```
L K _ _ _ _ _ L J
```

Choice (A) seems possible, but don't test it. With "could be true" questions, it's usually faster and more effective to eliminate the answers you know must be false. Eliminate first, and only test answer choices when you have to. (B) doesn't work because if Manny stocked aisle 7, there'd be no room for Olga. Since Jill stocks aisle 9, she can't stock both of her aisles before Olga and she can't stock only even-numbered aisles. That eliminates (C) and (D). Finally, Larisa and Jill already both stock aisles numbered higher than Olga, so there can't be just one clerk stocking a higher numbered aisle that Olga. That eliminates (E), confirming (A) as the correct answer.

6. E

Placing Jill in aisle 3 further limits the placement of bloc MKM. Now, it can only be placed in aisles 4-5-6 or 5-6-7. That means that, no matter what, Manny and Kurt must stock aisles 5 and 6. That leaves no room of Olga in aisle 6, making (E) the correct answer.

7. B

Once in a while, the LSAT will change the rules of the game. When it's happened, it has always been the last question of the question set. Sometimes these questions can be very time consuming. In this case, the changed rule simply allows us to definitively place L in both aisles 1 and 9. Everything else stays the same. Now with three aisles filled, the remaining aisles will be filled with the MKM bloc, O, and both of Jill's aisles. You need to recall Rule 4, which says that Jill can't stock consecutive aisles. With no further deductions, you should simply test the answer choices. (A) certainly seems possible, as long as Jill doesn't stock aisle 4, too. If Olga stocked aisle 6, that would place MKM in 3-4-5, leaving only aisles 7 and 8 for Jill. That's two consecutive aisles, which violates Rule 4. Therefore, choice (B) cannot be true, and is the correct answer.

PRACTICE SETS

Directions: Each group of questions is based on a set of conditions. It may be useful to draw a rough diagram to answer some questions. Choose the response that most accurately and completely answers each question.

Game 4

There are exactly seven houses on a street. Each house is occupied by exactly one of seven families: the Kahns, Lowes, Muirs, Newmans, Owens, Piatts, Rutans. All the houses are on the same side of the street, which runs from west to east.

> The Rutans do not live in the first or the last house on the street.
>
> The Kahns live in the fourth house from the west end of the street.
>
> The Muirs live next to the Kahns.
>
> The Piatts live east of both the Kahns and the Muirs, but west of the Lowes.

1. Which one of the following families could live in the house that is farthest east?

    (A) the Kahns
    (B) the Muirs
    (C) the Newmans
    (D) the Piatts
    (E) the Rutans

2. Which one of the following families CANNOT live next to the Kahns?

    (A) the Lowes
    (B) the Newmans
    (C) the Owens
    (D) the Piatts
    (E) the Rutans

3. If the Muirs live west of the Kahns, the Rutans CANNOT live next to both

    (A) the Kahns and the Piatts.
    (B) the Lowes and the Piatts.
    (C) the Muirs and the Piatts.
    (D) the Muirs and the Owens.
    (E) the Muirs and the Newmans.

4. If the Newmans live immediately west of the Kahns, which one of the following statements must be false?

    (A) The Owens live next to the Newmans.
    (B) The Owens live next to the Rutans.
    (C) The Piatts live next to the Newmans.
    (D) The Piatts live next to the Muirs.
    (E) The Rutans live next to the Newmans.

5. If the Owens live east of the Muirs, which one of the following statements must be true?

    (A) The Kahns live east of the Muirs.
    (B) The Kahns live west of the Rutans.
    (C) The Owens live west of the Lowes.
    (D) The Owens live east of the Piatts.
    (E) The Owens live west of the Piatts.

6. If the Owens live east of the Kahns, which one of the following pairs of families must live next to each other?

    (A) the Kahns and the Piatts
    (B) the Lowes and the Owens
    (C) the Muirs and the Newmans
    (D) the Newmans and the Rutans
    (E) the Owens and the Piatts

Game 5

Exactly seven different trains—Quigley, Rockville, Sunnydale, Tilbury, Victoria, Wooster, and York—arrive at Middlebrook Station on Saturday. The following conditions govern their arrival:

The trains arrive one at a time.

Either the York or the Wooster arrives fourth.

The Sunnydale arrives at some time after the Wooster but at some time before the York.

Both the Tilbury and the Victoria arrive at some time after the Rockville.

The Tilbury does not arrive next after the Victoria; nor does the Victoria arrive next after the Tilbury.

1. Which one of the following could be the order in which the trains arrive, from first to last?

   (A) Rockville, Tilbury, Victoria, Wooster, Sunnydale, York, Quigley

   (B) Rockville, Wooster, Quigley, York, Tilbury, Sunnydale, Victoria

   (C) Rockville, Tilbury, Quigley, Wooster, Sunnydale, York, Victoria

   (D) Quigley, Rockville, Wooster, Sunnydale, Victoria, York, Tilbury

   (E) Tilbury, Rockville, Quigley, Wooster, Sunnydale, York, Victoria

2. If the Wooster arrives at some time before the Rockville, then exactly how many different orders are there in which the seven trains could arrive?

   (A) four
   (B) five
   (C) six
   (D) seven
   (E) eight

3. Which one of the following must be true?

   (A) The first train to arrive is the Rockville.

   (B) The Quigley arrives at some time before the Sunnydale.

   (C) The Rockville arrives some time before the Wooster.

   (D) The Victoria arrives some time before the York.

   (E) The Wooster arrives some time before the York.

4. Which one of the following could be true?

   (A) The Sunnydale is the next train to arrive after the Quigley.

   (B) The Rockville is the next train to arrive after the Sunnydale.

   (C) The Rockville is the next train to arrive after the Tilbury.

   (D) The Quigley is the next train to arrive after the Sunnydale.

   (E) The Quigley is the next train to arrive after the Wooster.

5. If exactly one of the trains arrives after the Wooster, but before the York, then which one of the following could be true?

   (A) The sixth train to arrive is the Sunnydale.
   (B) The sixth train to arrive is the Tilbury.
   (C) The third train to arrive is the Rockville.
   (D) The second train to arrive is the Sunnydale.
   (E) The first train to arrive is the Rockville.

6. If the Quigley arrives at some time before the Rockville, the Wooster must arrive

   (A) second.
   (B) third.
   (C) fourth.
   (D) fifth.
   (E) sixth.

Game 6

Exactly seven professors—Madison, Nilsson, Orozco, Paton, Robinson, Sarkis, and Togo—were hired in the years 1989 through 1995. Each professor has one or more specialties, and any two professors hired in the same year or in consecutive years do not have a specialty in common. The professors were hired according to the following conditions:

Madison was hired in 1993, Robinson in 1991.

There is at least one specialty that Madison, Orozco, and Togo have in common.

Nilsson shares a specialty with Robinson.

Paton and Sarkis were each hired at least one year before Madison and at least one year after Nilsson.

Orozco, who shares a specialty with Sarkis, was hired in 1990.

1. Which one of the following is a complete and accurate list of the professors who could have been hired in the years 1989 through 1991?

    (A) Nilsson, Orozco, Robinson
    (B) Orozco, Robinson, Sarkis
    (C) Nilsson, Orozco, Paton, Robinson
    (D) Nilsson, Orozco, Paton, Sarkis
    (E) Orozco, Paton, Robinson, Sarkis

2. If exactly one professor was hired in 1991, then which one of the following could be true?

    (A) Madison and Paton share a specialty.
    (B) Robinson and Sarkis share a specialty.
    (C) Paton was hired exactly one year after Orozco.
    (D) Exactly one professor was hired in 1994.
    (E) Exactly two professors were hired in 1993.

3. Which one of the following must be false?

    (A) Nilsson was hired in 1989.
    (B) Paton was hired in 1990.
    (C) Paton was hired in 1991.
    (D) Sarkis was hired in 1992.
    (E) Togo was hired in 1994.

4. Which one of the following must be true?

    (A) Orozco was hired before Paton.
    (B) Paton was hired before Sarkis.
    (C) Sarkis was hired before Robinson.
    (D) Robinson was hired before Sarkis.
    (E) Madison was hired before Sarkis.

5. If exactly two professors were hired in 1992, then which one of the following could be true?

    (A) Orozco, Paton, and Togo share a specialty.
    (B) Madison, Paton, and Togo share a specialty.
    (C) Exactly two professors were hired in 1991.
    (D) Exactly two professors were hired in 1993.
    (E) Paton was hired in 1991.

6. If Paton and Madison have a specialty in common, then which one of the following must be true?

    (A) Nilsson does not share a specialty with Paton.
    (B) Exactly one professor was hired in 1990.
    (C) Exactly one professor was hired in 1991.
    (D) Exactly two professors were hired in each of two years.
    (E) Paton was hired at least one year before Sarkis.

Use this space for scratch work

Use this space for scratch work

Game 4 Answers and Explanations

Step 1: Overview

Situation: House on a street.

Entities: Seven families.

Action: Determined the order, or sequence, in which the families live on the street.

Limitation: Each house has exactly one family, so it's basic sequencing—seven families in seven houses.

Step 2: Sketch

As usual, draw and number seven slots left to right, and list your entities by initial. To avoid confusion, it's a good idea in a game like this to label the "west" (left) and "east" (right) sides of your sketch.

Step 3: Rules

The first rule dictates that the Rutans cannot be in the first or seventh house. Simply notate "No R" under those slots.

The second rule is the most concrete: the Kahns live in the fourth house from the west. This simply means that the Kahns live in house 4, so put that directly into the sketch.

The third rule states that the Muirs live next to the Kahns; however, it doesn't say on which side. Still, since the Kahns live in house 4, that means the Muirs are in either house 3 and/or house 5.

The last rule gives us a string of sequencing. First comes the MK (or KM) bloc, then P, then L.

Before going to the deductions, it's good to note that there are two floaters in this game: the Newmans and the Owens.

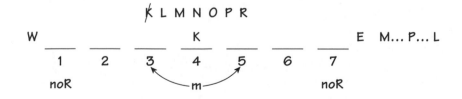

Step 4: Deductions

Knowing which house the Muirs are in can severely limit the placement of the Piatts and the Lowes. So, it's worth quickly exploring the limited options:

If the Muirs occupy house 5, that means the Piatts must be in house 6 and the Lowes in house 7. That fills up four slots. Then, knowing that the Rutans can't be first, the first slot must go to one of the floaters: the Newmans or the Owens.

If the Muirs occupy house 3, you can't definitely place the Piatts and the Lowes, but you know that those families will take up two of the last three houses in the sketch. Once again, the first slot must go to one of the floaters: the Newmans or the Owens.

The final sketches should look like so:

Option I: P ... L

N/O _____ M K _____ _____ _____

1   2   3   4   5   6   7
                                                       No R

or

Option II

N/O _____ _____ K M P L

1   2   3   4   5   6   7

Step 5: Questions

1. C

The Lowes live in house 7 in the second option, but that's not a choice. However, we know the Kahns are in house 4, which eliminates (A). The Muirs are in house 3 or 5, which eliminates (B). The Piatts have to come before the Lowes, eliminating (D). And the first rule told us the Rutans can't be in house 7, eliminating (E). That leaves the choice (C) (one of the floaters!) as correct.

2. A

This question is based entirely on the interpretation of rule 4 that the Piatts live between the Kahns and the Lowes. Therefore, there's no way that the Kahns can live next to the Lowes, making answer (A) the correct answer.

3. C

This "if" question puts the Muirs in house 3, which refers to the first option. That option is less complete, so you just have to check the choices. (A) seems possible if the Rutans are in house 5 and the Piatts are in house 6. (B) also seems possible with the Piatts in 5, the Rutans in 6 and the Lowes in 7. For the remaining three choices, if the Rutans were next to the Muirs, they would have to be in house 2 (since the Kahns are in house 4). That would put them next to either the Newmans or the Owens, but never the Piatts—making (C) the correct choice.

4. **A**

This "if" question puts the Newmans in house 3, which puts the Muirs in house 5. This leads to the second option, which you can redraw and fill in completely. Once the Newmans are in 3, that leaves the Rutans and the Owens for houses 1 and 2. And, since the Rutans can't be in house 1 (rule one), that leaves us with this final sketch:

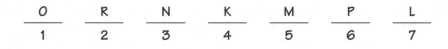

The Owens clearly do not live next to the Newmans, making choice (A) correct.

5. **A**

This "if" question puts the Owens somewhere east of the Muirs. If the Muirs lived in house 5, that wouldn't leave room on the east for the Owens (as the limited options clearly show). Therefore, the Muirs must live in house 3, leading to the first option. That means O, P, and L will occupy slots 5, 6, and 7. The two remaining entities, N and R, will therefore take houses 1 and 2, respectively (since the first rule prohibits R from being in house 1).

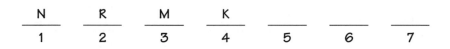

With that, the Kahns definitely live east of the Muirs, making choice (A) correct.

6. **D**

This "if" question puts the Owens somewhere east of the Kahns, which leads to the exact same scenario presented in the previous question. So, instead of redrawing the same sketch twice, use your previous scratch work to save time. The sketch from the previous question shows the Newmans and the Rutans next to each other, making (D) the correct choice.

Game 5 Answers and Explanations

Step 1: Overview

Situation: Trains arriving at a station.

Entities: Seven trains.

The action and limitations are not defined in the opening paragraph. It's not until the first rule that the setup of this game becomes clear. A quick glance at the first rule tells you:

Action: Arrange (sequence) them in order of arrival.

Limitations: Standard for a sequence game—all seven trains arrive, one at a time.

Step 2: Sketch

Nothing out of the ordinary. Seven slots, left to right. List the entities by initial.

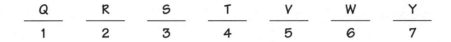

Q	R	S	T	V	W	Y
1	2	3	4	5	6	7

Step 3: Rules

The first rule provided the action and limitations of the game.

The second rule dictates that the fourth train will be either the Wooster or the York. You can fill in the fourth slot with W/Y for now, and consider limited options when you get to deductions.

The third rule provides a string of sequencing: Wooster, then Sunnydale, then York. Since both entities from rule two are mentioned in this rule, creating limited options is beginning to look like a good idea.

The fourth rule mentions that the Rockville train precedes both the Tilbury and Victoria trains, and does not provide an order for Tilbury and Victoria.

The final rule makes it clear that the Tilbury and Victoria have to be separated.

Note that Quigley is a floater, and move on to deductions.

Step 4: Deductions

As noted, deductions will begin with the relationship of Rules 2 and 3, since both involve the Wooster and York trains. Limited options definitely seem to be in order.

Place W in slot 4 for the first option, and Y in slot 4 for the second option. Starting with the first option: with the relationship from rule two, that means that Sunnydale and York will take up two of the last three slots. The relationship from rule four is limited by Rule 5. Because Tilbury and Victoria can't be next to each other, the first three slots can't be Rockville, Tilbury, and Victoria. Either Tilbury or Victoria is going to come after Wooster, forcing Quigley (a floater) to arrive before Wooster. Note as much as you can in the sketch, but don't feel you have to think through all the possibilities at this point.

In the section option, the relationship from Rule 2 places Wooster and Sunnydale into two of the first three slots. Once again, that leaves limited room for the sequence starting with Rockville from Rule 4. In this option, Rockville cannot arrive fifth because that would force Tilbury and Victoria to arrive consecutively. Therefore, Rockville is forced before York, giving it one of the first three spots along with Wooster and Sunnydale.

That means that the last three spots will contain Tilbury, Victoria, and Quigley. However, Tilbury and Victoria cannot be next to each other, so they must be split up into slots 5 and 7 (in either order), forcing Quigley (a supposed floater!) into slot 6!

Final sketches:

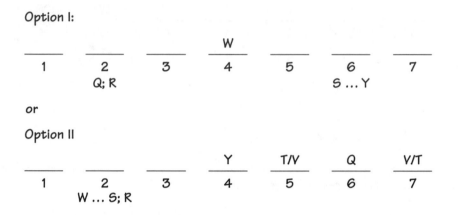

With all of this information, it's time to answer the questions.

Step 5: Questions

1.   C

An acceptability question. Quickly move through the rules. Choice (D) violates rule two by putting Sunnydale fourth. Choice (B) violates rule three by putting Sunnydale after York. Choice (E) violates Rule 4 by putting Rockville after Tilbury. And choice (A) violates the last rule by placing Tilbury and Victoria next to each other. That leaves choice (C) as correct.

2.   A

This "if" question places the Wooster before the Rockville, which can only happen in the section option. Therefore, York is fourth and Quigley is sixth. Now, with Wooster coming before Rockville *and* Sunnydale (Rule 2), that means Wooster must be first. From there, Rockville and Sunnydale will take up positions 2 and 3, in either order. Also, Tilbury and Victoria will take up positions 5 and 7, in either order. A quick count shows four possible orders:

WRSYTQV; WSRYTQV

WRSYVQT; WSRYVQT

That makes (A) the correct choice.

3.   E

This question can be answered exclusively on information from rule three. Since Wooster has to come before Sunnydale, which has to come before York, Wooster must come before York, making (E) the correct choice. All other answers are possible, but not "must be true."

4.   B

This question requires a little bit of testing. In both options, Quigley and Sunnydale fall on opposite sides of slot 4, which eliminates choices (A) and (D). Choice (B) seems possible in the second option (if the first three slots are W, S, R respectively), so that choice looks good. However, with "could be true" questions, it's good to make sure everything else is false. Choice (C) blatantly violates rule four. And even though Quigley is a floater, the options show that Wooster's limitations prevent Quigley from ever being immediately after it, which eliminates (E).

5.   E

This "if" question provides a solid bloc of entities. If only one train arrives between Wooster and York, it must be Sunnydale (per Rule 3). However, the WSY bloc could appear in either option, so they must both be drawn out. In the first option, W, S, and Y will be trains 4, 5, and 6, respectively. That leaves Tilbury or Victoria for the last slot. In the second option, W, S, and Y will be trains 2, 3, and 4, respectively, making Rockville the first train to arrive.

Option I:

			W	S	Y	T/V
1	2	3	4	5	6	7

or

Option II

R	W	S	Y	T/V	Q	V/T
1	2	3	4	5	6	7

The sixth train is either York or Quigley, so that eliminates choices (A) and (B). Sunnydale is either third or fifth, so that eliminates (D). Rockville can be first in the second option, so (E) is looking good. Sure enough, Rockville can't be third in the first option because it still needs to come before both Tilbury and Victoria. So (C) is no good, leaving (E) as correct.

6.   C

This "if" question places Quigley before Rockville. That can only happen in the first option, in which Wooster arrives fourth. That's choice (C).

Game 6 Answers and Explanations

Step 1: Overview

Situation: Professors being hired.

Entities: Seven professors.

Action: Determine the sequence (by year) in which the professors were hired.

Limitations: There are seven professors and seven years, but there's nothing here that says it's a strict 1:1 sequence. That means that there may be some years in which two or more professors were hired, and some years may not have a professor hired. In addition, there's the extra wrinkle about the "specialties." The specialties aren't listed, but the overview provides a rule for the game: any two professors hired in the same or consecutive years cannot share a specialty. For now, shorthand the rule and come back to it when you learn more information.

Before proceeding, note that the "specialties" rule refers to professors hired in consecutive years or *in the same year*. This is a subtle way of saying that there may be at least one year in which two professors were hired.

Step 2: Sketch

Despite the information about the specialties, this is still a sequencing game. However, since it's not necessarily one professor each year, you can't draw seven slots in a row. Instead, create a column for each year and add slots in each year as the rules dictate. Also, list the entities by initial:

M N O P R S T

89	90	91	92	93	94	95

Step 3: Rules

With a complicated overview, it's nice to get two concrete pieces of information in the first rule. Place M under 1993 and R under 1991.

The second rule tells us that Madison, Orozco, and Togo all share a specialty. Jot that to the side of the sketch for now, and that will probably be important to combine with the information from the overview later.

The same goes for the third rule, noting that Nilsson and Robinson share a specialty.

The fourth rule gives some general sequencing. Nilsson will come first, followed by Paton and Sarkis (in either order—maybe even the same year!), followed by Madison. Madison has already been established, so this sequence will be limited in its placement. For now, jot down the sequence (N…P…M and N…S…M) and come back to this during deductions.

The final rule definitively places Orozco in 1990 (so add that to the sketch), but also gives us another pair of professors who share a specialty—Orozco and Sarkis.

M̶ N Ø P R̶ S T

89	90	91	92	93	94	95
	O	R		M		

M, O, T share
N, R share
N... P... S
O, S share

Step 4: Deductions

Now it's time to put all the pieces together. According to the rule from the overview, any two professors who were hired in the same year or in consecutive years do not share a specialty. Combining that with the information from Rule 2 tells us that Madison, Orozco, and Togo (who all share a specialty) cannot be hired in the same or consecutive years. And Rules 1 and 5 have already established Madison and Orozco. Sharing a specialty with Orozco, Togo cannot be hired in 1989, 1990, or 1991. Sharing a specialty with Madison prohibits Togo from being hired in 1992, 1993, or 1994. That leaves just one year: 1995. So Togo was hired in 1995.

According to the second rule, Nilsson shares a specialty with Robinson. So, because Robinson was hired in 1991, Nilsson couldn't be hired in 1990, 1991, or 1992. Furthermore, Nilsson is limited by the sequence in Rule 4. According to that rule, Nilsson must come before Paton and Sarkis, both of whom have to come before Madison. So, Nilsson has to come before Madison, who was hired in 1993. Being excluded from 1990–1992, that means Nilsson must have been hired in 1989.

Now, all that's left are Paton and Sarkis, both of whom have to be hired after Nilsson and before Madison. According to the last rule, Sarkis shares a specialty with Orozco, who was hired in 1990. So Sarkis couldn't be hired in 1989, 1990, or 1991. That leaves just one year for Sarkis in between Nilsson and Madison: 1992. So Sarkis was hired in 1992.

All that's left is Paton, who (according to rule four) must be hired after Nilsson and before Madison. That means Paton was hired in either 1990, 1991, 1992.

So, despite a complex overview, careful analysis of the rules and solid deductions have led to six of the seven entities being definitively placed and only one unknown: which year Paton was hired (which itself is only limited to three possibilities!). Furthermore, a quick review indicates that 1994 winds up being a year with no one hired. So, feel free to X out 1994.

89	90	91	92	93	94	95
N	O	R	S	M	✕	T

P = 90, 91, or 92

With so much information established, the questions should be much easier to work with.

Step 5: Questions

1. C

Note that this question asks for a complete list of any professor who **could have been** hired from 1989 to 1991. So, in addition to the established professors Nilsson, Orozco, and Robinson, the correct answer must also include Paton, who could be hired in that time frame as well. Choice (C) provides the **complete** and accurate list.

2. A

This "if" question states that only one professor was hired in 1991. According to the sketch, that one professor would be Robinson. Therefore, Paton must have been hired in 1990 (with Orozco) or in 1992 (with Sarkis). If it's the former, then Paton's hiring year is far enough away from Madison's that they could share a specialty, making (A) seem possible. Choice (B) can never be true since Robinson and Sarkis were hired in consecutive years. For this question, only Robinson can be hired in 1991, so choice (C) is incorrect. Nobody was hired in 1994 and only one professor (Madison) could ever be hired in 1993, so (D) and (E) are likewise false. Therefore, choice (A) is correct.

3. E

A quick glance at the sketch showed choice (E) to be impossible since no one was hired in 1994. That makes it the correct choice.

4. D

Again, a quick glance at the sketch verifies that Robinson was hired the year before Sarkis, making choice (D) correct. Choices (A) and (B) are only possible, and choices (C) and (E) are demonstrably false.

5. A

This "if" question dictates that two professors were hired in 1992. Sarkis is already there, and the only entity left to place there is Paton. So, the two professors in 1992 must be Sarkis and Paton. If you draw that out, choice (A) definitely seems possible, with Orozco in 1990, Paton in 1992, and Togo in 1995. Just to be sure, choice (B) is impossible, since Madison and Paton are hired in consecutive years. Choices (C) and (D) don't work because only one year can ever have two professors hired, and that one is 1992 here. Finally, since it was determined that Paton was hired in 1992 for this question, choice (E) is out. That leaves (A) as the correct choice.

6. E

This "if" question makes Paton and Madison share a specialty. Based on the information from the overview, that means Paton can no longer be hired in 1992. So, Paton must have been hired in either 1990 or 1991. That means Paton must have been hired in an earlier year than Sarkis, making (E) the correct choice. For the record, choice (A) doesn't have to be true since Paton could be hired in 1991, allowing a shared specialty with Nilsson. Since Paton is hired in 1990 or 1991, either of those years could have two professors hired, so neither choice (B) nor choice (C) need to be true. And (D) has never been possible since every professor's hiring date was set, and in separate years, except for Paton's. Only one year could possibly have had two professors hired.

Chapter 5:
Loose Sequencing Games

In this second type of sequencing game, a **loose** sequencing game, your job is to rank the entities only in relation to one another. The best way to figure out if a game is a loose or strict sequencing game is to read the rules of the game. In a loose sequencing game, the rules deal with the relationships between different entities, not between entities and specific slots. As a result, both your scratch work and much of your reasoning will be very different from that used in a strict sequencing game.

GAME 1: THE METHOD

Once again, work through the first game, focusing on applying Kaplan's 5-Step Method. Note how the sketch for a loose sequencing game differs from the sketch for a typical strict sequencing game.

<u>Questions 1–7</u>

A car drives into the center ring of a circus and exactly eight clowns—Q, R, S, T, V, W, Y, and Z—get out of the car, one clown at a time. The order in which the clowns get out of the car is consistent with the following conditions:

   V gets out at some time before both Y and Q.

   Q gets out at some time after Z.

   T gets out at some time before V, but at some time after R.

   S gets out at some time after V.

   R gets out at some time before W.

Step 1: Overview

Situation: Clown car at a circus.

Entities: Eight clowns.

Action: Determine the order, or sequence, in which the clowns get out of the car.

Limitations: Eight clowns, in order, one at a time.

Step 2: Sketch

You may have started writing eight spaces, numbered 1 through 8. Looking at the rules, however, tells you those spaces won't help you. The rules are all "loose sequencing" rules. As such, you won't be able to make use of the typical sequencing sketch. Instead, simply list the entities and go to the rules.

Step 3: Rules

As you saw in the previous chapter, the following are the key issues in sequencing games.

Typical Sequencing Game Issues

Issue	Wording of Rule
Which entities are concretely placed in the ordering?	X is third.
Which entities are forbidden from a specific position in the ordering?	Y is not fourth.
Which entities are next to, adjacent to, or immediately preceding or following one another?	X and Y are consecutive. X is next to Y. No event comes between X and Y. X and Y are consecutive in the ordering.
Which entities cannot be next to, adjacent to, or immediately following one another?	X does not immediately precede or follow Z. X is not immediately before or after Z. At least one event comes between X and Z. X and Z are not consecutive in the sequence.
How far apart in the ordering are two particular entities?	Exactly two events come between X and Q.
What is the relative position of two entities in the ordering?	Q comes before T in the sequence. T comes after Q in the sequence.

Start by visualizing each rule. The first condition in Game 1 states that V gets out at some time before both Y and Q. You aren't told anything about the number of space between the entities, just the general order. Visualize V before both Y and Q. Remember, you don't know anything about the relationship between Y and Q, just that they both come after V.

Be careful here with the second condition. Even though Q is mentioned before Z in the rule, the rule states that Q comes *after* Z. Rushing through the rule leads to careless misinterpretations. You want Z first, then Q:

$$Z - Q$$

The third condition states that T gets out before V, but after R. That means R first, then T, then V:

$$R - T - V$$

The fourth condition states that S gets out after V. Again, don't rush the interpretation:

$$V - S$$

The final condition states that R gets out before W:

$$R - W$$

Step 4: Deductions

In Loose Sequencing games, the bulk of your deductions are going to come from combining rules that share entities (duplicates). In this game, V is in Rules 1, 3, and 4. Combing the information, V comes after T (which comes after R), and V comes before Q, Y, and S. Adding Rule 2 to the mix, Z can be added before Q. Finally, the last rule places W after R. The final sketch should incorporate all of the rules:

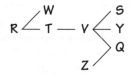

You can determine the relationship between entities only when you can travel from one to the other in one direction. For example, can you say whether R comes out before Y? Yes. You can tell because you can travel straight from R to T to V to Y. R definitely comes out before Y. Can you say whether R comes out before Z? No. To go from R to Z, you would have to travel right to Q, then back up left to Z. Once you're forced to change direction, a definite relationship cannot be determined. R could come about before or after Z.

Before proceeding to the questions, always ask two questions:

What could be first? To determine this, look for any entity that has no direct connection before it. In this case, either R or Z can be first. R seems pretty clear, but it's not as apparent that Z could be first. However, consider that the only thing you know about Z is that it comes before Q. It doesn't *have* to come after anyone. So it certainly can be first.

What could be last? Similarly, look for any entity that has no direct connection after it. In this case, there are four possibilities: Q, S, W, and Y. Again, W is not immediately apparent, but it only has to come after R, with nobody required to come after it.

Finally, note that all eight entities are bound to some condition, so there are no floaters. Now, move on to the questions.

Step 5: Questions

Here's the first question for Game 1. Take a moment to consider how you would approach it.

1. Which one of the following could be the order, from first to last, in which the clowns get out of the car?

    (A) T, Z, V, R, W, Y, S, Q
    (B) Z, R, W, Q, T, V, Y, S
    (C) R, W, T, V, Q, Z, S, Y
    (D) Z, W, R, T, V, Y, Q, S
    (E) R, W, T, V, Z, S, Y, Q

As with any other game, acceptability questions are handled best by going through the rules, one condition at a time, and eliminating any answer that violates that condition.

The first condition is that V gets out before Y and Q. Choice (B) violates that by having V get out after Q. The second condition that Q gets out after Z is violated by choice (C). Since T gets out before R in (A), that choice violates the third condition, which requires that T get out after R. Neither of the remaining answers violates the fourth condition, but R gets out after W in choice (D), which violates the fifth and final condition. That leaves (E) as the only answer choice that doesn't violate any of the conditions, which makes it acceptable. Don't take time to make sure it works. With everything else categorically eliminated, choice (E) must be correct.

2. Which one of the following could be true?

    (A) Y is the second clown to get out of the car.
    (B) R is the third clown to get out of the car.
    (C) Q is the fourth clown to get out of the car.
    (D) S is the fifth clown to get out of the car.
    (E) V is the sixth clown to get out of the car.

For this question, you will need to refer to your original "tree" sketch. To determine an entity's possible positions, follow the straight-line paths, in one direction only, before and after that entity. For example, Y has no connections after it, which means that the latest it could get out of the car is last (eighth). Before it, V must get out, which in turn has T, then R before it. With three entities in a straight line before it, that means the earliest Y could get out is fourth. In loose sequencing, as long as there are no blocs or established entities, an entity can be placed in any position between its earliest and latest possible position. That means Y can get out of the car at any time from fourth to eighth. That means it can't get out second, so choice (A) is out of the question.

No clown has to get out before R, which means it could get out as early as first. However, the sketch shows that W has to get out after R, as does T. After T comes V, and after V come Y, S, and Q. All told, that's six clowns that must get out after R. Therefore, R can get out second at latest, meaning choice (B) can be eliminated.

Before Q gets out, R, T, V, and Z must all get out. That means the earliest Q gets out is fifth. Choice (C) is no good.

Before S gets out, R, T, and V must all get out. That means that the earliest S can get out is fourth. And, since no clown has to get out after S, the latest S can get out is eighth. That means that S can get out of the car any time from fourth to eighth—including fifth. Therefore, (D) is the correct choice.

Just to make sure, look at choice (E). V has to get out of the car before Y, S, and Q. That means that V can get out no later than fifth. Therefore, (E) is eliminated and (D) is the only choice that isn't impossible.

3. If Z is the seventh clown to get out of the car, then which one of the following could be true?

   (A) R is the second clown to get out of the car.

   (B) T is the fourth clown to get out of the car.

   (C) W is the fifth clown to get out of the car.

   (D) V is the sixth clown to get out of the car.

   (E) Y is the eighth clown to get out of the car.

In this "if" question, one of the entities is established in a position. In a question like this, you can draw slots and fill in whatever entities you can. Place Z in position seven. There's one entity that has to come after Z, and that's Q. Therefore, Q must be eighth. Now that Z is seventh, R is the only entity left that could be first. Therefore, R is first. After that, either W or T could be second, so it's time to look at the answers.

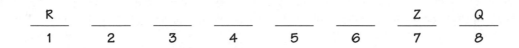

We know R is first and M is eighth, so choices (A) and (E) are quickly eliminated. T still needs V, Y and S to come after it. If T were fourth, there wouldn't be room for all three. Therefore choice (B) is incorrect. The only thing known about W is that it has to come after R. With R being first, that means W could be in any of the remaining open positions, including fifth. Therefore, (C) is correct. To be sure, V can't be sixth because it would still need Y and S to come after it, so choice (D) is impossible.

4. If T is the fourth clown to get out of the car, then which one of the following must be true?

   (A) R is the first clown to get out of the car.

   (B) Z is the second clown to get out of the car.

   (C) W is the third clown to get out of the car.

   (D) V is the fifth clown to get out of the car.

   (E) Y is the seventh clown to get out of the car.

Once again, one of the entities is established. Draw eight slots and place T in position four. The only entity that has to come before T is R, so you know that R will be in one of the first three positions. However, after T has to come V, which has to have Y, S, and Q after it. Therefore, those four clowns must get out in positions five through eight. And, since

V has to get out before Y, S, and Q, that means V is fifth, with Q, S, and Y jockeying for the last three slots. With the last four slots filled, that leaves W and Z to fill in the first three slots with R.

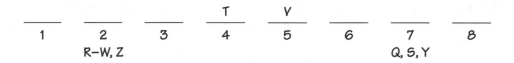

The only entity that can be established for sure is V in position five, which matches choice (D).

5. If Q is the fifth clown to get out of the car, then each of the following could be true EXCEPT:

(A) Z is the first clown to get out of the car.

(B) T is the second clown to get out of the car.

(C) V is the third clown to get out of the car.

(D) W is the fourth clown to get out of the car.

(E) Y is the sixth clown to get out of the car.

Again, draw eight slots and place Q in position five. R, T, V, and Z must all come before Q, meaning that those four clowns take up the first four positions. That means the remaining clowns (W, Y, and S) must all take up the three positions after Q.

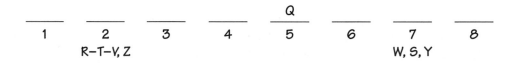

Even without determining definite positions, choice (D) stands out as the correct answer since W is forced to get out of the car after Q.

6. If R is the second clown to get out of the car, which one of the following must be true?

(A) S gets out of the car at some time before T does.

(B) T gets out of the car at some time before W does.

(C) W gets out of the car at some time before V does.

(D) Y gets out of the car at some time before Q does.

(E) Z gets out of the car at some time before W does.

For this question, R is established as the second clown. Every clown has to get out after R except for Z. Therefore, Z must be the first clown. From there, the rest of the order remains uncertain. Still, since Z gets out first, Z must get out before W does, making (E) the correct choice.

7. If V gets out of the car at some time before Z does, then which one of the following could be true?

   (A) R is the second clown to get out of the car.
   (B) T is the fourth clown to get out of the car.
   (C) Q is the fourth clown to get out of the car.
   (D) V is the fifth clown to get out of the car.
   (E) Z is the sixth clown to get out of the car.

Unlike the previous "if" questions, this question provides a new relative relationship instead of establishing an entity. In this case, a strict set of slots will still be relatively unhelpful. Therefore, the best plan of attack is to draw out the new condition and add the remaining entities as dictated by the original sketch.

In this case, start out by drawing V before Z. The entities before V don't change, so add R and T before V. Similarly, the entities after Z don't change, so add Q after Z. The remaining entities should be added as appropriate. W gets replaced after R, and Y and S must branch off after V.

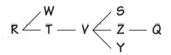

Quickly scanning the new sketch, R must be first, but either T or W could be second. And W, Y, Q, and S can all still be last. It's time to go the choices.

Choice (A) can't be true because R definitely gets out first. V, S, Y, Z, and Q must all get out after T; meaning T can't possibly be fourth. That eliminates (B). As always, R, T, V and Z must all get out before Q, so Q can't be fourth. That eliminates (C). S, Y, Q, and Z all have to get out after V, so V can't be sixth. That eliminates (D). R, T, and V have to get out before Z, so the earliest Z can get out is fourth. Q is the only clown that has to get out after Z, so Z can be seventh at latest. That means Z can get out at any time from fourth to seventh. That includes sixth, making (E) the correct choice.

GAME 2: PRACTICE

Now try Game 2 on the following page on your own before looking at the explanations. As always, focus on the method and strategy in this game, not on your pacing yet.

Questions 1–6

A law firm has exactly nine partners: Fox, Glassen, Hae, Inman, Jacoby, Kohn, Lopez, Malloy, and Nassar.

> Kohn's salary is greater than both Inman's and Lopez's.
>
> Lopez's salary is greater than Nassar's.
>
> Inman's salary is greater than Fox's.
>
> Fox's salary is greater than Malloy's.
>
> Malloy's salary is greater than Glassen's.
>
> Glassen's salary is greater than Jacoby's.
>
> Jacoby's salary is greater than Hae's.

1. Which one of the following partners cannot have the third highest salary?

   (A) Fox
   (B) Inman
   (C) Lopez
   (D) Malloy
   (E) Nassar

2. If Malloy and Nassar earn the same salary, at least how many partners must have lower salaries than Lopez?

   (A) 3
   (B) 4
   (C) 5
   (D) 6
   (E) 7

3. The salary rankings of each of the nine partners could be completely determined if which one of the following statements were true?

   (A) Lopez's salary is greater than Fox's.
   (B) Lopez's salary is greater than Inman's.
   (C) Nassar's salary is greater than Fox's.
   (D) Nassar's salary is greater than Inman's.
   (E) Nassar's salary is greater than Malloy's.

4. If Nassar's salary is the same as that of one other partner of the first, which one of the following must be false?

   (A) Inman's salary is less than Lopez's
   (B) Jacoby's salary is less than Lopez's
   (C) Lopez's salary is less than Fox's
   (D) Lopez's salary is less than Hae's
   (E) Nassar's salary is less than Glassen's

5. What is the minimum number of different salaries earned by the nine partners of the firm?

   (A) 5
   (B) 6
   (C) 7
   (D) 8
   (E) 9

6. Assume that the partners of the firm are ranked according to their salaries, from first (highest) to ninth (lowest), and that no two salaries are the same. Which one of the following is a complete and accurate list of Glassen's possible ranks?

   (A) fifth
   (B) fifth, sixth
   (C) fifth, seventh
   (D) fifth, sixth, seventh
   (E) fifth, sixth, seventh, eighth

Use this space for scratch work

Game 2 Answers and Explanations

Step 1: Overview

Situation: A law firm.

Entities: Nine partners.

The action and limitations are not defined in the opening paragraph. It's not until the first rule that the setup of this game becomes clear. A quick glance at the first rule tells you:

Action: Rank (or sequence) the partners based on salary.

Limitations: There are no limitations stipulating that each partner must receive a different salary. Therefore, some partners may actually make the same salary.

Step 2: Sketch

As is typical for loose sequencing games, list out the entities and go to the rules.

Step 3: Rules

The first rule states that Kohn's salary is greater than Inman's and Lopez's. Since the salaries are ranked from highest to lowest, a vertical tree might look more natural than a horizontal tree:

The second rule states that Lopez's salary is higher than Nassar's. You can draw this rule separately at first, or you can simply add N below L in your original sketch.

If you drew out the remaining rules first before adding them to your sketch, that would be fine. However, you may notice that the remaining rules simply dictate the order of salaries below Inman: Inman, then Fox, then Malloy, then Glassen, then Jacoby, then Hae.

Step 4: Deductions

Since most of the deductions were easily built into the sketch while running through the rules, the only thing left to do before going to the questions is to consider two things.

First, who could have the highest salary? In this case, it has to be Kohn. Kohn is the only partner who doesn't have another partner above him. The second highest salary can belong to either Inman or Lopez (or both—remember that there's no limitation that two partners can't have the same salary).

Second, who could have the lowest salary? In this case, it could be either Nassar or Hae, neither of whom have any partner ranked lower.

Step 5: Questions

1.   D

In order to have the third highest salary, a partner can have no more than two partners with higher salaries. However, Malloy's salary is lower than Kahn's, Inman's and Fox's, meaning Malloy can have the fourth highest salary at best. Therefore, (D) is the correct choice.

2.   C

This "if" question tells us that Malloy and Nassar earn the same salary. You can redraw the sketch by putting M and N together as a bloc, then adding the remaining entities:

From there, you simply have to count the number of entities connected in a straight line lower than Lopez. From Lopez, there's Malloy (1) and Nassar (2), then Glassen (3), Jacoby (4), and Hae (5). That makes (C) the correct choice. While Inman and Fox *could* have lower salaries, the question is looking for partners that *must* have lower salaries.

3.   D

The reason why it's impossible to tell the complete ranking is because there are two branches down from Kahn. Either Lopez or Inman can have the second highest ranking. The correct answer will determine the second highest ranking, as well as all of the other rankings. Choices (A) and (C) place Lopez and Nassar before Fox, but still doesn't resolve the issue of who has the second highest ranking. The same goes for choice (E), which places Nassar before Malloy, but doesn't resolve the second-place issue. By placing Lopez and Nassar above Inman, choices (B) and (D) both solidify Lopez as having the second-highest salary. However, if only Lopez has a higher salary than Inman, then Nassar can still have any rank from third to ninth. That doesn't help completely determine the rankings. Therefore, (B) is no good, leaving (D) as the correct choice. In that case, with Nassar ranking higher than Inman, you know that Kahn is first, Lopez and Nassar must be second and third, then Inman leads the rest of the ranking down the straight line from fourth to ninth (Hae).

4.   D

For this "if" question, Nassar's salary will be the same as one other partner's. It could be any partner in the straight line from Inman down to Hae. Regardless of whom, Lopez will always make a higher salary. Therefore, Lopez could never have a lower salary than Hae, making (D) the correct choice.

5.   C

This is a question that requires careful attention to the limitations and the rules. Remember that two partners can have the same salary, so it's certainly possible to have fewer than nine different salaries. Starting with the longest string, you know that Kahn has to be higher than Inman, who has to be higher than Fox, then Malloy, then Glassen, then Jacoby, then Hae. Since the rules dictate that each salary is higher than (therefore different from) the next, this string requires seven different salaries. The remaining two partners (Lopez and Nassar) can share any two of these salaries. So the fewest number of salaries required is seven, making (C) the correct choice.

6.   D

This final question provides the limitation that was probably expected from the beginning—no ties. Now the sketch can be treated like any standard loose sequencing sketch. As always, to determine the possible positions for an entity, simply count the number of connected entities in one direction above and below that entity. Going up the line, four partners must make higher salaries (Malloy, Fox, Inman and Kohn). So, Glassen can be fifth highest at best. Going down the line, Jacoby and Hae have to make lower salaries, so Glassen can be seventh highest at worst. As always, once you've determined the highest and lowest position, as long as there are no blocs or established entities, Glassen can be ranked in any position in between. Therefore, Glassen can be ranked fifth, sixth, or seventh, making (D) the correct choice.

GAME 3: PACING

Allow yourself no more than 12 minutes for the following game, keeping in mind that your goal is to average under 9 minutes per game on test day.

Especially when you are working on timing, it's important to be in a comfortable space where you can work without interruption for 15–20 minutes: 12 minutes for the game, and sufficient time to review the explanation thoroughly while the game is still clear in your mind.

Pushing yourself to stay within reasonable time limits is essential, even early in your practice. Always be looking for the way that gets you through quickest. There is no payoff in staying with a problem regardless of time, until you get the answer. Learning when to move on and not let a question bog you down is as much a part of the strategy for Logic Games as knowing how to work methodically. You must develop a sense of what 9 minutes feels like and the pace you have to maintain to achieve that goal.

Questions 1–6

A soft drink manufacturer surveyed consumer preferences for exactly seven proposed names for its new soda: Jazz, Kola, Luck, Mist, Nipi, Oboy, and Ping. The manufacturer ranked the seven names according to the number of votes they received. The name that received the most votes was ranked first. Every name received a different number of votes. Some of the survey results are as follows:

> Jazz received more votes than Oboy.
>
> Oboy received more votes than Kola.
>
> Kola received more votes than Mist.
>
> Nipi did not receive the fewest votes.
>
> Ping received fewer votes than Luck, but more votes than Nipi, and more votes than Oboy.

1. Which one of the following could be an accurate list of the seven names in rank order from first through seventh?

    (A) Jazz, Luck, Ping, Nipi, Kola, Oboy, Mist

    (B) Jazz, Luck, Ping, Oboy, Kola, Mist, Nipi

    (C) Luck, Ping, Jazz, Nipi, Oboy, Kola, Mist

    (D) Luck, Ping, Nipi, Oboy, Jazz, Kola, Mist

    (E) Ping, Luck, Jazz, Oboy, Nipi, Kola, Mist

2. Which one of the following statements must be true?

    (A) Jazz received more votes than Nipi.

    (B) Kola received more votes than Nipi.

    (C) Luck received more votes than Jazz.

    (D) Nipi received more votes than Oboy.

    (E) Ping received more votes than Kola.

3. If the ranks of Ping, Oboy, and Kola were consecutive, then which one of the following statements would have to be false?

    (A) Jazz received more votes than Luck.

    (B) Jazz received more votes than Ping.

    (C) Nipi received more votes than Oboy.

    (D) Nipi received more votes than Mist.

    (E) Oboy received more votes than Nipi.

4. What is the total number of soft drink names whose exact ranks can be deduced from the partial survey results?

    (A) one

    (B) two

    (C) three

    (D) four

    (E) five

5. What is the maximum possible number of soft drink names any one of which could be among the three most popular?

    (A) three

    (B) four

    (C) five

    (D) six

    (E) seven

6. If Ping received more votes than Jazz, what is the maximum possible number of names whose ranks can be determined?

    (A) two

    (B) three

    (C) four

    (D) five

    (E) six

Use this space for scratch work

Use this space for scratch work

[]

Game 3 Answers and Explanations

Step 1: Overview

Situation: Soda manufacturer survey.
Entities: Seven soda names.
Action: Rank (sequence) the names in order from most votes to least.
Limitations: Each name received a different number of votes.

Step 2: Sketch

Simply list the seven entities by first initial and go through the rules.

Step 3: Rules

The first three rules provide a quick string of sequencing. Jazz is higher than Oboy (rule one), which is higher than Kola (rule two), which is higher than Mist (rule three).

The fourth rule incorporates a strict sequencing rule into a loose sequencing game. Make a note to the side that Nipi cannot be seventh, and move on.

The final rule provides a lot of information. Ping must be lower than Luck. Also, Ping must be higher than Nipi and Oboy (which can be in either order).

Step 4: Deductions

As usual with Loose Sequencing, the most important thing to do is combine all of the rules as much as possible using the duplicated entities. In this case, the major duplicated entity is Oboy, which allows the sequencing string from the first three rules to be combined with the major information in the last rule. Combining everything result in the following tree:

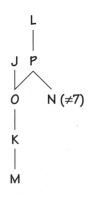

As always with loose sequencing, see if you can establish any entities. What name can have the most number of votes? Either Jazz or Luck, since neither one has any entities definitively listed higher. What name can have the least number of votes? Typically, based on the sketch, it would appear that either Mist or Nipi could have the least number of votes, since neither one of them has any entities definitively listed lower. However, the fourth rule explicitly prohibits

Nipi from being last, so that means Mist must be seventh. With one entity established, see how far you can go up the chain. What can be sixth? It could be Kola, but it could also be Nipi. So, only one entity can be established for sure, but that's good enough for now. Time for the questions.

Step 5: Questions

1. C

A typical acceptability question. Going through the rules, choice (D) violates the first rule by giving Oboy more votes than Jazz. Choice (A) violates the second rule by giving Kola more votes than Oboy. None of the remaining choices violates the third rule, but choice (B) violates the fourth rule by placing Nipi last. Finally, choice (E) violates the last rule by giving Ping more votes than Luck. That leaves (C) as the only choice that doesn't violate any rule, making it the correct choice.

2. E

The last rule tells us that Ping received more votes than Oboy, which (according to Rule 2) received more votes than Kola. That means Ping had to receive more votes than Kola, making (E) the correct choice. This is also seen in the master sketch because you only have to travel along the tree in one direction (down) to get from Ping to Kola. All of the other choices have relationships that require moving in at least two directions to get from one entity to the other.

3. C

This "if" question gives us a strict bloc of entities: POK. Start by drawing that bloc and adding in the remaining entities as dictated by the master sketch. Remember that Ping, Oboy, and Kola have to be consecutive, so no entities can fit in between. Therefore, any entity that has to be higher than Oboy (e.g., Jazz) now has to he higher than the entire POK bloc. So, Jazz and Luck have to be higher than the bloc and Mist and Nipi have to be lower. Jazz and Luck could be in any order, but Nipi can't be last (Rule 4), so Mist must be last, making Nipi sixth:

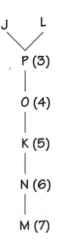

Choices (B), (D), and (E) are all true, and choice (A) is uncertain, so it doesn't have to be false. However, Nipi definitely receives fewer votes than Oboy, making choice (C) definitely false, and therefore the correct choice.

4. A

Having taken time at the beginning of the game to consider established entities, this question can be answered immediately. Only Mist was established at a definite rank, so there's only one name that can be completely determined. That's answer choice (A).

5. B

In order to be in the top three, an entity cannot have more than two entities ranked higher. Going through the entities, Jazz and Luck can be first, so they can both be in the top three. Ping only ranks lower than Luck, so it can be second at best. And Nipi only ranks lower than Luck and Ping, so Nipi can be ranked third at best. Oboy has to rank lower than Jazz, Ping and Luck, meaning Oboy is fourth at best—never in the top three. And since Kola and Mist rank lower than Oboy, they'll never make the top three, either. So, the final list of contenders for the top three spots is Jazz, Luck, Nipi, and Ping—that's four possible names in the top three, and that's choice (B).

6. B

This "if" question provides a new relative relationship. Start by drawing Ping ranking higher than Jazz, then add in the remaining entities. Luck still has to rank higher than Ping. Oboy, Kola, and Mist still have to rank lower than Jazz. (Oboy also has to rank lower than Ping, but having Ping higher than Jazz, which is higher than Oboy, automatically implies that.) The only entity left is Nipi, which still needs to rank lower than Ping, and that's all.

Now, consider what can be established. Luck is the only entity that has no names ranked higher, so Luck must be first. Then, Ping must be second. Either Jazz or Nipi can be third, so that's where the strict sequence ends. And this doesn't change the fact that Mist has to be last. But either Nipi or Kola could be sixth, so that's all that can be established. Luck is first, Ping is second, and Mist is seventh. That's three established entities, making (B) the correct choice.

PRACTICE SETS

Directions: Each group of questions is based on a set of conditions. It may be useful to draw a rough diagram to answer some questions. Choose the response that most accurately and completely answers each question.

Game 4

The eight partners of a law firm are Gregg, Hodges, Ivan, James, King, MacNeil, Nader, and Owens. In each of the years 1961 through 1968, exactly one of the partners joined the firm.

Hodges joined the firm before Nader.

King joined the firm before James.

Nader and James joined the firm before Gregg.

Nader joined the firm before Owens.

James joined the firm before MacNeil.

Gregg joined the firm before Ivan.

1. Which one of the following CANNOT be true?

    (A) Hodges joined the law firm in 1961.
    (B) Hodges joined the law firm in 1963.
    (C) Gregg joined the law firm in 1964.
    (D) MacNeil joined the law firm in 1964.
    (E) Owens joined the law firm in 1964.

2. If James joined the firm in 1962, which one of the following CANNOT be true?

    (A) Hodges joined the law firm in 1963.
    (B) MacNeil joined the law firm in 1963.
    (C) Hodges joined the law firm in 1964.
    (D) Nader joined the law firm in 1964.
    (E) Owens joined the law firm in 1964.

3. Of the following, which is the latest year in which James could have joined the firm?

    (A) 1962
    (B) 1963
    (C) 1964
    (D) 1965
    (E) 1966

4. If Owens joined the firm in 1965 and MacNeil joined it in 1967, one can determine the years in which exactly how many of the other partners joined the firm?

    (A) 1
    (B) 2
    (C) 3
    (D) 4
    (E) 5

5. Assume that Owens joined the law firm before MacNeil. Of the following, which one is the earliest year in which MacNeil could have joined it?

    (A) 1963
    (B) 1964
    (C) 1965
    (D) 1966
    (E) 1967

KAPLAN

Game 5

On the basis of an examination, nine students—Fred, Glen, Hilary, Ida, Jan, Kathy, Laura, Mike, and Nick—are each placed in one of three classes. The three highest scores are placed in the level 1 class; the three lowest scores are placed in the level 3 class. The remaining three are placed in the level 2 class. Each class has exactly three students.

Ida scores higher than Glen.

Glen scores higher than both Jan and Kathy.

Jan scores higher than Mike.

Mike scores higher than Hilary.

Hilary scores higher than Nick.

Kathy scores higher than both Fred and Laura.

1. How many different combinations of students could form the level 1 class?

   (A) one
   (B) two
   (C) three
   (D) four
   (E) six

2. Which one of the following students could be in the level 2 class, but cannot be in the level 3 class?

   (A) Fred
   (B) Glen
   (C) Jan
   (D) Kathy
   (E) Nick

3. Which one of the following students could be placed in any one of the three classes?

   (A) Fred
   (B) Jan
   (C) Kathy
   (D) Laura
   (E) Mike

4. The composition of each class can be completely determined if which one of the following pairs of students is known to be in the level 2 class?

   (A) Fred and Kathy
   (B) Fred and Mike
   (C) Hilary and Jan
   (D) Kathy and Laura
   (E) Laura and Mike

5. Which one of the following pairs of students cannot be in the same class as Fred?

   (A) Hilary and Nick
   (B) Jan and Laura
   (C) Kathy and Laura
   (D) Jan and Mike
   (E) Laura and Mike

Game 6

Six hotel suits—F, G, H, J, K, L—are ranked from most expensive (first) to least expensive (sixth). There are no ties. The ranking must be consistent with the following conditions:

  H is more expensive than L.

  If G is more expensive than H, then neither K nor L is more expensive than J.

  If H is more expensive than G, then neither J nor L is more expensive than K.

  F is more expensive than G, or else F is more expensive than H, but not both.

1. Which one of the following could be the ranking of suites, from most expensive to least expensive?

  (A) G, F, H, L, J, K

  (B) H, K, F, J, G, L

  (C) J, H, F, K, G, L

  (D) J, K, G, H, L, F

  (E) K, J, L, H, F, G

2. If G is the second most expensive suite, then which one of the following could be true?

  (A) H is more expensive than F.

  (B) H is more expensive than G.

  (C) K is more expensive than F.

  (D) K is more expensive than J.

  (E) L is more expensive than F.

3. Which one of the following CANNOT be the most expensive suite?

  (A) F

  (B) G

  (C) H

  (D) J

  (E) K

4. If L is more expensive than F, then which one of the following could be true?

  (A) F is more expensive than H.

  (B) F is more expensive than K.

  (C) G is more expensive than H.

  (D) G is more expensive than J.

  (E) G is more expensive than L.

5. If H is more expensive than J and less expensive than K, then which one of the following could be true?

  (A) F is more expensive than H.

  (B) G is more expensive than F.

  (C) G is more expensive than H.

  (D) J is more expensive than L.

  (E) L is more expensive than K.

Use this space for scratch work

Use this space for scratch work

Game 4 Answers and Explanations

Step 1: Overview

Situation: Law firm.

Entities: Eight partners.

Action: Determine the order (or sequence) in which the partners were hired.

Limitations: Exactly one of the eight partners was hired each year from 1961 through 1968.

Step 2: Sketch

Since this game is loose sequencing, there's no need to draw slots. Simply list the eight entities by initial and move to the rules.

Step 3: Rules

Since the rules are all relative, simply sketch out each rule separately and combine them during deductions.

The first rule states that Hodges joined before Nader. That's straightforward: H–N.

The second rule states than King joined before James: K–J.

The third rule states that Nader and James both joined the firm before Gregg. Remember, the rule doesn't state an order between Nader and James: N–G and J–G.

The fourth rule states that Nader joined before Owens: N–O.

The fifth rule states that James joined the firm before MacNeil: J–M.

The last rule states that Gregg joined the firm before Ivan: G–I.

Step 4: Deductions

Now is the time to combine all of the rules using the duplicated entities. You can start with any rule, but the third rule is a good place to start here since it gives you the most to work with. Start by setting N and J before G. Based on the first rule, add H before N. Based on the second rule, add K before J. Based on the fourth rule, add O after N (making sure not to assume any relationship between O and G). Similarly, add M after J for the fifth rule. Finally, add I after G for the last rule, and your final sketch should look like so:

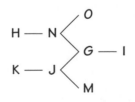

Before moving on, take a moment to review the sketch. What entities could have joined the firm in 1961? Hodges and King are the only entities that aren't below an entity, so either Hodges or King must have joined in 1961. What entities could have joined in 1968? Ivan, Owens, and MacNeil are the only partners with no entities below them, so they're the only ones who could have joined in 1968.

Step 5: Questions

1. C

In a loose sequence game like this (when all the entities are in the master sketch), just check each choice against the sketch, using the sketch to figure out the choice that is impossible. It's already been determined that Hodges could have joined in 1961, so choice (A) isn't right. If King joined in 1961 and James in 1962, then Hodges could have joined in 1963, so choice (B) isn't the answer. Four entities (Hodges, King, James, and Nader) are all before Gregg in the sketch, so at least four partners joined the firm before Gregg. The earliest that Gregg could have joined the firm is 1965. Therefore, Gregg couldn't have joined in 1964, making choice (C) correct.

Quickly, here is why choices (D) and (E) can be true: Only two partners had to be hired before MacNeil (King and James), and nobody had to be hired after MacNeil, so MacNeil could have joined the firm anytime from 1963 to 1968. The same can be said for Owens (who only had to be hired after Hodges and Nader).

2. E

The "if" for this question states that James joined in 1962. Exactly one partner joined earlier, and that must be King. So, King joined in 1961. That's all that can be established, so it's time to check the choices. Either Hodges or MacNeil could have joined in 1963, so that gets rid of choices (A) and (B). If MacNeil joined in 1963, then Hodges could have joined in 1964, so that gets rid of choice (C). And, if Hodges joined in 1963, then Nader could have joined in 1964. That eliminates choice (D), leaving choice (E) as the correct answer. Having established King and James in 1961 and 1962, at least Hodges and Nader must have joined before Owens. So, the earliest Owens could have joined was in 1965.

3. D

To determine the latest year in which James could have been hired, you look at the master sketch for partners that *must* have been hired after James. Looking at the sketch and following straight lines in only one direction, only Gregg, Ivan, and MacNeil were definitely hired after James. Therefore, the latest that James could have joined the firm was 1965, which is choice (D).

4. B

For this "if" question, draw out a strict sketch and add the two new conditions: Owens in 1965 and MacNeil in 1967 (to save time, simply label the slots 1 through 8). Based on the deductions, Ivan is the only entity left that could have joined in 1968. Therefore, Ivan must have joined the firm in 1968. Of the remaining five entities, Gregg has to have been hired after all of the others. Therefore, Gregg must have been hired in 1966. The remaining pairs (Hodges–Nader and King–James) can each occupy two of the four slots from 1961 to 1964. Thus, Gregg and Ivan are the only other entities whose slots can be determined, making choice (B) correct.

Note: Never relax your critical thinking skills. The question stem asked for the *other* entities—i.e., not counting MacNeil and Owens—whose positions can be determined. If you glossed over this fact and counted MacNeil and Owens in your final tally, your work would have been wasted and you would have missed this point.

5. D

In this question, a new relative relationship is added to the equation: Owens joined the firm before MacNeil. Start by drawing the new condition, then add the remaining information from the master sketch. Hodges and Nader joined the firm before Owens, and King and James joined the firm before MacNeil.

H — N — O ⁊ M
        K — J ⁄

Adding Gregg and Ivan can be complicated, but this question is asking for the earliest year in which MacNeil could have joined the firm. Since Gregg and Ivan have no relationship to MacNeil, there's no need to add them to this sketch. To determine the earliest year in which MacNeil could have joined the firm, count the number of entities that must come before MacNeil in a straight line, in one direction. That means Owens, Nader, Hodges, James, and King. That makes a total of five partners that must have joined the firm before MacNeil, meaning the earliest that MacNeil could have joined the firm is 1966. That's choice (D).

Game 5 Answers and Explanations

Step 1: Overview

Situation: Classes.

Entities: Nine students.

Action: Sequence the students in order of their scores, separating them into three classes based on their ranking.

Limitations: Once the sequence is determined, the students will be split up into three classes of exactly three students each: the top three in class 1, the next three in class 2, the bottom three in class 3.

Step 2: Sketch

Simply start by listing the nine entities by initial. You can list nine slots from top to bottom and separate them into three groups, but the loose sequencing rules will preclude the need to do so.

Step 3: Rules

With all of the rules, simply draw out each relationship and wait until deductions to combine. The first rule places Ida higher than Glen. The second rule places Glen higher than both Jan and Kathy (in either order). The third rule places Jan higher than Mike. The fourth rule places Mike higher than Hilary. The fifth rule places Hilary higher than Nick. And the final rule places Kathy higher than both Fred and Laura (in either order).

Step 4: Deductions

The rules are laid out in perfect order in a sequence of decreasing scores. The first two rules combine to set Ida higher than Glen, and Glen higher than Jan and Kathy. The next three rules provide a string of sequencing down from Jan to Mike, then Hilary, then Nick. The final rule adds a fork beneath Kathy down to Fred and Laura.

It's time to consider what entities can be established. Every score is below Ida's, and every score other than Ida's is below Glen's. Therefore, Ida has the top score, and Glen the second highest. That means Ida and Glen have to be in class 1. The only students that could possibly have the third highest score are Jan and Kathy. Therefore, rounding out class 1 must be either Jan or Kathy. Nick, Fred, and Laura all have no students ranked lower, so any one of them could be last. Moreover, none of them have to be in class 3. Class 3 could consist of Kathy, Fred, and Laura (placing Nick in class 2) or it could consist of Mike, Hilary and Nick (placing Fred and Laura in class 2). So, only Ida and Glen are established, and it's time to go to the questions.

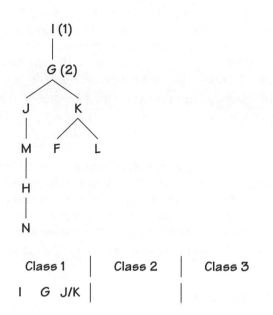

Step 5: Questions

1.　B

Ivan and Glen are fixtures of class 1, while the final spot will go to either Jan or Kathy. That makes for two possible combinations of students for this class, making (B) the correct choice.

2.　C

As determined during deductions, Fred and Nick could be ranked last, so they could both be in class 3, eliminating choices (A) and (E). Furthermore, Glen must be in class 1 only, so that eliminates choice (B). Because there are three students (Mike, Hilary, and Nick) whose scores must be lower than Jan's, the lowest rank Jan could have is sixth. That means Jan could be in class 2, but never class 3, making (C) the correct answer. As for Kathy, only Fred and Laura need to be ranked lower. As was considered during deductions, Kathy could be in class 3 because she can be ranked as low as seventh.

3.　C

The first student you should cross off is Jan, choice (B), who can't be in class 3 as determined by the previous question. The only student besides Jan who can join Ida and Glen in the top class is Kathy. At this point, there's no need to even check whether she can be in the other two classes; she's the only student among the remaining choices eligible for class 1, and that's enough evidence to take choice (C) and move on. Nonetheless, as has been determined a number of times already, Kathy could rank anywhere from third (class 1) to seventh (class 3) and anywhere in between (including class 2).

4.   C

In order to completely determine the ranking, you'd have to know whether Jan or Kathy was in class 2 (thereby forcing the other entity into class 1). Choices (B) and (E) don't include Jan or Kathy, so that won't help completely determine the ranking. The rest of the answers are best tested individually.

For choice (A), placing Fred and Kathy in class 2 puts Jan into class 1. However, either Mike or Laura could take up that third spot in class 2, so this doesn't help completely determine the class compositions. For choice (C), if you place Hillary and Jan in class 2, then Mike, whose score comes between theirs, must also be in class 2. Furthermore, with Jan in 2, Kathy is the only eligible student to join Ida and Glen in class 1. This leaves Nick, Fred, and Laura in class 3. So, by placing Hillary and Jan in class 2, the class compositions are completely determined, making choice (C) correct.

For the record, similar to choice (A), placing Kathy and Laura in class 2 per choice (D) leaves Fred and Mike to float between classes 2 and 3.

5.   E

Once again, this question requires testing of the answer choices. Hilary and Nick could be placed in class 3 along with Fred, so choice (A) is no good. Place Kathy in class 1 and Mike, Hilary and Nick in class 3, and Fred could be in class 2 with Jan and Laura, eliminating choice (B). Swap Kathy and Jan, and you can eliminate choice (C) as well. Place Kathy in class 1, and Jan and Mike can easily join Fred in class 2 (with Hilary, Nick, and Laura in class 3). That eliminates choice (D). However, if Laura and Mike were with Fred, there would be too few students (just Hilary and Nick) for the bottom class, and too many (Ida, Glen, Jan, and Kathy) for the top class. Therefore, (E) is the correct choice.

Game 6 Answers and Explanations

Step 1: Overview

Situation: Suites in a hotel.

Entities: The suites: F, G, H, J, K, and L.

Action: Ranking them from most expensive to least expensive: Sequencing.

Limitations: None of the suites cost the same amount (no ties). The most expensive suite is ranked first, and the cheapest is ranked sixth.

Step 2: Sketch

Since this is a Loose Sequencing game, simply jot down a list of entities.

Step 3: Rules

The first rule provides the first loose relationship: H is more expensive than L. Jot this down: H–L

The next pair of rules is a bit of a twist for Loose Sequencing games, which don't usually involve Formal Logic. But they're no more complicated than the rules you'd usually expect to see, and they actually set up a pair of alternate situations. The second rule states that if G is more expensive than H, neither K nor L is more expensive than J. Turn the negatives in this rule into positives before you write it out. If G is more expensive than H, then K and L are less expensive than J. The third rule provides the alternate situation: If H is more expensive than G, then J and L are less expensive than K.

The final rule is another dichotomy. F is more expensive than either G or H, but not both. Again, think before you write the rule. If F is more expensive than G, then it will be less expensive than H, and vice versa. This translates to: H–F–G or G–F–H.

Step 4: Deductions

As usual, most of the Deductions in Loose Sequencing games come from duplications. But there's a twist here in that Rules 2 and 3 also set up Limited Options: 1) If G is more expensive than H, or 2) if H is more expensive than G. Start by drawing out those two results. Then, Rule 4 provides even more information by cementing F in between G and H in both options. Finally, build each Option by adding in the "H…L" from Rule 1. The Final Visualization:

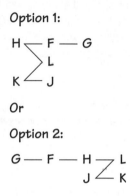

Take a moment to think about who could be first or last in each Option. In Option 1, either H or K could be first and any of G, J, or L could be last; In Option 2, either G or J could be first and either L or K could be last. Unfortunately, there are no established entities. Still, there's enough information here to tackle the questions.

Step 5: Questions

1. B

Quickly eliminate wrong answer choices in Acceptability questions by knocking out anything that violates a rule. Choice (E) has L before H, so it violates Rule 1. Rule 4 is the next easiest to check, and it knocks out choice (D), which has F after both G and H. Rule 2 knocks out choice (A), which has G before H, but L before J; and Rule 3 gets rid of (C), which has H before G and J before K. Only choice (B) remains, and must be correct.

2. C

When an "If" rule in a Loose Sequencing game gives you an established position, try making a Strict Sequencing sketch. Here, just draw out the slots and drop G into the second one. In Option 1, both H and F have to come before G. That can't happen here, so you can only work with Option 2. In Option 2, the only entity that can come before G is J:

Unfortunately, that's the only other entity that can be established. The rest of the sequence will have F before H and H before L, but K could drop in anywhere from third to sixth without breaking a rule. So look through the choices and find the one that could be true, eliminating the four choices that must be false. H can't be more expensive than F without violating Rule 4, so choice (A) is out; and only J is more expensive than G here, so choice (B) is out. K could be third and F could be fourth without breaking any rules, so choice (C) looks good. Nothing is more expensive than J in this sequence, so (D) must be false; and you can eliminate (E) because once G is more expensive than F, Rule 4 states that F is more expensive than H and Rule 1 states that H is more expensive than L.

3. A

It's often easiest to eliminate the four wrong choices in a "CANNOT be true" question. If the correct answer is the suite that cannot be the most expensive, then all four of the wrong answers are suites that could be the most expensive. This type of question is often easiest to answer last, once you have several sketches to work from. But here, the Limited Options provide a quick answer. Option 1 shows that either H or K could be first, eliminating choices (C) and (E); Option 2 shows that either G or J could be first, eliminating choices (B) and (D). Choice (A) remains, and is correct. In fact, Rule 4 provides proof: F cannot be more expensive than both G and H, so it must be less expensive than one of them. Therefore, it can never be the most expensive.

4. D

This "if" question states that L is more expensive than F. That can only happen in Option 1. Why? H must be more expensive than L, so it must also be more expensive than F. This means that G is less expensive than F, that K is more expensive than L, and that J is less expensive than K. All that looks like this:

$$H \diagdown L — F — G$$
$$K \diagdown J$$

In this sketch, F is less expensive than both H and K, which eliminates choices (A) and (B). G is less expensive than H and L, eliminating (C) and (E). That makes choice (D) the correct answer.

5. D

This "if" question provides a new string of sequencing: K–H–J. Checking the two options, this order can only happen in Option 1. Add in the remaining entities based on that sketch:

$$K — H \diagup F — G$$
$$\diagdown J$$
$$\diagdown L$$

With this new sketch, K must be the most expensive suite, which eliminates (E). F is less expensive than H and more expensive than G, which eliminates (A), (B), and (C). That leaves (D) as the correct choice—J and L don't have a clear relationship to each other, so J could be more expensive than L, or vice versa.

Chapter 6: **Selection Games**

In grouping games of **selection**, you are given the cast of characters and told to select a smaller group based on the rules. For example, a game may include eight DVDs from which you must choose four.

Sometimes the test makers specify an exact number for the smaller group, sometimes they don't. In an occasional variation, the initial group of entities is itself broken into subgroups at the start of the game: an example would be a zookeeper choosing three animals from a group of three apes and five lizards.

GAME 1: THE METHOD

Start, as usual, with a game setup, and work your way through applying Kaplan's 5-Step Method. As your confidence improves, be sure to stop and work on your own sketch based on the stimulus and rules before reading further, and work out the answer to each question before reading its explanation.

> A fruit stand carries at least one kind of the following kinds of fruit: figs, kiwis, oranges, pears, tangerines, and watermelons. The stand does not carry any other kind of fruit. The selection of fruits the stand carries is consistent with the following conditions:
>
> > If the stand carries kiwis, then it does not carry pears.
> >
> > If the stand does not carry tangerines, then it carries kiwis.
> >
> > If the stand carries oranges, then it carries both pears and watermelons.
> >
> > If the stand carries watermelons, then it carries figs or tangerines or both.

Step 1: Overview

Situation: Fruits being offered at a stand.

Entities: figs, kiwis, oranges, pears, tangerines, watermelons.

Action: To select the fruits to be offered.

Limitations: At least one of these fruits is offered, and no other fruits are offered.

Step 2: Sketch

The key to the master sketch for a selection game is a roster of all of the entities. If there are no specific numbers, as in this game, circle the entities as they are selected and cross them out when they're rejected. Some games, though, will require the selection of a specific number of the entities (ie: six of nine). When the numbers are specific, blanks can help make the limitations explicit and keep them clear.

F K O P T W

Step 3: Rules

The following is a list of the key issues in grouping games of selection, each followed by a corresponding rule—in some cases, with several alternative ways of expressing the same rule. These rules all refer to a scenario in which you are to select a subgroup of four from a group of eight entities—Q, R, S, T, W, X, Y, and Z:

Typical Selection Game Issues

Issue	Wording of Rule
Which entities are definitely chosen?	Q is selected.
Which entities trigger the selection of another entity?	If X is selected, then Y is selected. X will be selected only if Y is selected. X will not be selected unless Y is selected.
Which entities must be chosen together, or not at all?	If Y is selected, then Z is selected, and if Z is selected, then Y is selected. Y will not be selected unless Z is selected, and vice versa.
Which entities cannot both be chosen?	If R is selected, then Z is not selected. If Z is selected, then R is not selected. R and Z won't both be selected.

Note that a rule like "If X is selected, then Y is selected" works only in one direction. If X is chosen, Y must be, but if Y is chosen, X may or may not be.

Rule 1: If the stand carries kiwis, then it does not carry pears (and the contrapositive):

$$K \rightarrow No\ P \qquad P \rightarrow No\ K$$

Rule 2: If the stand does not carry tangerines, then it carries kiwis (and the contrapositive):

$$No\ T \rightarrow K \qquad No\ K \rightarrow T$$
$$\text{(always T or K)}$$

Rule 3: If the stand carries oranges, then it carries both pears and watermelons (and the contrapositive):

$$O \rightarrow P + W \qquad No\ P\ or\ No\ W \rightarrow No\ O$$

Rule 4: If the stand carries watermelons, then it carries figs or tangerines or both:

$$W \rightarrow F \text{ or } T \text{ or } FT \qquad \text{No } F \text{ and No } T \rightarrow \text{No } W$$

Step 4: Deduction

Selection games often employ a number of conditional rules, and combining those rules with common entities to see the "chain reactions" the selection or rejection of a single entity can set off is one of the most common deductions you'll find in selection games.

For example, Rules 1 and 3 both involve pears. When they're combined, you find:

$$P \rightarrow \text{No } K \rightarrow \text{No } O \qquad O \rightarrow P + W \rightarrow \text{No } K$$

The really powerful deductions, though, are the concrete ones—the ones that aren't conditional. This game, like many with all conditional rules, doesn't have any.

Step 5: Questions

1. Which one of the following could be a complete and accurate list of the kinds of fruit the stand carries?

    (A) oranges, pears

    (B) pears, tangerines

    (C) oranges, pears, watermelons

    (D) oranges, tangerines, watermelons

    (E) kiwis, oranges, pears, watermelons

This is a standard acceptability question and you'll attack it rule by rule, as always. In a nebulous game like this, in which you don't even know how many fruits are going to be selected, it's all the more important to be strictly methodical. Rule 1 eliminates (E) because K and P can't be together. Rule 2 eliminates both (A) and (C) because the correct answer must include either K or T (or both). Rule 3 knocks out (D) because it gives us O without the required P + W (and if we hadn't already eliminated (A), Rule 3 would have taken it out as well). (B) is correct.

2. Which one of the following could be the only kind of fruit the stand carries?

    (A) figs

    (B) oranges

    (C) pears

    (D) tangerines

    (E) watermelons

This question is a great example of the power of thoroughly working the rules up front. We already know that there's one sure requirement—we must select either K or T. Therefore, if we're going to select only one kind of fruit, it has to be one or the other. Either could be the right answer, but only T appears as an option in correct answer choice (D).

3. Which one of the following CANNOT be a complete and accurate list of the kinds of fruit the stand carries?

    (A) kiwis, tangerines

    (B) tangerines, watermelons

    (C) figs, kiwis, watermelons

    (D) oranges, pears, tangerines, watermelons

    (E) figs, kiwis, oranges, pears, watermelons

"Which of the following cannot be a complete and accurate list…" translates to an acceptability/EXCEPT question. Rather than eliminating the answer choices that violate rules, we're looking for the one that does. Work your way through the rules just as you would in an acceptability question. In this case, you don't have to look far: Rule 1 answers the question, since correct answer choice (E) includes the forbidden K + P combination.

4. If the stand carries no watermelons, then which one of the following must be true?

    (A) The stand carries kiwis.

    (B) The stand carries at least two kinds of fruit.

    (C) The stand carries at most three kinds of fruit.

    (D) The stand carries neither oranges nor pears.

    (E) The stand carries neither oranges nor kiwis.

A new sketch makes this question clear and concrete. You know from Rule 3 that if the stand doesn't carry W, it also doesn't carry O. That leaves just four fruits available:

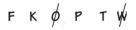

Rule 1 tells you that you can never select both K and P, so that means that at most the fruit stand can carry three fruits: F, T, and either K or P. That's correct answer choice (C).

5. If the stand carries watermelons, then which one of the following must be false?

    (A) The stand does not carry figs.

    (B) The stand does not carry tangerines.

    (C) The stand does not carry pears.

    (D) The stand carries pears but not oranges.

    (E) The stand carries pears but not tangerines.

The correct answer must be false, which means the four wrong answer choices could be true. The stem tells you that W is chosen, so on your new sketch, circle W.

Next, check your rules to see what the selection of W triggers. Rule 4 says that means F or T or both. Sketch the possibilities:

$$(F) \quad K \quad O \quad P \quad \not{T} \quad (W)$$

$$\not{F} \quad K \quad O \quad P \quad (T)(W)$$

$$(F) \quad K \quad O \quad P \quad (T)(W)$$

Make any additional deductions you can. In the first scenario, you know that K must be selected; every acceptable line-up has either K or T, and you've crossed out T. And what else does that mean? No P, according to Rule 1.

$$(F)(K) \quad O \quad \not{P} \quad \not{T} \quad (W)$$

Now check the choices, but don't dig too deep—before you start playing out anything that looks okay at a glance, check for an answer choice that contradicts all three of your possibilities. Answer choice (E) does—there's no line-up in which P is selected but T is not.

6. If the condition that if the fruit stand does not carry tangerines then it does carry kiwis is suspended, and all other conditions remain in effect, then which one of the following CANNOT be a complete and accurate list of the kinds of fruit the stand carries?

    (A) pears
    (B) figs, pears
    (C) oranges, pears, watermelons
    (D) figs, pears, watermelons
    (E) figs, oranges, pears, watermelons

When a rule is rescinded for purposes of a single question, you can't rely on your past sketches. It's no longer necessary to choose either K or T. That twist aside, this is simply another acceptability/EXCEPT question. Given the change in the rules, all of the answer choices are possible but one—so find the one that violates one of the remaining rules. Rule 1 is no help: none of the answer choices include both P and K. Rule 2 is out of the equation. None of the choices violate Rule 3. However, correct answer choice (C) violates Rule 4 by including W without either F or T.

GAME 2: PRACTICE

Now that you have a good sense of the issues you can face in a game of selection, try working methodically through the next game on your own. By this time, you should be picking up some speed—allow yourself no more than 11 minutes, always keeping in mind that your goal is an average of less than 9 minutes per game.

However, don't focus on timing at the expense of your primary goal—in this game be sure you use the right strategies. Use the extra space provided to keep your scratch work clear, and check all aspects of your own work against the explanations provided to see where you went wrong or could have worked more efficiently.

Questions 1–7

The coordinator of an exhibition will select at least four and at most six rugs from a group of eight rugs made up of two oval wool rugs, three rectangular wool rugs, one oval silk rug, and two rectangular silk rugs according to the following conditions

At least two oval rugs must be selected.

The number of wool rugs selected can be neither less than two nor more than three.

If the oval silk rug is selected, at least one rectangular silk rug must be selected.

1. Which one of the following is an acceptable selection of rugs for the exhibition?

   (A) one oval silk rug, one oval wool rug, and two rectangular wool rugs
   (B) one oval silk rug, one rectangular wool rug, and two rectangular silk rugs
   (C) two oval wool rugs, one rectangular silk rug, and two rectangular wool rugs
   (D) two oval wool rugs, one rectangular silk rug, and one rectangular wool rug
   (E) two rectangular silk rugs and three rectangular wool rugs

2. If three wool rugs are selected, then any of the following could be a complete and accurate list of the other rugs selected EXCEPT:

   (A) one oval silk rug.
   (B) one rectangular silk rug.
   (C) two rectangular silk rugs.
   (D) one oval silk rug and one rectangular silk rug.
   (E) one oval silk rug and two rectangular silk rugs.

3. The rugs selected for the exhibition can include any of the following EXCEPT:

   (A) one oval silk rug.
   (B) two oval wool rugs.
   (C) three oval rugs.
   (D) two rectangular wool rugs.
   (E) three rectangular wool rugs.

4. If only one silk rug is selected for the exhibition, then the other rugs selected must be a group made up of

   (A) one oval rug and two rectangular rugs.
   (B) two oval rugs and one rectangular rug.
   (C) two oval rugs and two rectangular rugs.
   (D) two oval rugs and three rectangular rugs.
   (E) three rectangular rugs.

5. If exactly four rugs are selected, then the rugs selected could be

   (A) one oval rug and three rectangular wool rugs.
   (B) two oval rugs and two rectangular wool rugs.
   (C) three oval rugs and one rectangular silk rug.
   (D) three oval rugs and one rectangular wool rug.
   (E) two rectangular silk rugs and two rectangular wool rugs.

6. If all three silk rugs are selected, then each of the following could be a complete and accurate list of the other rugs selected EXCEPT:

   (A) one oval wool rug.
   (B) two oval wool rugs.
   (C) one oval wool rug and one rectangular wool rug.
   (D) one oval wool rug and two rectangular wool rugs.
   (E) two oval wool rugs and one rectangular wool rug.

7. If exactly six rugs are selected, they must include

   (A) exactly one of the oval rugs.
   (B) the two oval wool rugs.
   (C) the two rectangular silk rugs.
   (D) exactly three of the rectangular rugs.
   (E) all three rectangular wool rugs.

Use this space for scratch work

Game 2 Answers and Explanations

Step 1: Overview

Situation: A rug exhibition.

Entitities: two oval wool rugs (OW), three rectangular wool rugs (RW), one oval silk rug (OS), and two rectangular silk rugs (RS).

Action: Select the rugs to be exhibited.

Limitations: Four to six of eight rugs will be selected.

Step 2: Sketch

When there are multiple entities of the same type, list them separately: selection games play out by circling and crossing out entities, so you can't work effectively with your roster if entities are lumped together.

OW   OW   RW   RW   RW   OS   RS   RS

Step 3: Rules

Rule 1: At least two oval rugs must be selected (that's two out of three available). That means:

Oval rugs = 2 or 3

Rule 2: The number of wool rugs selected can be neither less than two nor more than three:

Wool rugs = 2 or 3

Rule 3: If the oval silk rug is selected, at least one rectangular silk rug must be selected:

OS → RS   No RS → No OS

Step 4: Deductions

There are only three oval rugs (OW, OW, OS), and you must select two or three of them. That means the possible combinations are OW + OW, OW + OS, or OW + OW + OS—in any of the three possibilities, at least one OW is selected.

(OW) OW   RW   RW   RW   OS   RS   RS

That deduction triggers another. Because at least one of the two or three wool rugs selected must be oval, at most two rectangular wool rugs may be selected. That means you can cross off one rectangular wool rug.

(OW) OW   RW   RW   ~~RW~~   OS   RS   RS

Whenever numerical rules appear, look for deductions about the numerical possibilities of the game. In this case, you know that 4–6 rugs are chosen, that 2–3 of the rugs must be oval, and that 2–3 of the rugs must be wool. In addition,

KAPLAN

there are only two possible shapes and only two possible materials. That means that any rug that isn't wool is silk, and any rug that isn't oval is rectangular.

Break down the possibilities. If two wool rugs are chosen, 2–3 silk rugs must be chosen. If three wool rugs are chosen, you must choose 1–3 silk rugs:

Wool	Silk
2	2–3
3	1–3

The same sort of deduction can be made regarding the shape of the rugs chosen.

Oval	Rectangular
2	2–3
3	1–3

There's a further deduction available if there are three oval rugs, too—since that would mean at least one was the oval silk, at least one rectangular silk would be required as well.

Step 5: Questions

1.   D

Work your way through the rules. Rule 1 requires at least two oval rugs, but answer choice (B) includes only one and (E) none—eliminate. Rule 2 says you must select either two or three wool rugs, knocking out answer choice (C), where we find four. Rule 3 says if the oval silk rug is selected, you must select at least one rectangular silk, but answer choice (A) lists the oval silk with no rectangular silk. That leaves only correct answer choice (D).

2.   A

If three wool rugs are selected, you may select 1–3 silk rugs; that doesn't help identify the unacceptable grouping among the answer choices. Work the rules. Rule 1 doesn't make any eliminations and Rule 2 is irrelevant since you're told that three wool rugs are selected. Rule 3 says that if the oval silk rug is selected, you must also select at least one rectangular silk rug—but answer choice (A) makes the oval silk rug the only silk rug chosen.

3.   E

"Could include any of the following except" means that there's one selection here that violates the rules. Here's where you directly earn points for making deductions up front. The sketch tells you that all three rectangular wool rugs cannot be selected, which means that answer choice (E) isn't possible.

4.   B

The new "rule" provided here triggers a lot of new information. The first step is to make the information given concrete. You're told that only one silk rug is chosen, but you want to nail that down as clearly as possible. Which silk rug? You know that if the oval silk rug is chosen, the rectangular silk rug is chosen as well, so if there's only going to be one, it has to be rectangular.

Your numerical deductions tell you that if only one silk rug is chosen, three wool rugs must be chosen. One, an oval wool, has already been identified, but there are three remaining wool rugs to choose from. But that isn't all the numerical deductions tell you. You also know that you must choose either two or three oval rugs. Since the oval silk is out of the running, you must choose both oval wool rugs. That's only two wool rugs, though, so you'll have to choose one of the rectangular wool rugs as well.

5. C

At a glance, this question looks tougher than it really is. The mixed answer choices, giving partial information, don't give you much concrete to work with…if you start with the answer choices. Fortunately, you know by now to work by the rules, not by the choices. Rule 1 requires at least two oval rugs—that eliminates answer choices (A) and (E). Rule 3 eliminates answer choice (D), since the presence of all three oval rugs means that the oval silk rug has been selected—but that requires a rectangular silk rug, which doesn't appear in this listing. It takes a deduction to knock out answer choice (B): Combining Rule 2 and Rule 3, the oval silk rug can't be chosen unless you've chosen a rectangular silk rug, but leaving out the oval silk rug would mean four wool rugs, violating Rule 2.

6. A

A new sketch will quickly illustrate the possibilities when all three silk rugs are chosen:

OW OW RW RW RW (OS)(RS)(RS)

Knowing that all three silks are chosen, you have enough silk rugs, enough rectangular rugs, and enough oval rugs. However, you need 2–3 wool rugs, and you've only selected one. That's not enough—which quickly identifies answer correct choice (A) as the unacceptable listing.

7. C

Your numerical deductions up front tell you that if six rugs are chosen, three must be wool and three silk. There are only three silk rugs, so they must all be selected. That makes correct answer choice (C) a must.

GAME 3: PACING

Finally, try a selection game on your own under test-like conditions.

Work on all aspects of your timing. For example, allowing an average of only 1 minute per question for 6 questions, in order to finish the game in 8.75 minutes you must do your overview, sketch, and deductions in under 3 minutes. Notice where you're losing time, and focus on improving there.

Allow yourself no more than 10 minutes for this game. If you're still having trouble finishing in time, try to identify patterns in your work that are holding you back: Are you missing key deductions or an opportunity to use a contrapositive to your advantage? If you can recognize what's slowing you down, you can make sure you focus on that in future practice.

Questions 1–5

A panel of five scientists will be formed. The panelists will be selected from among three botanists—F, G, and H—three chemists—K, L, and M—and three zoologists—P, Q, and R. Selection is governed by the following conditions: The panel must include at least one scientist of each of the three types.

If more than one botanist is selected, then at most one zoologist is selected.

F and K cannot both be selected.

K and M cannot both be selected.

If M is selected, both P and R must be selected.

1. Which one of the following is an acceptable selection of scientists for the panel?

    (A) F, G, K, P, Q
    (B) G, H, K, L, M
    (C) G, H, K, L, R
    (D) H, K, M, P, R
    (E) H, L, M, P, Q

2. If M is the only chemist selected for the panel, which one of the following must be true?

    (A) F and G are both selected.
    (B) G and H are both selected.
    (C) H and P are both selected.
    (D) F, G, and H are all selected.
    (E) P, Q, and R are all selected.

3. If four of the scientists selected are F, L, Q, and R, which one of the following must be the fifth scientist selected?

    (A) G
    (B) H
    (C) K
    (D) M
    (E) P

4. If P is the only zoologist selected, which one of the following must be true?

    (A) If K is selected, G cannot be selected.
    (B) If L is selected, F cannot be selected.
    (C) If exactly one chemist is selected, it must be K.
    (D) If exactly two chemists are selected, F cannot be selected.
    (E) If exactly two chemists are selected, G cannot be selected.

5. If both G and H are among the scientists selected, then the panel must include either

    (A) F or else K.
    (B) F or else M.
    (C) K or else M.
    (D) M or else Q.
    (E) P or else Q.

Use this space for scratch work

Game 3 Answers and Explanations

Step 1: Overview

Situation: Formation of a panel from a larger group.

Entities: Botanists F, G, H; Chemists K, L, M; Zoologists P, Q, R.

Action: To select the members of the panel.

Limitations: Choose five of nine, which means rejecting four. One scientist must be chosen from each category.

Step 2: Sketch

Your entities in this game are broken into categories. Your roster should keep them clearly divided.

Bot	Chem	Zoo
F G H	k l m	p q r

Step 3: Rules

Rule 1: The panel must include at least one scientist of each of the three types:

With a total of five panel members, at least one from each of three groups, there are only two possible number combinations—2:2:1 and 3:1:1.

Rule 2: If more than one botanist is selected, then at most one zoologist is selected:

$$2 \text{ or } 3 \text{ Bot} \rightarrow 1 \text{ Zoo}$$
$$2 \text{ or } 3 \text{ Zoo} \rightarrow 1 \text{ Bot}$$

(Note that although the rule says "at most one zoologist", you know that means "exactly one botanist" because the introductory paragraph requires at least one scientist from each group.)

Rule 3: F and K cannot both be selected:

$$F \rightarrow No \ k$$
$$k \rightarrow No \ F$$
$$(Never \ Fk)$$

Rule 4: K and M cannot both be selected:

$$k \rightarrow \text{No } m$$
$$m \rightarrow \text{No } k$$
$$(\text{Never km})$$

Rule 5: If M is selected, both P and R must be selected:

$$m \rightarrow p + r$$
$$\text{No } p \text{ or No } r \rightarrow \text{No } m$$

Step 4: Deduction

With the exception of Rule 1, everything here is conditional, and you should already have worked out the number combinations. There's no big deduction to be had, so move right on to working the questions.

Step 5: Questions

1.   C

A standard acceptability question: just work the rules. Rules 1 and 2 don't help you, but Rule 3 eliminates answer choice (A), which combines F and k. Rule 4 eliminates both (B) and (D), since both place k and m together. Rule 5 knocks out (E), which includes m but not *r*. That leaves only correct answer choice (C).

2.   E

If m is the only Chemist, then you know which number combination you're working with: Rule 2 doesn't allow for a 2:2 split between the Botanists and the Zoologists. So you'll need three of one and one of the other. Selecting m also means that both *p* and *r* are selected; that's two Zoologists, so you'll need the third (*q*) as well—and that's correct answer choice (E).

3.   E

Create a new sketch and incorporate the new information:

Bot	Chem	Zoo
(F) G H	k (l) m	p̶ (q) (r)

Now, apply the rules to find additional information. For instance, Rule 1 tells you that if F is chosen, k cannot be. Cross out k. You also know that if m were chosen, both *p* and *r* would have to be chosen—but that would be six scientists, and you can only select five. So, you can eliminate both k and m as possibilities.

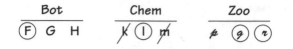

That means only one Chemist is chosen, which means either three Botanists and one Zoologist or vice versa. But you've already got two Zoologists, so you must select the third (*p*) as well.

4. D

Create a new sketch and apply the rules. If *p* is the only Zoologist chosen, that means *q* and *r* are not chosen. The contrapositive of Rule 5 tells us that if *r* isn't selected, m can't be selected. That leaves three Botanists and two Chemists from whom to choose your remaining four panelists, in either a 2:2 or 3:1 split.

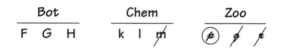

If/then answer choices are usually time-consuming, but you have a lot of information to work with. There's no reason that k and G cannot be selected together, nor l and F. There's also no reason that l can't be selected along with all three Botanists. Answer choice (D) is the first to veer away from concrete entities—whenever possible, turn the general concrete. "If exactly two chemists are selected", who will they be? K and l, of course. They're the only Chemists available. The selection of k triggers Rule 1, which says that k and F can't be together—so answer choice (D) is correct.

5. A

G and H are both Botanists, so you know that you can only select one Zoologist. That means either three Botanists and a Chemist or two Botanists and two Chemists, with F, k, l and m to choose among. Those entities bring two rules into play. First, Rule 3 says no F and k. And Rule 5 takes m out of the running, since m would require additional Zoologists. Since F and k can't be chosen together, you've got two choices: FGHl plus a Zoologist or GHkl plus a Zoologist. Each of these possibilities includes either F or k, so answer choice (A) is correct.

PRACTICE SETS

<u>Directions:</u> Each group of questions is based on a set of conditions. It may be useful to draw a rough diagram to answer some questions. Choose the response that most accurately and completely answers each question.

Game 4

<u>Questions 1–5</u>

The organizer of a reading club will select at least five and at most six works from a group of nine works. The group consists of three French novels, three Russian novels, two French plays, and one Russian play. The organizer's selection of works must conform to the following requirements:

> No more than four French works are selected.
>
> At least three but no more than four novels are selected.
>
> At least as many French novels as Russian novels are selected.
>
> If both French plays are selected, then the Russian play is not selected.

1. Which one of the following could be the organizer's selection of works?

    (A) one French novel, two Russian novels, one French play, one Russian play

    (B) two French novels, one Russian novel, two French plays one Russian play

    (C) two French novels, two Russian novels, two French plays

    (D) three French novels, one Russian novel, two French plays

    (E) three French novels, two Russian novels, one Russian play

2. Which one of the following could be true about the organizer's selection of works?

    (A) No Russian novels are selected.

    (B) Exactly one French novel is selected.

    (C) All three plays are selected.

    (D) All three Russian novels are selected.

    (E) All five French works are selected.

3. If the works selected include three French novels, which one of the following could be a complete and accurate list of the remaining works selected?

    (A) one Russian novel

    (B) two French plays

    (C) one Russian novel, one Russian play

    (D) one Russian novel, two French plays

    (E) two Russian novels, one French play

4. The organizer must at least select

    (A) one French novel and one French play

    (B) one French novel and one Russian play

    (C) one Russian novel and one French play

    (D) two French novels

    (E) two Russian novels

5. Any one of the following could be true about the organizer's selections of works EXCEPT:

    (A) No Russian novels and exactly one play are selected.

    (B) Exactly one Russian novel and both French plays are selected.

    (C) Exactly two French novels and the Russian play are selected.

    (D) Exactly two French novels and exactly two plays are selected.

    (E) Exactly two Russian novels and exactly one play are selected.

Game 5

<u>Questions 1–6</u>
A park contains at most five of seven kinds of trees—
a firs, laurels, maples, oaks, pines, spruces, and yews—
consistent with the following conditions:

> If maples are in the park, yews are not.
>
> If firs are in the park, pines are not.
>
> If yews are not in the park, then either laurels or oaks, but not both, are in the park.
>
> If it is not the case that the park contains both laurels and oaks, then it contains firs and spruces.

1. Which one of the following could be a complete and accurate list of the kinds of trees in the park?

    (A) firs, maples
    (B) firs, laurels, oaks
    (C) firs, laurels, pines, spruces
    (D) firs, laurels, spruces, yews
    (E) firs, maples, oaks, spruces, yews

2. If neither maples nor spruces are in the park, then which one of the following could be true?

    (A) Exactly four kinds of trees are in the park.
    (B) Exactly five kinds of trees are in the park.
    (C) Laurels are not in the park.
    (D) Oaks are not in the park.
    (E) Yews are not in the park.

3. Which one of the following could be true?

    (A) Neither firs nor laurels are in the park.
    (B) Neither laurels, oaks, nor yews are in the park.
    (C) Neither laurels nor spruces are in the park.
    (D) Neither maples nor yews are in the park.
    (E) Neither oaks nor spruces are in the park.

4. If firs are not in the park, then which one of the following must be true?

    (A) Maples are not in the park.
    (B) Spruces are not in the park
    (C) Yews are not in the park.
    (D) Pines are in the park.
    (E) Spruces are in the park.

5. If pines are in the park, then which one of the following must be true?

    (A) Exactly four kinds of trees are in the park.
    (B) Exactly five kinds of trees are in the park.
    (C) Neither firs nor maples are in the park.
    (D) Neither firs nor oaks are in the park.
    (E) Neither laurels nor maples are in the park.

6. Each of the following could be an accurate, partial list of the kinds of trees in the park EXCEPT:

    (A) oaks, spruces.
    (B) oaks, yews.
    (C) firs, laurels, oaks.
    (D) firs, maples, oaks.
    (E) laurels, maples, oaks.

Game 6

<u>Questions 1–5</u>
This morning, a bakery makes exactly one delivery, consisting of exactly six loaves of bread. Each of the loaves is exactly one of three kinds: oatmeal, rye, or wheat, and each is either sliced or unsliced. The loaves that the bakery delivers this morning must be consistent with the following:

> There are at least two kinds of loaves.
>
> There are no more than three rye loaves.
>
> There is no unsliced wheat loaf.
>
> There is at least one unsliced oatmeal loaf.
>
> If two or more of the loaves are unsliced, then at least one of the unsliced loaves is rye.

1. Which one of the following could be a complete and accurate list of the loaves that the bakery delivers?

    (A) six unsliced oatmeal loaves
    (B) five unsliced oatmeal loaves, one sliced rye loaf
    (C) five unsliced oatmeal loaves, one unsliced wheat loaf
    (D) four unsliced oatmeal loaves, two unsliced rye loaves
    (E) four unsliced oatmeal loaves, two sliced wheat loaves

2. Each of the following could be a complete and accurate list of the unsliced loaves that the bakery delivers EXCEPT:

    (A) three oatmeal loaves.
    (B) three oatmeal loaves, one rye loaf.
    (C) two oatmeal loaves, two rye loaves.
    (D) two oatmeal loaves, three rye loaves.
    (E) one oatmeal loaf, one rye loaf.

3. Which one of the following statements CANNOT be true?

    (A) The only unsliced loaves are oatmeal loaves.
    (B) The only sliced loaves are rye loaves.
    (C) The only unsliced loaves are rye loaves.
    (D) The number of sliced loaves is exactly one greater than the number of sliced oatmeal loaves.
    (E) The number of unsliced loaves is exactly one greater than the number of unsliced oatmeal loaves.

4. Which one of the following statements must be true?

    (A) At least one of the loaves is rye.
    (B) At least one of the loaves is wheat.
    (C) At least one of the loaves is sliced.
    (D) No more than four oatmeal loaves are sliced.
    (E) No more than four wheat loaves are sliced.

5. If the bakery delivers exactly four wheat loaves, then the bakery could also deliver

    (A) one sliced rye loaf and one unsliced rye loaf.
    (B) one sliced oatmeal loaf and one unsliced oatmeal loaf.
    (C) two unsliced rye loaves.
    (D) two unsliced oatmeal loaves.
    (E) two sliced oatmeal loaves.

Use this space for scratch work

Use this space for scratch work

Game 4: Answers and Explanations

Step 1: Overview

Situation: Organizing a reading club.

Entities: French and Russian novels and plays.

Action: The works being read must be selected.

Limitations: This game is all about numbers—specifically, about making vague arithmetic assertions concrete. Note that the opening paragraph tells you, as well, that you will pick at least 5, but no more than 6, of the books.

Step 2: Sketch

Remember that for a selection game, the sketch is just a list of the entities. Make the novels capital letters and the plays in lower case, so your sketch will simply be:

$$\text{F F F R R R f f r}$$

Step 3: Rules

Rule 1 says that you can choose at most four French works. This means, of course, that at least one Russian work must be chosen (two Russian works if we pick six of the entities). Either way, at most four F's and f's.

Rule 2 requires you to select three or four novels (and thus between 1 and 3 plays). Jot this down as well.

Rule 3 indicates that there are at least as many French works as Russian. It might be easiest to use mathematical notation to shorthand this rule.

Rule 4, though written as a Formal Logic rule, actually indicates that all three plays can never be picked—if both French plays are chosen, the Russian play can't be. Thus, the easiest way to add this information is to eliminate the possibility of all three plays.

$$\text{F F F R R R f f r}$$
pick 5 or 6
at most 4 F/f
3 or 4 novels
1-2 plays
F/f ≥ R/r

Step 4: Deductions

There's not a lot to go on here. One Russian work must be chosen, but it could be a play or a novel. At least three novels are chosen, but they could be all French or all Russian. Thus, it's time to move on to the questions.

Step 5: Questions

1. C

A proper selection of works cannot include more than four French works—but (D) does. It cannot include more than four novels of any type—but (E) does. It cannot let the Russian novels outnumber the French ones, yet they do in (A). And it cannot include all three plays, as (B) does. Through this process of eliminating the losers, the winner—(C), in this case—is quickly revealed.

2. A

The correct answer *could* be true, meaning the four wrong choices cannot be true, and your best bet here is either to try out each choice until you find the winner, or skip the question for now. The former option works out well here, because we discern (A) as possible right away. If no Russian novels are selected, we can still get an acceptable group like so: F F F f r. Having seen that as possible, we can quickly ascertain the problems with the others because they violate rules almost as quickly as the wrong answers in a standard Acceptability question:

(B) Choosing one French novel means choosing one Russian one (Rule 3), so we couldn't meet the quota of three novels mandated by Rule 2. At this point we might notice that F F will be part of every acceptable group; how much more pleasant to notice it this way, in passing, then to agonize it out of the original rules.

(C) is forbidden by Rule 4, as we have already noted.

(D) Choosing R R R would also mean choosing F F F (Rule 3), a violation of Rule 3.

(E) is a blatant violation of Rule 1.

3. C

In a new roster for this question you could circle F F F and build from there, realizing that either we choose zero or one R's (two is impossible, given Rule 2). Or you could put the rules up against the choices, Acceptability-style, and realize that:

(A) involves a total of four works, unacceptable; the total must be five or six.

(B), **(D)** each account for a total of five French works, a violation of Rule 1.

(E) means a total of five novels, a violation of Rule 2.

But **(C)** is O.K. in all particulars, an acceptable total of five and no rule violations.

4. D

The very appearance of this question might have suggested to you, at the outset, that there's at least one fact about the selection process that is inferable from the rules alone. But whether you worked it out up front or now, when question 10 came along, the fact is that we can never choose fewer than two French novels, as correct choice (D) states. How come? Because to choose a single French novel would restrict us to a single Russian novel (Rule 3), and that plus Rule 4 would ensure that we could never meet our quota of five works mandated in the opening para. At most we'd be restricted to four: the French novel, the Russian novel, and two plays. In order to meet the requirement of five works minimum, we must choose at least two French novels at all times. And if you look back over the first three questions, we've done just that all along.

(A), (B), (C), (E) Speaking of looking back, notice that the correct answer to question 9 proves that neither (A) nor (C) nor (E) has to be part of any acceptable group. And question 7's correct answer (C) knocks out this question's (B) and (C) all by itself.

5.   A

Four of the five choices are acceptable, and one is not, meaning that one of these schoices violates a rule. Now that you undoubtedly know this game's rules so well, the quickest approach might be to use your pencil to work out each choice. Doing so reveals (A) right off. If, in line with (A)'s dictates, you list the nine entities and cross off all the R's while circling only one lower-case letter, you should realize very quickly that you're stuck. At best you can have a total of four—the three French novels and the one play. But that won't cut it, so (A) is correct.

(B), (D) If the group consists of F F R f f, we have violated no rules and proven that both (B) and (D) are possible.

(C) A group of F F R R r proves that both (C) and (E) are possible.

Game 5: Answers and Explanations

Step 1: Overview

Situation: A park.

Entities: Trees in the park—firs, laurels, maples, oaks, pines, spruces, and yews.

Actions: Selecting which trees will go in the park.

Limitations: At most five of the trees will be selected.

Step 2: Sketch

Once again, a simple roster of the entities, with a reminder to pick at most 5, will suffice.

at most 5

F L M O P S Y

Step 3: Rules

Rule 1 gives us a pair of entities that are mutually exclusive: maples and yews. Easier than writing the "if/then" statement and contrapositive is simply stating "never MY."

Rule 2 creates another mutually exclusive pair of trees—firs and pines.

Rule 3 is a bit more complicated, and a good argument for always thinking in complete sentences. If yews are not in the forest, either laurels or oaks (but not both laurels and oaks) are in the park. We can translate the rule as "if no Y, then L or O but not LO." Keep thinking in complete sentences. The contrapositive is a bit complicated, but says if both laurels and oaks are in the forest, or if neither laurels nor oaks are in the forest, yews must be.

Rule 4 also requires us to decipher more difficult Formal Logic statements. Be careful translating the trigger of this rule: "if it is not the case that the park contains both laurels and oaks," which really means, "if the park is missing either laurels or oaks." If we're missing either, we must have firs and spruces. If we're missing either firs or spruces, we must have laurels and oaks. So, you must have either the pair of laurels and oaks, or the pair of firs and spruces (or both pairs even).

at most 5

F L M O P S Y

never MY
never FP
no Y → L or O, but not LO
LO or no L and no O → Y
FS or LO

Step 4: Deductions

Notice that you figured out that either firs and spruces or laurels and oaks were selected. That means the game breaks down one of two ways—and knowing that we have either pair would lead to further deductions. The game is ripe for limited options.

Create two sketches. In Option 1, select firs and spruces; in Option 2, laurels and oaks. Let's look at Option 1 first. If you select firs, you can't select pines. Add this to your sketch. In Option 2, selecting laurels and oaks means yews are selected…which means maples cannot be.

Ⓕ L M O P̶ Ⓢ Y   **at most 5**   F Ⓛ M̶ Ⓞ P S Ⓨ
                         never MY
                         never FP
                no Y → L or O but not LO
              LO or no L and no O → Y

Notice that by using limited options, each sketch is almost half complete; not bad before having even started the questions!

Step 5: Questions

1. D

We can treat this first question just like any Acceptability question, eliminating wrong answer choices because they violate a rule. This is because a complete and accurate list of trees selected must follow all the rules, just like the answer to an Acceptability question, while the wrong answers will violate at least one rule each.

Rule 1 eliminates (E), which selects both maples and yews. Rule 2 eliminates (C), which selects firs and pines together. Rule 3 eliminates (A) and (B), which both do not select yews; (A) selects neither laurels nor oaks, and (B) selects both laurels and oaks, both of which violate the trigger of this rule. (D) remains, and is correct.

2. A

Here, "neither maples nor spruces" points us to Option I. We know by looking back at our Master Sketch that rejecting spruces means that we must select laurels oaks, and yews:

$$\text{F} \;\textcircled{L}\; \text{M}\!\!\!\!/\; \textcircled{O}\; \text{P}\,\text{S}\!\!\!/\; \textcircled{Y}$$

We can't be sure whether firs or pines are selected, but at most one of them could be. Rule 2 tells us that both firs and pines cannot be selected. If one or the other of these two is selected, then four trees could be selected. Thus, (A) is correct.

(B) cannot be true. Once maples and spruces are eliminated, we cannot select the five remaining kinds of trees without violating Rule 2.

(C) and (D) cannot be true. Rule four tells us that laurels and oaks must be selected if spruces are not.

(E) cannot be true. We deduced in Option I that once spruces are rejected, yews must be selected.

3. D

Without an "if" clause to guide our work, we'll have to use trial and error to find the correct answer. Ordinarily, this process would be time-consuming and lead you to skip this question, but our options will make it quick.

(A) cannot be true in either option. We must have either firs (Option II) or laurels (Option I). Eliminate.

(B) cannot be true in either option. It's not quite as quickly eliminated as the others, since at first glance Option II doesn't have laurels, oaks, or yews; but the Rule 3 tells us that if yews are not selected, then either laurels or oaks must be. Eliminate.

(C) cannot be true in either option. We must select either laurels (in Option I) or spruces (in Option II). Eliminate.

(D) could be true. Rejecting yews puts us in Option II, and Rule 3 tells us we must also reject either laurels or oaks. There is no reason we couldn't also reject maples. (D) is correct. For the record:

(E) cannot be true in either option. We must either

select oaks (in Option I) or spruces (In Option II).

4. A

Knowing that firs are not in the park tells us that we must be in Option I. Even if we hadn't drawn out our Limited Options, "no firs" would trigger the contrapositive of Rule 4. Thus, we also know that the park must contain laurels and oaks, which means that it also must contain yews (Rule 3), but no maples (Rule 1). We can quickly see that (A) must be true, and is correct.

(B) and (E) could be false. Don't assume that firs and spruces are always together, whether they are in the park or outside it. Rule 4 only links these two entities when it is triggered—in other words, when either laurels or oaks are not in the park. We can't be certain whether or not spruces are in the park in this question.

(C) is false. If firs are not in the park, then yews must be. Read carefully to avoid being trapped by answer choices that are the opposite of what you should be looking for.

(D) could be false. This choice negates Rule 2 without reversing it, a classic formal logic error.

5.   C

The LSAT often includes rules that only apply to one or two situations in a game, then waits to test those rules until later questions. The test makers hope that examinees will forget about the rule they haven't used, and waste time on this question because of it. This game is no exception. We haven't really been forced to use Rule 2 since the Acceptability question, and it would have been easy to forget about it until now. A quick skim of the rules after every question or two will help you avoid this trap.

According to Rule 2, if pines are in the park, firs are not. Thus, laurels and oaks are both in the forest (Rule 4). This tells us that yews are in the forest (Rule 3), and that maples are not (Rule 1). The only type of tree that we can't definitely place is spruces: they could be in the park, or not. Only (C) must be true, and is correct.

(A) and (B) both could be true, but need not be, depending on whether or not spruces are in the park.

(D) must be false. Firs are not in the forest, but oaks definitely are.

(E) must be false. Maples are not in the forest, but laurels are.

6.   E

Four of the choices in this question are accurate partial lists of the trees in the park. In other words, four of the answer choices do *not* violate any rules. The correct answer is *not* an accurate partial list, which means that it must violate some rule. We should run through the choices to see if any of them violate the rules of the game. We can also use our previous work to eliminate choices: if we have seen any of the partial lists in a previous question, we can eliminate that choice.

(A) and (B) We saw that oaks and spruces or oaks and yews could be partial lists in Question 11. Eliminate these choices.

(C) If laurels and oaks are both in the park, then according to Rule 3, yews must also be in the park. This would mean that maples are not in the park, but it wouldn't tell us anything about whether or not firs are in the park. (C) doesn't violate any of the rules. Eliminate it, and move on.

(D) The only thing in (D) that will immediately trigger a rule is maples; Rule 1 tells us that if maples are in the forest, then yews are not. This also triggers Rule 3; if yews are not in the park, then either laurels or oaks are also in the park (but not both). According to (D), oaks are in the park, so laurels must not be. This would also trigger Rule 4, so that both firs and spruces must be in the park. Firs are in (D), so this choice follows the rules. Eliminate.

(E) must be correct, since it's the only one left! But let's see why. If maples are in the park, then yews are not (Rule 1); and according to Rule 3, if yews are not in the park, then both laurels and oaks cannot be. (E) violates this combination of rules, so it is not an accurate partial list.

Game 6: Answers and Explanations

Step 1: Overview

Situation: Baking loaves of bread.

Entities: Oatmeal, rye, and wheat; and sliced or unsliced.

Action: Selecting the loaves baked.

Limitation: Exactly six loaves will be baked.

Step 2: Sketch

Write out the possible types of loaves to create your entity list; You'll circle the loaves selected and cross out the loaves rejected. If you select multiple loaves of a particular type, you'll write that in above the loaf type.

6 total

OS Ou rs ru WS Wu

Step 3: Rules

Rule 1 indicates that at least two different kinds of loaves are made. Thus you can't have all oatmeal, or all rye, or all wheat. This rule is perhaps best marked in the test booklet, as it's difficult to shorthand.

Rule 2 caps the rye loaves at three. This means there must be at least three oatmeal and wheat loaves as well.

Rule 3 eliminates the unsliced wheat loaves.

Rule 4 indicates that unsliced oatmeal must be selected, just leaving the question of how many unsliced oatmeal loaves will be baked.

Rule 5 says that if there are two or more unsliced loaves, one of them must be unsliced rye (i.e., unsliced rye must be selected). The contrapositive? That if unsliced rye is not selected, there are less than two unsliced loaves.

6 total

OS (Ou) rs ru WS W̶u̶

at most 3

2t u → (ru)

r̶u̶ → u, 1 u

Step 4: Deductions

Remember that unsliced oatmeal is definitely selected, so it's impossible to select no unsliced oatmeal, thus if unsliced rye is not selected, there's only one unsliced loaf, and it's the oatmeal unsliced. There's nothing else definite to pin down, however, making it time to move on to the questions.

Step 5: Questions

1. D

As it turns out, Rule 5 eliminates all the wrong choices, but if you tackled the rules in order, here's what you would have found: Rule 1 kills (A), which has only oatmeal loaves. Rule 2 doesn't help, but Rule 3 kills (C), which has the forbidden unsliced wheat loaf. Rule 4 doesn't help, but Rule 5 knocks off (B) and (E), which each have two or more unsliced loaves but no unsliced rye loaf.

2. A

The reference to unsliced loaves should point you to Rules 3, 4, and 5. Each choice has at least one unsliced oatmeal loaf, and there's no unsliced wheat loaf among the choices, but (A) is a straightforward violation of Rule 5. With more than one unsliced loaf, (A) needs to have an unsliced rye loaf as well, but it isn't there. So (A) can't be a complete and accurate list of the unsliced loaves.

3. C

This one has to be handled choice by choice:

(A) is a little complicated. If the only unsliced loaves are oatmeal loaves, then only one loaf is unsliced (Rules 4 and 5). Could the other five be sliced? Sure, they could all be sliced wheat loaves, or some combination of sliced wheat and sliced rye, as long as we don't have more than three rye loaves. So (A) is possible.

(B) If the only sliced loaves are rye, then there's no wheat loaves at all (Rule 3). Can we still make an acceptable arrangement? Sure. We could, for example, have three unsliced oatmeal, one unsliced rye, and two sliced rye loaves.

(C) is a straightforward violation of Rule 4, so it's our answer. There's no need to check the other choices, but for the record:

(D) Yes, we could (for example) have no sliced oatmeal loaves, one sliced wheat loaf, two unsliced oatmeal loaves and three unsliced rye loaves.

(E) Yes, we could (for example) have one unsliced oatmeal loaf, one unsliced rye loaf, and four sliced wheat loaves.

4. D

This is another one that must be checked choice by choice, but you can (and should!) do so strategically. The best place to start is with the correct choice for Acceptability question 1: There we saw that we could have all unsliced loaves, and no wheat loaves, which proves that neither (B) nor (C) must be true.

(A), (E) We could have one unsliced oatmeal loaf and five sliced wheat loaves, so neither (A) nor (E) must be true.

(D) is therefore our winner: If we had more than four sliced oatmeal loaves—say five—then all six loaves would be oatmeal when we added in Rule 4's unsliced oatmeal loaf. A delivery consisting only of oatmeal loaves would violate Rule 1.

5. B

If four wheat loaves are delivered, then those wheat loaves are sliced (Rule 3). One unsliced oatmeal loaf is always included, and that kills (A), (C), and (E). So what could the sixth loaf be? It can't be an unsliced oatmeal, since that would violate Rule 5. That kills (D). So (B) must be correct. The sixth loaf could be a sliced oatmeal loaf.

Chapter 7: **Distribution Games**

In grouping games of **distribution**, you're concerned with who goes where, rather than who's chosen and who isn't. Sometimes, every entity will end up in a group—like placing eight marbles into two jars, four to a jar. Or a game might mandate the placement of three marbles in each jar, leaving two marbles out in the cold.

It's important to be aware of the numbers that govern each particular game, because although all grouping games rely on the same general skills, you have to adapt these skills to the specific situation. Like sequencing games, grouping games have a language all their own, and it's up to you to speak that language fluently.

To get started, work through Game 1.

GAME 1: THE METHOD

By this time, you should always make your own sketch and draw your own inferences based on the stimulus and rules before reading further. Respond to each question on your own, following Kaplan's Method, before continuing through the explanations below them. However, since the work done on one question may help on another, it's still useful in this first distribution game to make sure you understand each question and its explanation before moving on to the next.

Questions 1–5

In a certain recipe contest, each contestant submits two recipes, one for an appetizer and one for a main dish. Together the two recipes must include exactly seven flavorings—fenugreek, ginger, lemongrass, nutmeg, paprika, saffron, and turmeric—with no flavoring included in more than one of the two recipes. Each contestant's recipes must satisfy the following conditions:

The appetizer recipe includes at most three of the flavorings.

Fenugreek is not included in the same recipe as nutmeg.

Saffron is not included in the same recipe as turmeric.

Ginger is included in the same recipe as nutmeg.

Step 1: Overview

Situation: Submitting two recipes for a recipe contest.

Entities: Two recipes—appetizer and main dish—and seven flavorings: F, G, L, N, P, S, and T.

Action: Distribution—all seven flavorings must be included in one of two recipes.

Limitations: Each flavoring is to be used in exactly one of the two recipes.

Step 2: Sketch

No fancy sketch work here. It's always good to list the entities first to keep track of them. Then, under the list, make two headings, one for the appetizer and one for the main dish. You'll use these headings to track the distribution of flavorings to recipes.

F G L N P S T

Appetizer   Main Dish

Step 3: Rules

Here are the issues involved in grouping games of distribution—along with the rules that govern them. These rules refer to a scenario in which the members of another group of eight entities—Q, R, S, T, W, X, Y, Z—have to be distributed into three different classes:

Typical Issues—Grouping Games of Distribution

Issue	Wording of Rule
Which entities are concretely placed in a particular subgroup?	X is placed in Class 3.
Which entities are barred from a particular subgroup?	Y is not placed in Class 2.
Which entities must be placed in the same subgroup?	X is placed in the same class as Z.
Which entities cannot be placed in the same subgroup?	X is not placed in the same class as Y. Y is not placed in the same class as X. X and Y are not placed in the same class.
Which entity's placement depends on the placement of another entity?	If Y is placed in Class 1, then Q is placed in Class 2.

Rule 1: The appetizer recipe includes at most three of the flavorings. We'll consider this rule more closely in Deduction, but for now note that if the appetizer has a maximum of three flavorings, then the main dish has a minimum of four flavorings (remember that all seven flavorings must be used).

Rule 2: Fenugreek is not included in the same recipe as nutmeg. Use a big NO to help you remember this rule:

NO FN

Rule 3: Saffron is not included in the same recipe as turmeric. Identical situation as Rule 2:

NO ST

Rule 4: Ginger is included in the same recipe as nutmeg. You can use a block to note this rule:

G N

Step 4: Deduction

Since F and N can never be in the same recipe, and since S and T can never be in the same recipe, we know that each recipe must have one of F and N and one of S and T. Putting "F/N" and "S/T" under each recipe will be a great visual reminder of this deduction. Next, you can take advantage of the fact that nutmeg appears in Rules 2 and 4. Since F is never with N, and G is always with N, F can never be with G. This means that one recipe will have F, and the other will have G and N.

Review the numbers one more time before going to the questions. Number limitations figure prominently in Grouping Games of Distribution, and this one is no different. Since each recipe has one of the F/N pair and one of the S/T pair, the appetizer must include at least two flavorings. Remember that Rule 1 also tells us that the appetizer can include no more than three flavorings. This means that the main dish, which already has a minimum of four flavorings, now also has a maximum of five. Note this in the sketch:

F G L N P S T

2–3	4–5
<u>Appetizer</u>	<u>Main Dish</u>
F/GN	F/GN
S/T	S/T

Notice that the rules seemed very vague initially. But finding the positive implications of negatively phrased rules like Rules 2 and 3 helps crack open big deductions. Now you're ready for the questions.

Step 5: Questions

1. Which one of the following could be a complete and accurate list of the flavorings included in one contestant's main-dish recipe?

    (A) fenugreek, lemongrass, saffron
    (B) fenugreek, ginger, nutmeg, turmeric
    (C) ginger, lemongrass, nutmeg, paprika
    (D) ginger, nutmeg, paprika, turmeric
    (E) lemongrass, nutmeg, saffron, turmeric

Think of this as a "partial acceptability" question, which allows you to use the rules to eliminate answer choices. Use your deductions to zip through these answer choices even more quickly. You already know that the main dish has to include four or five flavorings. You can therefore eliminate choice (A), which only includes three. Next, turn your attention to the flavorings themselves. You know that each recipe has to include exactly one of the F/N pair and exactly one of the S/T pair. Choice (C) has neither saffron nor turmeric, and choice (E) has both of them, so those can be eliminated as well. Choice (B) violates Rule 2 by including both F and N, so only choice (D) is left.

2. If a contestant's appetizer recipe does not include fenugreek, then the contestant's appetizer recipe must include

    (A) ginger.
    (B) lemongrass.
    (C) paprika.
    (D) saffron.
    (E) turmeric.

With new "if" questions, your instinct should be to redraw your master sketch. Don't think you will be saving time by skipping this redrawing. If you don't redraw, you will waste time trying to figure out what is "master sketch" info and what is only good for the question you just finished.

But some questions are easy enough that they don't require redrawing. Use your deduction to make short work of this question. We know from the final sketch that a recipe not including F must include N. We don't see N in the answer choices, but knowing that G must always be with N makes choice (A) automatically correct.

3. Which one of the following could be a list of all the flavorings included in one contestant's appetizer recipe?

    (A) fenugreek, saffron
    (B) ginger, nutmeg
    (C) fenugreek, nutmeg, turmeric
    (D) lemongrass, nutmeg, saffron
    (E) fenugreek, lemongrass, paprika, turmeric

Another partial acceptability question. Again, start with the numbers. Since the appetizer recipe must include two or three flavorings, (E) can be eliminated quickly. Then follow the same process as you did for Question 1: the F/N and

S/T pairs must each have one representative in each recipe. Choice (B) leaves out both S and T. Finally, choices (C) and (D) each leave out G, which you know must always be included with N. This leaves choice (A) as the correct answer.

4. If a contestant includes lemongrass in the same recipe as paprika, which one of the following is a flavoring that must be included in the contestant's main-dish recipe?

(A) ginger
(B) lemongrass
(C) nutmeg
(D) saffron
(E) turmeric

You have to place L and P now. But the question doesn't tell you which recipe includes them. You only know that they are to be included in the same recipe. Once again, your number deduction is going to hand you the answer here. Each recipe must include one of the F/N pair and one of the S/T pair. So each recipe has those two flavorings to start. Add in L and P and you're already up to four flavorings. Looking at the number limitations, you know that's too many flavorings for the appetizer. So L and P must be included in the main dish. This makes choice (B) correct.

5. If the condition that requires ginger to be included in the same recipe as nutmeg is suspended but all of the other original conditions remain in effect, then which one of the following could be a list of all of the flavorings included in one contestant's main-dish recipe?

(A) ginger, lemongrass, nutmeg, paprika
(B) ginger, lemongrass, paprika, turmeric
(C) fenugreek, ginger, lemongrass, paprika, saffron
(D) fenugreek, ginger, lemongrass, saffron, turmeric
(E) fenugreek, lemongrass, nutmeg, paprika, saffron

A rule change: Rule 4 is eliminated. Normally, rule changes make questions difficult and time-consuming, since they force you to re-evaluate your deductions. However, it's not as difficult here—just revise the sketch so that G and N are no longer in a block:

2–3	4–5
Appetizer	Main Dish
F/N	F/N
S/T	S/T

From here, check the rules as you would for any other acceptability question. Rule 1 doesn't eliminate any choices, since there aren't any main-dish recipes in the choices with three or fewer flavorings. Rule 2 eliminates (E), which has both F and N, and (B), which has neither and would therefore force FN into the appetizer. Rule 3 eliminates (D), which has both S and T, and (A), which has neither and would therefore force ST into the appetizer. (C) remains and is correct.

GAME 2: PRACTICE

Now that you're familiar with the issues you'll face in distribution games, try the following one on your own, using the extra space we've provided for your sketches and notes. By this time, you should be doing all practice games under timed conditions, so allow youself no more than 10 minutes.

Questions 1–6

Seven job applicants—Feng, Garcia, Herrera, Ilias, Weiss, Xavier, and Yates—are hired to fill seven new positions at Chroma, Inc. One position is in the management department, three are in the production department, and three are in the sales department. The following conditions must apply:

Herrera is hired for a position in the same department as Yates.

Feng is hired for a position in a different department from Garcia.

If Xavier is hired for a sales position, then Weiss is hired for a production position.

Feng is hired for a production position.

1. Which one of the following could be a complete and accurate matching of the applicants with the departments in which they were hired?

    (A) management: Weiss; production: Feng, Herrera, Yates; sales: Garcia, Ilias, Xavier

    (B) management: Weiss; production: Garcia, Ilias, Xavier; sales: Feng, Herrera, Yates

    (C) management: Xavier; production: Feng, Garcia, Herrera; sales: Ilias, Weiss, Yates

    (D) management: Xavier; production: Feng, Herrera, Ilias; sales: Garcia, Weiss, Yates

    (E) management: Xavier; production: Feng, Ilias, Weiss; sales: Garcia, Herrera, Yates

2. Which one of the following is a complete and accurate list of the applicants, each of whom CANNOT be hired for a production position?

    (A) Feng, Ilias, Xavier

    (B) Garcia, Herrera, Yates

    (C) Herrera, Yates

    (D) Garcia

    (E) Ilias

3. It can be determined in which department each of the seven applicants is hired if which one of the following statements is true?

    (A) Feng and Weiss are both hired for production positions.

    (B) Garcia and Yates are both hired for sales positions.

    (C) Ilias and Weiss are both hired for sales positions.

    (D) Ilias and Weiss are both hired for production positions.

    (E) Ilias and Xavier are both hired for production positions.

4. Each of the following could be an accurate partial list of the applicants hired for sales positions EXCEPT:

    (A) Garcia, Ilias.

    (B) Garcia, Xavier.

    (C) Garcia, Yates.

    (D) Herrera, Weiss.

    (E) Herrera, Xavier.

5. If Feng is hired for a position in the same department as Xavier, then each of the following could be true EXCEPT:

    (A) Garcia is hired for a sales position.

    (B) Herrera is hired for a production position.

    (C) Ilias is hired for a sales position.

    (D) Weiss is hired for the management position.

    (E) Weiss is hired a production position.

6. If Xavier is not hired for one of the production positions, then which one of the following could be true?

    (A) Feng and Herrera are both hired for sales positions.

    (B) Herrera and Weiss are both hired for sales positions.

    (C) Feng and Yates are both hired for production positions.

    (D) Garcia and Weiss are both hired for production positions.

    (E) Herrera and Weiss are both hired for production positions.

Use this space for scratch work

Use this space for scratch work

Use this space for scratch work

Game 2 Answers and Explanations

Step 1: Overview

Situation: Hiring new employees at Chroma, Inc.

Entities: Seven applicants and three types of positions.

Action: To distribute the applicants into groups based on department.

Limitations: The distribution of applicants is 1/3/3 for management/production/sales.

Step 2: Sketch

Use the standard sketch for a distribution game. You have the exact number distribution, so you can draw in the appropriate number of slots for each department. Don't forget to list the applicants, too.

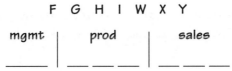

Step 3: Rules

Rule 1 tells us that we will place H + Y together in the same department (production or sales, of course), while Rule 2 tells us never to have F and G together. Notes off to the side can act as reminders of both:

Rule 3, like any if/then rule, needs to be understood as both itself and its contrapositive. Should we place X in the sales department, we must place W in production. And should W be somewhere other than production, X cannot be placed in sales.

$$X \text{ in sales} \rightarrow W \text{ in prod}$$

$$W \text{ not in prod} \rightarrow X \text{ not in sales}$$

Rule 4 can be built right into the master sketch. If F must be in production, you can fill up one of the production slots right away.

KAPLAN

Step 4: Deduction

The key to good deduction is combining rules to push the data to the definite, and this game is no exception. You can combine the most definite rule here, Rule 4, with Rule 1 to plug more entities into the sketch. Since H and Y must be in the same department, you know they can't be in management—there simply isn't room. The H/Y pair must therefore either be hired for production or sales positions. Sketch out the possibilities:

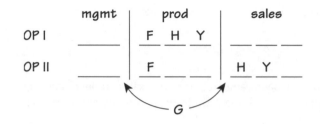

And it turns out that there's one more deduction you can make for the first option. If you incorporate Rule 3 and its contrapositive, you can deduce that since W is not going to production (there's no room left), X is not going to sales. The only place left for X is management, leaving W, G, and I for the three sales positions. Now the first option is complete:

	mgmt	prod	sales
OP I	X	F H Y	W G I

Step 5: Questions

1. E

Compare the rules to the choices. Rule 1 is violated by (C) and (D), each of which separates H and Y. Rule 2 is violated by (C), although we threw out that choice already. Rule 3 knocks out (A), which has X in sales and hence should have W in production, but doesn't. Rule 4 allows us to throw out (B). F must be in production, not sales. (E), the only non-violator, is correct.

2. D

This one can be approached in several ways, but the simplest is to check the master sketch to see that given F in production and the requirements of Rule 2, G is certainly on the "no production" list, meaning that the right answer is (B) or (D). And then, since Option I clearly places H and Y together in production, (B) can be eliminated, leaving (D) as correct.

3. C

The right answer is a fact which, when combined with the rules, creates one and only one distribution. You may need to work with each choice, using the pencil and abandoning the choice once more than one possibility is confirmed.

(A)—If F and W go into production, you'd be in Option II, where several possibilities emerge for the remaining entities.

(B)—Even with G joining Y (and H) in sales in Option II, more than one distribution is possible.

(C) places I and W in sales, which means Option I, and the contrapositive of Rule 3 kicks in: since W is not in production, X can't be in sales, meaning that X must be the management person. G, forced by Rule 2 not to interact with F, goes into sales, with two slots in production remaining to the two applicants H and Y. The distribution is complete and (C) is correct.

(D)'s placing I and W in production (Option II) still leaves G and X ambiguous, with one in management and the other in sales.

(E), like (D), leaves two placements ambiguous; this time it's G and W.

4. B

Use previous work whenever possible. In correct choice (E) for Question 1 you saw (C)'s pair in sales, and in Option I you saw (A)'s pair. So those choices can be discarded: they are clearly possible partial lists for the sales department. (B), when tried, yields the right answer. With X in sales, Rule 3 forces W into production, and now you must separate H and Y in violation of Rule 1. Unacceptable.

(D) and (E) can quickly be seen as possible, for example: "G management; F, X, I, production; H, W, Y sales" confirms (D), and merely switch W and X in that distribution, and you confirm (E).

5. B

F and X can share a department, the production department (Rule 4), only in Option II, where H and Y are in sales—and that makes (B) correct. It's impossible for H to be in production here.

6. C

Turn negatives into positives whenever possible, and work out possibilities with your pencil. If X doesn't work in production, then X works in management or sales. Work out each possibility, remembering that F is always in production. If X is the management person, then G goes into sales (Rule 2), and the remaining slots go to two interchangeable pairs: "H + Y" (Rule 1) and "I + W" (the two left over):

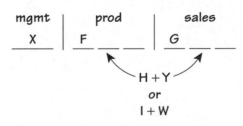

If you go by the first arrangement, (C) is confirmed as possible and your work is over. You don't even have to work out what happens if Herrera and Yates go into sales, or if G goes into management.

If necessary, you can solve this question by working out each answer choice until you find a rule violation. (A) is clearly wrong, since F can't leave the production department. If you put H and W in sales, as in (B), you need to accommodate Y in sales also, but then there's no room for either G or X, one of whom also must go to sales. (D) puts G in production with F, who's always there—thus violating Rule 2. (E) puts H and W in production with F, leaving no room for Y to tag along with H.

GAME 3: PACING

Now do another, in test-like conditions. You should be pushing yourself to spend no more than an *average* of 9 minutes on each game.

Questions 1–6

A reporter is trying to uncover the workings of a secret committee. The committee has six members—French, Ghauri, Hsia, Irving, Magnus, and Pinsky—each of whom serves on at least one subcommittee. There are three subcommittees, each having three members, about which the following is known:

> One of the committee members serves on all three subcommittees.
>
> French does not serve on any subcommittee with Ghauri.
>
> Hsia does not serve on any subcommittee with Irving.

1. If French does not serve on any subcommittee with Magnus, which one of the following must be true?

   (A) French serves on a subcommittee with Hsia.
   (B) French serves on a subcommittee with Irving.
   (C) Irving serves on a subcommittee with Pinsky.
   (D) Magnus serves on a subcommittee with Ghauri.
   (E) Magnus serves on a subcommittee with Irving.

2. If Pinsky serves on every subcommittee on which French serves and every subcommittee on which Ghauri serves, then which one of the following could be true?

   (A) Magnus serves on every committee on which French serves and every subcommittee on which Ghauri serves.
   (B) Magnus serves on every subcommittee on which Hsai serves and every subcommittee on which Irving serves.
   (C) Hsia serves on every subcommittee on which French serves and every subcommittee on which Ghauri serves.
   (D) French serves on every subcommittee on which Pinsky serves.
   (E) Hsia serves on every subcommittee on which Pinsky serves.

3. If Irving serves on every subcommittee on which Magnus serves, which one of the following could be true?

   (A) Magnus serves on all of the subcommittees.
   (B) Irving serves on more than one subcommittee.
   (C) Irving serves on every subcommittee on which Pinsky serves.
   (D) French serves on a subcommittee with Magnus.
   (E) Ghauri serves on a subcommittee with Magnus.

4. Which one of the following could be true?

   (A) French serves on all three subcommittees.
   (B) Hsia serves on all three subcommittees.
   (C) Ghauri serves on every subcommittee on which Magnus serves and every subcommittee on which Magnus serves.
   (D) Pinsky serves on every subcommittee on which Irving serves and every subcommittee on which Magnus serves.
   (E) Magnus serves on every subcommittee on which Pinsky serves, and Pinsky serves on every subcommittee on which Magnus serves.

5. Which one of the following must be true?

   (A) Ghauri serves on at least two subcommittees.
   (B) Irving serves on only one subcommittee.
   (C) French serves on a subcommittee with Hsia.
   (D) Ghauri serves on a subcommittee with Irving.
   (E) Magnus serves on a subcommittee with Pinsky.

6. Which one of the following must be true?

   (A) Every subcommittee has either French or Ghauri as a member.
   (B) Every subcommittee has either Hsia or Irving as a member.
   (C) No subcommittee consists of French, Magnus, and Pinsky.
   (D) Some committee member serves on exactly two subcommittees.
   (E) Either Magnus or Pinsky serves on only one subcommittee.

KAPLAN

Use this space for scratch work

Use this space for scratch work

Game 3 Answers and Explanations

Step 1: Overview

Situation: An investigation into the membership of subcommittees within a "secret committee."

Entities: The six people who sit on those subcommittees.

Action: To distribute them into the subcommittees.

Limitations: Each committee member serves on at least one subcommittee; three subcommittees, three members per subcommittee.

Step 2: Sketch

In the nine slots, you'll place the six entities plus three repeats, whatever they are. The Master Sketch is a standard one for Grouping games of Distribution:

Step 3: Rules

Rule 1 gives you an important bit of clarification: one of the six appears on every subcommittee. You can't determine who this person is—yet—but for now, suffice it to say that there is a "Triple": someone who takes three slots.

Rule 2 and Rule 3 seem to add little more than detail when they name members who can't serve together. You can never see "F G" in any subcommittee, nor "H I." The members of those pairs have to be separated.

Step 4: Deduction

First of all, remember the governing number rules: there are nine slots; six people, all of whom must be used; and one person who is the holder of three slots. For the purposes of these explanations, let's call that person "the Triple." Well, with one person taking three slots, and each of the other five taking one, that would add up to only eight slots. So besides the Triple and all the Singles, there must be a Double here; that is, a member who occupies exactly two slots. As for the identity of the Triple, it cannot be F, G, H, or I, because each of them has a rule preventing them from serving with some other member. Therefore, the Triple has to be Magnus or Pinsky. One of them will serve on every subcommittee. As for the other, he will either be a Single or the Double; there is no way to tell at this point.

That's all the deduction you can do for now, because there are very few rules to combine. However, working with the numbers pays off in virtually every Distribution games. So with our deductions made, the final visualization looks something like this:

F G H I M P   1 Triple: M or P
                      1 Double, 4 Singles
                      Never F G
                      Never H I

$$\underline{}\ \underline{}\ \underline{}\ /\ \underline{}\ \underline{}\ \underline{}\ /\ \underline{}\ \underline{}\ \underline{}$$

Step 5: Questions

1. C

Use your number deduction to handle this question. If F and M never serve together on a subcommittee, it means that M isn't the Triple, because if M were, he would be serving on a subcommittee with everyone. If M is not the Triple, then of course P is, which means that everyone else will share some subcommittee with P and, therefore, that (C) is correct.

2. C

According to the stem, P serves on every subcommittee on which F serves and every committee on which G serves. Note that F and G are always (Rule 3) on different subcommittees. And now you can deduce that P is the Triple, because if M were the Triple, notice that H and I would be left together on a subcommittee, a violation of Rule 3 And the remaining four slots are left for H, I, and M. M will serve with H or I to separate them from each other:

$$\underline{P}\ \underline{F}\ \underline{}\ /\ \underline{P}\ \underline{G}\ \underline{}\ /\ \underline{P}\ \underline{M}\ \underline{H/I}$$

We can now attack the choices, confident that one and only one is possible, while the other four are false. (A) is impossible, because putting M on the same subcommittees as P, F, and G would force a violation of Rule 3. (B) is also impossible. M certainly serves with either H or I, but cannot serve with both. (C) If H is the Double, which he can be, then he could serve with both F and G, and the distribution would be:

$$\underline{P}\ \underline{F}\ \underline{H}\ /\ \underline{P}\ \underline{G}\ \underline{H}\ /\ \underline{P}\ \underline{M}\ \underline{I}$$

No problem there, so (C) is possible and therefore correct. For the record, (D) and (E) would each propose a second Triple—a second person, F or H, to serve along with P on all three subcommittees. That's clearly impossible.

3.   B

As mentioned earlier, there's only one Triple (either M or P), and there's only one Double, identity unknown. That leaves things fairly wide open, but this question narrows them significantly. I can serve on every M subcommittee, as the question demands, only if M serves on exactly one subcommittee. (If it were two subcommittees, I would have to be either a second Double, or the Triple.) With M on one subcommittee, P would be the Triple:

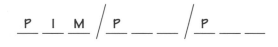

The Double can be anyone but M or P. (A) can be eliminated almost immediately, because if M were the Triple, then I would have to be a Triple as well. This can't happen. But as for (B), there's nothing stopping I from being the Double— I can serve on M's subcommittee and one other. The distribution could go like so:

$$\underline{P} \ \underline{I} \ \underline{M} \Big/ \underline{P} \ \underline{G} \ \underline{I} \Big/ \underline{P} \ \underline{F} \ \underline{H}$$

Note that this arrangement violates no rules and follows the question's "if" as well. Thus (B) is possible and correct. Of the wrong choices, because P is the Triple, I is restricted to two subcommittees, making (C) incorrect, and M's single appearance in a "P I M" subcommittee renders (D) and (E) impossible.

4.   D

Use your deductions and previous work to help yourself narrow answer choices quickly. Eliminate (A), since F can't be the Triple. And neither can H, which eliminates (B). (C) is also wrong, since we know that M or P is the Triple, and for G to serve on all of M and P's committees would make G a second Triple, which is impossible. (D) This would be true— has been true in the previous three questions, in fact—whenever P is the Triple, because then P serves with everyone. (D) is the choice that "could be true." (E) contradicts the fact that one—and only one—of M and P can be the Triple.

5.   E

Evaluate each choice in turn. G serves on one subcommittee or two, and never three, so (A) is far from a true statement. (B) is possible but by no means certain. As we saw in question 3, it's also possible that I is the Double. The arrangement we worked out in question 3 demonstrates that F and H need not always serve together, so you can eliminate (C). The same is true for (D). No rules require that G and I ever be paired up on a subcommittee. (E), as the last choice remaining, must be correct. Of course, because M or P is the Triple, obviously they will serve together on a subcommittee, so (E) must be true.

6.   D

(A) would be true if either F or G had to be the Triple or Double. Because neither one can be the Triple, and there are no restrictions on the Double, there are many possible distributions in which a subcommittee includes neither F nor G. For example:

$$\underline{M} \;\; \underline{F} \;\; \underline{H} \Big/ \underline{M} \;\; \underline{G} \;\; \underline{H} \Big/ \underline{M} \;\; \underline{P} \;\; \underline{I}$$

You can use the same logic to eliminate (B). Here's one possible distribution in which (B) is false:

$$\underline{P} \;\; \underline{G} \;\; \underline{H} \Big/ \underline{P} \;\; \underline{G} \;\; \underline{I} \Big/ \underline{P} \;\; \underline{F} \;\; \underline{M}$$

There are others. And notice that in the arrangement just mentioned, (C) is contradicted as well. (D) simply states a truth we realized at the very beginning. For the slots to add up to 9, we need a Triple, four Singles, and a Double. (D) must be true. For the record, (E) has been proven untrue several times so far: one of either M or P could be the Triple, and the other the Double. As long as you split up the forbidden pairs (F and G, H and I), such an arrangement is perfectly acceptable.

PRACTICE SETS

<u>Directions:</u> Each group of questions is based on a set of conditions. It may be useful to draw a rough diagram to answer some questions. Choose the response that most accurately and completely answers each question.

Game 4

Each of two boats, boat 1 and boat 2, will be assigned exactly four people. Exactly eight people, three adults—F, G, and H—and five children—V, W, X, Y, and Z—must be assigned to the boats according to the following conditions:

Each boat is assigned at least one adult.
If F is assigned to boat 2, G is assigned to boat 2.
If V is assigned to boat 1, W is assigned to boat 2.
X and Z are assigned to different boats.

1. Which one of the following is an acceptable assignment of people to boat 1?

   (A) F, G, H, X
   (B) F, H, W, Y
   (C) F, H, Y, Z
   (D) F, V, W, X
   (E) G, H, X, Y

2. If F is assigned to boat 2, which one of the following is a pair of people who could be assigned to the same boat as each other?

   (A) F and Y
   (B) G and H
   (C) G and Y
   (D) V and W
   (E) Y and Z

3. If exactly three children are assigned to boat 1, which one of the following is a pair of people who could both be assigned to boat 2?

   (A) F and H
   (B) G and Y
   (C) H and W
   (D) V and W
   (E) W and Y

4. If G is assigned to boat 1, which one of the following must be true?

   (A) H is assigned to boat 2.
   (B) V is assigned to boat 2.
   (C) Exactly one adult is assigned to boat 1.
   (D) Exactly two adults are assigned to boat 2.
   (E) Exactly two children are assigned to boat 2.

5. If V and W are assigned to the same boat as each other, which one of the following is a pair of people who must also be assigned to the same boat as each other?

   (A) F and H
   (B) F and Y
   (C) G and X
   (D) W and X
   (E) Y and Z

6. If H is assigned to a different boat than Y, which one of the following must assigned to boat 1?

   (A) F
   (B) G
   (C) H
   (D) V
   (E) Y

7. If exactly one adult is assigned to boat 1, which one of the following must be true?

   (A) F is assigned to boat 1.
   (B) G is assigned to boat 2.
   (C) H is assigned to boat 2.
   (D) V is assigned to boat 1.
   (E) Z is assigned to boat 2.

Game 5

Planes 1, 2, 3, and 4—and no others—are available to fly in an air show.

> Pilots Anna, Bob, and Cindy are all aboard planes that are flying in the show and they are the only qualified pilots in the show.
>
> Copilots Dave, Ed, and Fran are all aboard planes that are flying in the show and they are the only qualified copilots in the show.
>
> No plane flies in the show without a qualified pilot aboard.
>
> No one but qualified pilots and qualified copilots flies in the show.
>
> Anna will only fly in either plane 1 or plane 4.
>
> Dave will only fly in either plane 2 or plane 3.

1. If Anna flies in plane 4 and Dave flies in plane 2, which one of the following must be true?

    (A) Cindy flies in either plane 1 or plane 3.

    (B) If Cindy flies in plane 3, Bob flies in plane 2.

    (C) Bob and one other person fly in plane 1.

    (D) If Bob is aboard plane 4, Cindy flies in plane 3.

    (E) If Cindy is in plane 2, Bob flies in plane 3.

2. If Bob and Anna fly on the same plane, which one of the following must be true?

    (A) Cindy flies with Dave and Ed.

    (B) Cindy flies with Ed.

    (C) Dave flies with Cindy.

    (D) Dave flies with Cindy, Ed, and Fran.

    (E) Fran flies with Ed.

3. If Cindy and Fran are the only people in one of the planes, which one of the following must be true?

    (A) Bob flies with Anna.

    (B) Dave flies with Ed.

    (C) Dave and Ed fly with Bob.

    (D) Dave flies with Bob.

    (E) Ed flies with Anna.

4. If plane 1 is used, its crew could consist of

    (A) Anna, Bob, Cindy, Fran.

    (B) Anna, Bob, Ed, Fran.

    (C) Bob, Cindy, Ed, Fran.

    (D) Bob, Cindy, Dave, Ed.

    (E) Bob, Dave, Ed, Fran.

5. If as many of the pilots and copilots as possible fly in plane 4, that group will consist of

    (A) exactly two people.

    (B) exactly three people.

    (C) exactly four people.

    (D) exactly five people.

    (E) three pilots and two copilots.

KAPLAN

Game 6

A newly formed company has five employees—F, G, H, K, and L. Each employee holds exactly one of the following positions: president, manager, or technician. Only the president is not supervised. Other employees are each supervised by exactly one employee, who is either the president or a manager. Each supervised employee holds a different position than his or her supervisor. The following conditions apply:

There is exactly one president.

At least one of the employees whom the president supervises is a manager.

Each manager supervises at least one employee.

F does not supervise any employee.

G supervises exactly two employees.

1. Which one of the following is an acceptable assignment of employees to the positions?

	President	Manager	Technician
(A)	G	H, K, L	F
(B)	G	H	F, K, L
(C)	H	F, G	K, L
(D)	H, K	G	F, L
(E)	K	F, G, H, L	----

2. Which one of the following must be true?

   (A) There are at most three technicians.
   (B) There is exactly one technician.
   (C) There are at least two managers.
   (D) There are exactly two managers.
   (E) There are exactly two employees who supervise no one.

3. Which one of the following is a pair of employees who could serve as managers together?

   (A) F, H
   (B) F, L
   (C) G, K
   (D) G, L
   (E) K, L

4. Which one of the following could be true?

   (A) There is exactly one technician.
   (B) There are exactly two managers.
   (C) There are exactly two employees who are not supervised.
   (D) There are more managers than technicians.
   (E) The president supervises all of the other employees.

5. If F is supervised by the president, which one of the following must be true?

   (A) G is the president.
   (B) H is the president.
   (C) L is a technician.
   (D) There is exactly one manager.
   (E) There are exactly two technicians.

6. If K supervises exactly two employees, which one of the following must be true?

   (A) F is supervised by K.
   (B) G is a manager.
   (C) L is supervised.
   (D) There are exactly two managers.
   (E) There are exactly two technicians.

Use this space for scratch work

Use this space for scratch work

Use this space for scratch work

Game 4 Answers and Explanations

Step 1: Overview

Situation: A boat trip.

Entities: Eight people—three adults and five children.

Action: To distribute the eight people into the two boats.

Limitations: Each boat is assigned exactly four people.

Step 2: Sketch

Just list the two boats and draw four dashes under each to represent the four people that will go in each boat. List the adults and children off to the side and you're all set. It will help to differentiate visually between adults and children. One way to do so is to list the adults in uppercase and the children in lowercase:

<u>adult</u>	<u>child</u>
F G H	v w x y z
1	2
__ __ __ __	__ __ __ __

Step 3: Rules

According to Rule 1, of the four dashes under each boat, at least one must be filled by a capital letter. A boat filled with four children is not allowed. Anyhow, as a reminder, make a note of this under one dash in each boat in your sketch: one adult per boat, minimum.

Rule 2 restricts the possibilities further. This is a conditional rule, so take care when interpreting it and its contrapositive. If F (an adult) is in boat 2, then G (another adult) must also be in boat 2. Likewise, the contrapositive: If G is not in boat 2, then F cannot be in boat 2. But do not leave the information there, because you always want to turn negative statements positive. Since there are only two boats, "not in boat 2" means exactly the same thing as "in boat 1." Here's how it would look:

if F in 2 → G in 2

if G in 1 → F in 1

Be careful, though: you cannot infer from this rule that F and G must always be in the same boat. If G is in boat 2, F could occupy boat 1; if F is in boat 1, G could occupy boat 2. You can't, remember, simply flip the terms of an if/then statement and be sure that the statement remains true.

Rule 3 is another conditional rule so, once again, take care when interpreting it. This time you're dealing with two children, v and w. If v occupies boat 1, then w occupies boat 2. Likewise—here's the contrapositive—if w is not in boat 2, then v is not in boat 1; and again, we can take that a step further: It means that if w is in boat 1, then v is in boat 2:

$$\text{if } v \text{ in } 1 \rightarrow w \text{ in } 2$$

$$\text{if } w \text{ in } 1 \rightarrow v \text{ in } 2$$

Again, you cannot impulsively deduce that v and w must always be separated. Not so; v and w could happily share boat 2.

Rule 4 eliminates the possibility of x and z in the same boat. The rule demands that x (a child) and z (a child) occupy different boats. And this can be built right into your sketch: Since x and z must be separated, there must be a place in each boat for one member of that pair. Set those places aside by jotting down x/z in one seat per boat.

Step 4: Deduction

Look for entities which appear in more than one rule. Here there are none, which might be taken as a hint that there are no deductions to be made. But don't stop there. As with all Distribution games, take the time to get the numbers under control. Take Rule 1 for example. Each of the two boats must carry at least one adult. There are three adults and five children, so consider the possible breakdowns of adult and child to boat. You'll see that there is only one possibility: One boat must contain one adult and three children, while the other boat must contain two adults and two children. Another way to seek out deductions is to consider the rules in light of each other; that is, see how the rules affect each other. Take Rule 1 and Rule 2 together. Rule 2 provides two cases in which two of the three adults are in the same boat: If F's in boat 2, so is G; If G's in boat 1, so is F. Now, Rule 1 says that each boat must have at least one adult. So in each of the two cases mentioned in Rule 2, the other adult—who of course is H—must occupy the other boat, the boat that F and G are not in. See how this works? Therefore, if F's in boat 2, then so is G in boat 2, meaning that H must occupy boat 1. This realization also deepens your understanding of the contrapositive of Rule 2—take your time with it. If either of the "then" clauses is false—if, in other words, G occupies boat 1 or H occupies boat 2—then F must occupy boat 1. Here's how you might symbolize it all:

$$\text{If F in 2} \rightarrow \text{G in 2 } \underline{and} \text{ H in 1}$$

$$\text{If } G \text{ in 1 } \underline{or} \text{ H in 2} \rightarrow \text{F in 1 } \underline{and} \text{ H in 2}$$

It is also a good idea during Step 4 to check for "floaters," those entities not mentioned in any rule or deduction. These entities will fill in the remaining slots after all of the other entities have been placed. Here y is the only floater in the game—and y will certainly play an important role in the questions that follow.

So here's the final sketch:

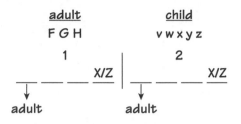

if F in 2 → G in 2 <u>and</u> H in 1

if G in 1 <u>or</u> H in 2 → F in 1 <u>and</u> H in 2

if v in 1 → w in 2

if w in 1 → v in 2

Step 5: Questions

1. C

This is an acceptability question dealing with boat 1, so just eliminate those choices that violate rules. Rule 1 is violated by choice (A), which places all three adults in the same boat without leaving an adult for the other boat. Rule 2 is violated by choice (E), which places F in boat 2 but keeps G in boat 1. Choice (D) places v in boat 1 with w, a direct violation of Rule 3. Rule 4 is violated by choice (B)—that one is tricky; you have to see that (B) fails to mention either x or z, thus leaving x and z together by default in boat 2. Anyway, only (C), the correct answer, remains.

2. E

You need to find a pair of people who can occupy the same boat, meaning that the four wrong choices will contain pairs that have to be separated. The stem places F in boat 2, and Rule 2 says that therefore G must also occupy boat 2. Create a new basic sketch and enter what we now know. Since every boat needs an adult (Rule 1), H must be inserted into boat 1. Your sketch reminds you that x and z have slots reserved, one per boat. Thus you can see that two slots are left in boat 1 and one in boat 2. And v, w, and y are left.

Since v and w can't both occupy boat 1 (Rule 3), one slot in each boat must be reserved for one of them. There's only one slot left, and y, the "floater," must take it; it's in boat 1. Here's what the seating looks like:

$$\underline{\text{H}} \quad \underline{\text{Y}} \quad \underline{\text{v/w}} \quad \underline{\text{x/z}} \quad \Big| \quad \underline{\text{F}} \quad \underline{\text{G}} \quad \underline{\text{x/z}} \quad \underline{\text{v/w}}$$

Armed with this new sketch, it's a simple matter to skim the choices for the pair of entities that can share a boat; y and z can share boat 1, so (E) is the answer.

3.   C

Since three children are placed in boat 1 here, we know that one adult accompanies them in boat 1, leaving two adults and two children for boat 2. And G cannot be the sole adult in boat 1, because the contrapositive of Rule 2 says that if G sits in boat 1, then so must F, but we have room for only one adult in boat 1. Therefore, G must occupy boat 2. The adult in boat 1 will be either F or H. The adult not in boat 1 will join G in boat 2. Boat 2 contains only two children, and one of them is x or z (Rule 4). We're left with two slots in boat 1 and one slot in boat 2, and this is exactly where you were at the end of the last question, with 3 slots available for v, w, and y. Rule 3 demands that v and w not take both slots in boat 1, so one slot in each boat has to be given over to the v/w pair. This leaves only one slot left, and y is left to fill it in boat 1:

$$
\begin{array}{cccc|cccc}
& 1 & & & & 2 & & \\
\underline{F/H} & \underline{Y} & \underline{v/w} & \underline{x/z} & \underline{G} & \underline{F/H} & \underline{v/w} & \underline{x/z}
\end{array}
$$

Now, it's just a matter of finding the pair that could share boat 2. H and w could do so, and thus (C) is the answer.

4.   A

If you place G in boat 1 as the stem demands, you'll recognize that F must be there, too (contrapositive of Rule 2). Each boat must have an adult (Rule 1), so H must occupy boat 2, and (A) is the answer. If you did continue, you'd have seen that (C), (D), and (E) are all impossible, while (B) is only <u>possible</u>—v could be assigned to either boat.

5.   B

If v and w are both in the same boat, that boat cannot be boat 1 (remember, Rule 3 says that if v sits in boat 1, then w sits in boat 2). So, they must both be assigned to boat 2. Now recognize that that's three slots in boat 2 taken up by children (v, w, and x or z). The fourth slot there will go to an adult, leaving two children—y, and either x or z—and two adults for boat 1. The adult in boat 2 cannot be F; if F sits in boat 2, so must G (Rule 2). So F must be in boat 1:

$$
\begin{array}{cccc|cccc}
& 1 & & & & 2 & & \\
\underline{F} & \underline{G/H} & \underline{y} & \underline{x/z} & \underline{G/H} & \underline{v} & \underline{w} & \underline{x/z}
\end{array}
$$

You're looking for the pair of entities who must share a boat. F and y must both sit in boat 1, so (B) is the answer. The pairs in (A), (C), (D), and (E) all could share a boat, but need not.

6. A

H and y are in different boats, but you're not told which boat each is in. So there are two options: one in which H takes boat 1 while y takes boat 2, and the other in which y is in boat 1 while H is in boat 2. Take the time to work out each option, keeping in mind that you're looking for the entity that must occupy boat 1—in other words, the entity that is definitely assigned to boat 1 in both options.

Option 1: With H in boat 1 and y in boat 2, the x/z pair are, as always, occupying one seat in each boat. Use your rules to go further, starting with v and w. They cannot both be assigned to boat 1 (if v is in boat 1, Rule 3 tells us, then w is in boat 2); and if they were both assigned to boat 2, boat 2 would contain no adult. So there's no way around it: v and w cannot travel together, so one slot in each boat will be taken up by a member of the v/w pair. This leaves one slot in each boat, with F and G left to fill them. Can F be assigned to boat 2? No way; Rule 2 says that if F sits in boat 2, so must G. Therefore, F must take the last seat in boat 1, and G must fill out boat 2. Option 1 looks like this:

$$
\begin{array}{ccc|ccc}
\multicolumn{3}{c|}{\mathbf{1}} & \multicolumn{3}{c}{\mathbf{2}} \\
\underline{F} & \underline{H} & \underline{v/w}\ \underline{x/z} & \underline{G} & \underline{y} & \underline{v/w}\ \underline{x/z}
\end{array}
$$

You might stop at this point to make the happy discovery that the correct answer has to be (A) or (C), since in this option, F and H are the only two people who must occupy boat 1. Thus they are the only two people eligible for the correct answer here. We're looking for someone who "must be assigned to boat 1," and we know now it can only be F or H because, as shown by this option, G, v, and y could take boat 2. And in the other option, y takes boat 1 while H takes boat 2. Clearly, it cannot be H who must be assigned to boat 1. Therefore, the answer must be F, answer choice (A).

7. B

Exactly one adult sits in boat 1; thus we know that boat 1 contains one adult and three children, while boat 2 contains two adults and two children. Who could be that lone adult in boat 1? Clearly not G, because the contrapositive to Rule 2 says that if G sits in boat 1, so must F. Therefore, G must occupy boat 2, and again, don't do more work than you have to—(B) is the answer. The other four choices are possible only, but with any luck at all you never went far enough to notice that.

Game 5 Answers and Explanations

Step 1: Overview

Situation: An air show.

Entities: Six people—three pilots and three copilots.

Action: To distribute the six people among four planes.

Limitations: Only these six people fly in the show; more limitations to come in the rules.

Step 2: Sketch

Keep this setup simple; four circles or columns, numbered 1 to 4, can represent the planes. Then list the pilots and copilots off to the side. As with Game 4, it may help to list the copilots in lowercase:

<u>PILOT</u> <u>copilot</u>
A B C   d e f

1   2   3   4

Step 3: Rules

You most likely already used Rules 1 and 2 to get a handle on the entities. However, some test takers overlooked a key element of these rules—that the pilots and copilots "are all aboard planes that are flying in the show." This means that everyone flies. Selecting who flies isn't an issue; they're all up in the air. The only question here is which plane each person is in.

Rule 3 tells you that every plane that's flying needs one pilot—at least one. This rule says nothing about copilots, nor does it imply that only one pilot may fly in a particular plane. So far, it's quite possible that exactly one pilot flies a plane without a copilot, just as it's possible for more than one pilot to fly in one plane.

Rule 4 is basically a loophole closer to ensure that no one from the audience or anywhere else rushes out and pilots a plane.

According to Rule 5, Anna will only fly in plane 1 or plane 4. Since everyone is flying in the show, we know that one of these planes must be used. To build this into our master sketch, write "A" with arrows pointing to planes 1 and 4.

Rule 6 tells us something similar—that Dave only flies in plane 2 or plane 3—"d" with arrows to 2 and 3 takes care of this:

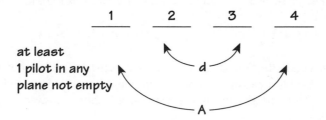

Step 4: Deduction

There isn't much in the way of deductions, but there are a few issues that are worth working out before hitting the questions. First, the numbers: No plane flies without a qualified pilot aboard. But we have only three qualified pilots, which means that a maximum of three of the four planes are flying; at least one is going to remain empty and on the ground. Also, since a plane can't fly without a pilot (Rule 3), we know that one of the pilots must join Dave (a copilot) in either plane 2 or plane 3. It can't be Anna, since she's in plane 1 or 4, so Dave must fly with either B or C, in plane 2 or 3.

So here's the final sketch:

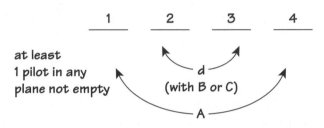

Step 5: Questions

1. B

Anna is in plane 4 and Dave is in plane 2. Well, we knew we'd have to focus on the Dave situation, and here it is right off the bat. Since Bob or Cindy (or both) needs to accompany Dave, Cindy in 3 forces Bob into 2 with Dave. (A) doesn't have to be true, because there's no reason why Cindy couldn't fly in plane 2 with Dave. (C) can also be eliminated, because Bob could fly in plane 2. (D) is downright impossible; if Bob flies in plane 4, Cindy would have to fly with Dave in plane 2. (E) could be false; if Cindy flies in plane 2 with Dave, then Bob is free to fly in any of the planes.

2. C

Anna can't fly with Dave (Rules 5 and 6). If Bob joins Anna, he can't fly with Dave. So Cindy would have to fly with copilot Dave, choice (C). Choices (A), (B), (D), and (E) all could be true, but none of them must be true. Don't be surprised when the test makers use one or two basic concepts as the key to the majority of the questions (like running out of pilots to place with Dave).

3. D

Cindy and Fran fly alone, Anna never flies with Dave, so Bob must fly with Dave—choice (D). (A) is dead wrong, and (B), (C), and (E) are merely possible. Unless you're unsure of the workings of the game and you need to test you thinking, you should never continue checking the choices after you've found the answer. Trust your work, and save yourself some precious time.

4. B

This is very much like a standard acceptability question. (D) and (E) can be eliminated thanks to Rule 6. Dave can't fly in 1 but must have a pilot with him in plane 2 or 3, so any prospective plane 1 crew that included all three pilots would be impossible. That eliminates Choice (A). (C) leaves only Anna to join Dave, which isn't possible. That leaves us with (B)—Anna, Bob, Ed, and Fran—a perfectly acceptable crew for plane 1, with Cindy and Dave in plane 2 or 3. It is important to learn to recognize acceptability questions even when they are not structured like normal acceptability questions. These questions are among the easiest on the test. If you were running short on time, a quick scan of the questions should have suggested starting with this one (which also helps to clarify the action of the game, as discussed above).

5. C

Start by thinking about who cannot be in plane 4. You know from Rule 6 that Dave has to be in plane 2 or plane 3. Since Dave is a copilot, he must also be accompanied by a pilot, which means that you now have two people that will not fly in plane 4. As for the other four (two pilots and two copilots), they can all pile into plane 4 without breaking any of the rules, so (C) is correct. This game may exaggerate the point, but some games are based around central elements, so much so that these elements play a big part in every single question. This game was all about getting a pilot to go along with Dave in 2 or 3. The games you'll see on your test will be based around other dominant issues. Attempt to seek them out; you'll be doing yourself a great favor.

Game 6 Answers and Explanations

Step 1: Overview

Situation: Assigning positions in a newly formed company.

Entities: Five new employees—F, G, H, K, and L.

Action: To distribute the five employees into their respective positions (president, manager, or technician).

Limitations: Except for the president (who remains unsupervised), each other employee is supervised by exactly one employee, who must be either the president or the manager.

Step 2: Sketch

This is not an easy setup to get a handle on, because you'll want to include not only the consideration of position, but also who supervises whom. One way is to mimic a "family tree" type of game, with entities placed above and below each other and connected by lines. This way you can place entities who supervise over those they supervise and connect them with lines, like so:

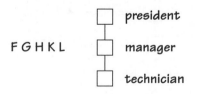

Step 3: Rules

This game has many vital rules built into the opening paragraph:

We're told that only the president is not supervised, and that each employee is supervised by one employee who is either the president or a manager. We can infer then that technicians cannot supervise anyone.

We're also told that the supervised employee has a different position than his or her supervisor. Since the supervised employee and the supervisor cannot hold the same position, this means that all managers are supervised by the president and all technicians are supervised by a manager or the president. These basic rules are just as important as the indented ones.

Rule 1 tells you that there can only be one president, which means that only one of our employees will go unsupervised. Note how Logic Games tend to reflect real life situations. It makes sense that there is only one president, just as it makes sense that the employees can only supervise those that are of a lower level.

According to Rule 2, at least one of the people that the president supervises will be a manager. Don't make the mistake of assuming that this rule means that the president must supervise more than one employee; that's not what the rule states. It's quite possible that the president supervises exactly one employee, a manager.

Rule 3 will prove vital. We know that the president is unsupervised (opening paragraph), and that a manager cannot supervise another manager (opening paragraph). So if each manager supervises at least one employee, we now know that there must be at least as many technicians as managers.

You learned from the setup that only technicians do not supervise anyone, so instead of simply rewriting Rule 4, we can put F directly into our diagram as one of the technicians.

You will want to make a note reminding yourself that G must supervise two employees, but once again, first stop and think about what this tells you. You can put G right into your diagram by noting that G must either be the president or at least a manager (since technicians do not supervise anyone).

After the rules, you should have the following:

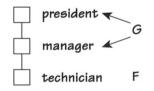

Step 4: Deduction

As usual, there's more to think about before moving on to the questions. With only five entities and one (F) solidly fixed to a group (Technician), you can bet that it would be worth your time to consider the numbers game and drive it to something concrete. With five entities, only one of whom can be president, the only possibilities for the number breakdown of president/managers/technicians are 1, 1, 3 and 1, 2, 2; we inferred from Rule 3 that the number of managers can't be greater than the number of technicians. We could even take this thinking one step further by combining it with Rule 5. If G is a manager, then the setup has to be 1, 1, 3, because if G is a manager, the requirement that G supervises at least two employees (technicians in this case), wouldn't leave any technicians for the other manager to supervise in the 1, 2, 2 setup. Going another step further, what if we know that there are two managers? Well, that means that the setup is 1, 2, 2, and G must be the president. G can only be the president or a manager, and we just showed that G can't be a manager unless she's the only one. This is quite a bit of deducing to do up front; don't get the idea that you couldn't have handled this game without working all of this out up front. But if you're able to deduce this far, it saves you a tremendous amount of time in the long run.

So here's what you should be armed with as you move on to the questions:

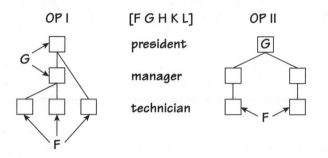

Step 5: Questions

1. B

You should eagerly anticipate these acceptability questions by now. Just check each rule against each choice. Rule 1 eliminates (D). Rule 3 cuts (A) and (E), which each have more managers than technicians (something we know is impossible). (C) can also easily be eliminated because it doesn't agree with our deduction that F is a technician. Only (B) remains as the correct answer.

2. A

Here's where the LSAT tests your deduction skills. This we already know: exactly 1 president (Rule 1), at least one manager (Rule 2), so a maximum of three technicians. A "must be true" question with no new information is always testing a deduction that you could have made up front. Sometimes (like here), that deduction is expressed in more abstract terms, but don't let that throw you.

3. E

This question asks for an acceptable pair of managers. You can cross off (A) and (B), thanks to your first deduction that F is a technician. You also should have deduced that if there are two managers, then the president must be G. Since G can't be one of two managers, we can cross off (C) and (D), leaving (E). If you hadn't made that second deduction, no problem; you're simply forced to make it now: If G is one of two managers, then there needs to be three technicians:

Two for G to supervise (Rule 5) and one for the other manager to supervise. This does not work, because it leaves no one to be president.

4. B

When a question like this provides no new information in the form of an "if" clause and also does not ask for a deduction by asking you what must be true, it's time to test the choices. (A) is absolutely impossible. From the beginning you've known that there have to be at least two technicians. But in the second option for the master sketch, (B) is certainly possible, as long as G is our president. On Test Day, mark (B) and go on, but to get some practice at spotting wrong answer choices, examine the other choices. (C) can't happen; the only employee who isn't supervised is the president, and there's only one president, so only one employee will go unsupervised. You know that the only two possibilities are 1, 1, 3 and 1, 2, 2. There can't be more managers than technicians, thanks to Rule 3, so (D) can be eliminated. And as for (E), Rule 2 said that at least one of the employees that the president supervises is a manager. Rule 3 says that every manager supervises at least one employee. Since every employee is only supervised by one employee, (E) is not possible. As you can see, even in situations like this where you have to try out each choice, the work you did up front still proves to be extremely valuable in quickly eliminating wrong answer choices.

5. D

Start by working with the new information. F (a technician) is supervised by the president, and we know (Rule 2) that the president also supervises at least one manager, so the president supervises at least two employees. But since F is supervised by the president, you must therefore be dealing with the 1, 1, 3 setup (the only setup in which the president supervises a technician), which gives you your answer, (D). (A) doesn't have to be true, since G could indeed be that one manager supervising two of the three technicians. And by the same token, G could be the president. H could either be the one manager or even one of the technicians, invalidating (B). For all you know, L could be the president or the manager, which eliminates (C). And if, as (E) says, there are exactly two technicians, we can no longer be in the first option (with the 1/1/3 ratio). This contradicts the new information from the question stem, so (E) cannot be correct.

6. C

So now K as well as G both supervise two employees. Since the maximum number of technicians is three, either K or G must be president while the other is a manager (if they were both managers, they'd need four technicians to supervise). And you must be dealing with the 1/1/3 setup because that is the only setup in which two people each supervise two other employees:

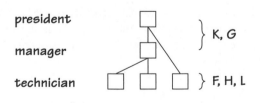

So K and G must be president and manager, in either order, and all of the other employees, including L, must be supervised technicians. As for the wrong answers: F can be supervised by either K or G, so (A) doesn't have to be true. Likewise, (B) only could be true, since G could just as easily be president. (D) is flat-out wrong, because according to the numbers, there can be only one manager. And once again, (E) contradicts the relevant sketch, which tells us that there are exactly three technicians.

Chapter 8: **Matching Games**

Matching games ask you to match up various characteristics—frequently more than a single type of characteristic—about a group of entities: perhaps three animals, each assigned a name, color, and size (the example used in chapter 1). The sheer numbers are often difficult to handle, unless you develop a methodical, organized approach, like a table or grid.

You already know you should help keep the entities and characteristics distinguished by using variations in your notations, such as lowercase and uppercase letters, subscripts—whatever works for you. To get the data under control, center your sketch around the most important characteristic—that is, the one with the most information attached to it. Going back to the animals example, don't assume that you should organize your sketch around the animals—there may be a better attribute, one that you know more about, that should take center stage. Visualize the action and create a mental picture or a sketch that puts the elements into a logical order. If you think through the scenarios and don't get scared off by their seeming complexity, you can find matching games accessible and even fun.

Most matching games require scratch work in the form of a list: grids work only when there are three types of entities and a low number of each type to match up—$3 \times 3 \times 2$ or $4 \times 2 \times 3$, say.

GAME 1: THE METHOD

Don't forget to pause and work through the setup and each question on your own, as much as possible, before reading on.

Questions 1–7
Three couples—John and Kate, Lewis and Marie, and Nat and Olive have dinner in a restaurant together. Kate, Marie, and Olive are women; the other three are men. Each person orders one and only one of the following kinds of entrees: pork chops, roast beef, swordfish, tilefish, veal cutlet. The six people order in a manner consistent with the following conditions:

The two people in each couple do not order the same kind of entree as each other.

None of the men orders the same kind of entree as any of the other men.

Marie orders swordfish.

Neither John nor Nat orders a fish entree.

Olive orders roast beef.

Step 1: Overview

Situation: Couples having dinner.

Entities: The couples (J and K, L and M, and N and O) and the entrees (pc, rb, sf, tf, vc).

Action: To match entrees with diners.

Limitations: Each diner orders exactly one entree.

Step 2: Sketch

Sketch out the list of diners, putting the couples next to each other, and include the list of entrees underneath. Don't forget to mark which member of each couple is a man, and which is a woman:

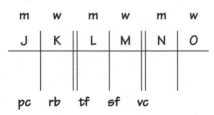

Step 3: Rules

The first rule states that the members of a couple must order different entrees. That doesn't reveal what anyone orders (yet), but is best written in the sketch. Rule 2, likewise, doesn't directly tell what anyone orders, but can be shorthanded under our sketch. Rules 3 and 5, however, state what Marie and Olive order, which can be drawn directly into the sketch. Rule 4 limits what John and Nat order; if they can't order fish, they are limited to ordering pork chops, roast beef, or the veal cutlet, and this can be written into the sketch.

	m ≠ w		m ≠ w		m ≠ w	
	J	K	L	M	N	O
	pc			sf	pc	rb
	rb				rb	
	vc				vc	
	pc	rb	vc	tf	sf	vc

J ≠ L ≠ N

Step 4: Deduction

Nat can't order the same entree as his date, which means roast beef isn't an option for him; he's restricted to pork chops or veal cutlet. Similarly, Lewis can't order swordfish, so he will have to choose between pork chops, veal cutlet, roast beef, or tilefish. Nothing is known about Kate; she can order any of the four entrees. With these deductions, your new sketch should look something like this:

J	K	L	M	N	O
pc		pc	sf	pc	rb
rb		vc		vc	
vc		rb			
		tf			

m ≠ w   m ≠ w   m ≠ w

pc   rb   tf   sf   vc

J ≠ L ≠ N

Step 5: Questions

1. Which one of the following is a complete and accurate list of the entrees any one of which Lewis could order?

    (A) pork chops, roast beef

    (B) pork chops, veal cutlet

    (C) pork chops, swordfish, veal cutlet

    (D) pork chops, roast beef, tilefish, veal cutlet

    (E) pork chops, roast beef, swordfish, tilefish, veal cutlet

This question can be answered right off the master sketch; it asks for all of the different entrees Lewis could order. A quick look at your sketch reveals that (D) gives the right list of entrees.

2. Which one of the following statements could be true?

    (A) John orders the same kind of entree as Marie does.

    (B) Kate orders the same kind of entree as Nat does.

    (C) Lewis orders the same kind of entree as Nat does.

    (D) Marie orders the same kind of entree as Olive does.

    (E) Nat orders the same kind of entree as Olive does.

This question asks you for a statement that is possible; any answer choices that are impossible will be eliminated. Examine each in turn. (A) can't be true, since Marie orders swordfish and John can't. (B), however, is possible; there are no rules that limit what Kate orders (other than ordering something different from John), and so she can certainly have the same thing as Nat. This is the correct answer. Rule 2 eliminated choice (C), Rules 3 and 4 together eliminated (D), and Rule 1 eliminated (E).

3. Which one of the following statements must be true?

    (A) One of the men orders pork chops or veal cutlet.

    (B) One of the men orders swordfish or veal cutlet.

    (C) Two of the women order tilefish.

    (D) None of the men orders a fish entree.

    (E) Exactly one of the women orders a fish entree.

Unlike Question 2, Question 3 asks for what must be true. Again, compare each choice to your sketch. Choice (A) must be true; one of the men, specifically Nat, can only order pork chops or veal cutlet.

4. If John orders veal cutlet, then which one of the following statements must be true?

    (A) Kate orders roast beef.

    (B) Kate orders swordfish.

    (C) Lewis orders tilefish.

    (D) Lewis orders veal cutlet.

    (E) Nat orders pork chops.

With new "if" questions, you should always redraw your master sketch. Don't think you will be saving time by skipping this redrawing. If you don't redraw, you will waste time trying to figure out what is "master sketch" info and what is only good for the question you just finished.

This question stipulates that John orders veal cutlet. Since the men all order different entrees, that leaves Nat with only pork chops, and Lewis, now unable to order pork chops or veal, is left to choose between roast beef and tilefish.

```
   m ≠ w      m ≠ w      m ≠ w

    J  | K  ||  L  | M  ||  N  | O
   ─────────────────────────────
   vc           rb   sf     pc   rb
                tf

        pc    rb    tf    sf    vc

            J ≠ L ≠ N
```

Since the question asks for what must be true, (E) is correct.

5. If none of the six people orders pork chops, then which one of the following statements must be true?

(A) John orders veal cutlet.
(B) Kate orders tilefish.
(C) Lewis orders tilefish.
(D) One of the men orders swordfish.
(E) One of the women orders tilefish.

This question requires another re-sketch. If no one orders pork chops, Nat must have the veal cutlet. If John can't have pork chops, and now can't have veal because Nat is having the veal, he must have roast beef. Lewis is left only the tilefish. Kate, who can't have pork chops or roast beef (because her date is having the roast beef), is left with a choice of tilefish, swordfish, or veal cutlets.

```
   m ≠ w      m ≠ w      m ≠ w

    J  | K  ||  L  | M  ||  N  | O
   ─────────────────────────────
   rb           tf   sf     vc   rb

        pc    rb    tf    sf    vc

            J ≠ L ≠ N
```

The question asks us for what must be true, and (C) fits the bill.

KAPLAN

6. If Lewis orders pork chops, then which one of the following is a complete and accurate list of the entrees any one of which John could order?

   (A) roast beef
   (B) veal cutlet
   (C) roast beef, veal cutlet
   (D) roast beef, swordfish
   (E) pork chops, roast beef, swordfish

One more "if" question, and we'll re-sketch. Lewis ordering pork chops means neither Nat nor John can order them, and this means Nat must have the veal cutlet. If Nat has veal, John can't, leaving John to have roast beef.

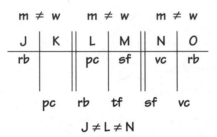

Choice (A) gives the correct list of possibilities.

7. Suppose that the people in each couple both order the same kind of entree as each other rather than order different kinds of entrees. If all other conditions remain the same, and no two women order the same kind of entree, then which one of the following statements could be true?

   (A) John orders roast beef.
   (B) John orders swordfish.
   (C) Kate orders roast beef.
   (D) Two of the people order pork chops.
   (E) Two of the people order tilefish.

The last question changes one of the original rules. Start from scratch and recreate your Master Sketch, paying attention to which rules still apply and which don't, but remember that the game still works the same as it has before, so you're not completely starting from the beginning.

Rule 1 is no longer in effect, and has been replaced with the couples ordering the same entree. Rule 3 and 5 are still in effect, and will still operate in the same way as before. But now, because the couples order the same dishes, we know Lewis orders swordfish and Nat orders roast beef. Rule 4, that John doesn't order fish, will limit him to pork chops, roast beef, or veal cutlets, but since he can't order the same dish as Nat, roast beef is not a possibility. Thus John (and Kate) must have pork chops or veal cutlet.

$$\begin{array}{c}
m = w \qquad m = w \qquad m = w \\[4pt]
\begin{array}{|c|c||c|c||c|c|}
\hline
J & K & L & M & N & O \\
\hline
pc & pc & sf & sf & rb & rb \\
vc & vc & & & & \\
\hline
\end{array}
\end{array}$$

$$J \neq L \neq N$$

Choice (D) is the only answer choice that is possible.

GAME 2: PRACTICE

As you can see, the work done up front organizing the data is especially important—and especially effective—in matching games. Now try a game on your own, focusing on applying Kaplan's Method and strategies, before reviewing the explanations.

Remember that all practice should include some emphasis on timing now: allow yourself 10 minutes for the following game. We're still allowing a lot of space for your scratch work, because we want you to be able to easily compare your scratch work with ours, but remember that you won't have that luxury on Test Day. Look for ways to make it smaller, quicker, and clearer as you perfect your approach to the games. It only has to be clear and legible while you work on that game.

Questions 1–5

A school has exactly four dormitories that are to be fully occupied—Richards, Tuscarora, Veblen, and Wisteria—each consisting entirely of a North wing and a South wing. The following rules govern assignment of students to dormitory wings:

> Each wing is assigned only male students or only female students.
>
> Exactly three wings have males assigned to them.
>
> Richards North and Tuscarora North are assigned females.
>
> If a dormitory has males assigned to one of its wings, then its other wing is assigned females.
>
> If males are assigned to Veblen South, then Wisteria
>
> North is assigned males.

1. If females are assigned to Veblen South and Veblen North, then which one of the following could be two other wings that are also assigned females?

    (A) Richards North and Tuscarora South

    (B) Richards South and Wisteria South

    (C) Richards South and Tuscarora North

    (D) Tuscarora North and Wisteria South

    (E) Tuscarora South and Wisteria South

2. It CANNOT be true that females are assigned to both

    (A) Richards South and Wisteria South.

    (B) Richards South and Tuscarora South.

    (C) Richards South and Veblen North.

    (D) Tuscarora South and Wisteria South.

    (E) Veblen North and Wisteria South.

3. If Wisteria North is assigned females, then females must also be assigned to which one of the following?

    (A) Richards South

    (B) Wisteria South

    (C) Tuscarora South

    (D) Veblen South

    (E) Veblen North

4. If males are assigned to Veblen South, which one of the following is a complete and accurate list of the wings that CANNOT be assigned males?

    (A) Richards North, Tuscarora North

    (B) Richards North, Tuscarora North, Veblen North

    (C) Richards North, Tuscarora North, Wisteria South

    (D) Richards North, Tuscarora North, Veblen North, Wisteria South

    (E) Richards North, Richards South, Tuscarora North, Veblen North, Wisteria South

5. If Tuscarora South is assigned females, then it could be true that females are assigned to both

    (A) Richards South and Wisteria North.

    (B) Richards South and Wisteria South.

    (C) Veblen North and Wisteria North.

    (D) Veblen South and Wisteria South.

    (E) Veblen South and Veblen North.

Use this space for scratch work

Game 2 Answers and Explanations

Step 1: Overview

Situation: A school's dormitories are in need of assignment.

Entities: Each of four dorms has a north and south wing, and the entities prove to the genders (though we don't realize this until Rule 1).

Action: To match up each wing with the gender of the students who reside in it.

Limitations: None, at least, that are revealed in the opening paragraph; as noted above, we don't realize what the entities are until the indented rules kick in. However, we know that there are eight wings (four North, four South), and whenever a game involves compass points, that's an invitation to take advantage of your sketch to build them in.

Step 2: Sketch

Sketch a quick rectangle or square for each dorm. With such a sketch, the concepts of "north" and "south" are ingrained, and there's no need to add any more labeling or symbols.

Step 3: Rules

Rule 1 clarifies what's going on here, in a way that the opening paragraph does in most other games. It's more than a loophole closer (closing off the possibility of co-ed wings): It tells us exactly what we're going to match to each wing. This is a perfect opportunity to use the universal symbols for male and female, so handy, so much more vivid than adding more letters to the game.

Rule 2: If there are exactly three "male wings," then there must be exactly five "female wings." By this point your basic setup can be established as:

Rule 3 should be entered directly into the sketch:

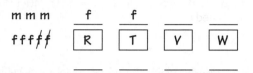

Rule 4: If a dorm has males in a wing, then its other wing gets females. But remember what we just learned, that there are exactly three male wings involved. It follows, then, that three of our four dorms will be male/female, and exactly one of the four dorms will be female/female.

Rule 5 is an if/then statement, which can be noted along with its contrapositive:

$$\text{If } VS_m \rightarrow WN_f$$
$$\text{If } WN_m \rightarrow VS_f$$

Step 4: Deductions

With the lack of concrete information (the only rule that matches genders to actual wings is a conditional one), we don't expect to be able to determine a lot up front, beyond knowing that three dorms will have one male and one female wing, and one dorm will be all females. Proceed to the questions.

Step 5: Questions

1. **E**

Re-sketch and add the new information. Seeing that Veblen is the all female dorm, we know the others must be male/female dorms, and the males definitely go in the south wings of Richards and Tuscarora. (E) gives us the possibility that could occur.

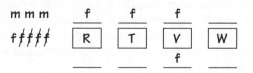

2.   B

The right answer is a pair to which females cannot both be assigned, so the four wrong choices are pairs that can both take females. This ends up being much easier than it looks. Since according to Rule 3, Richards North and Tuscarora North are female wings, and since as we deduced earlier, it's impossible to have more than one all-female dorm, then (B) is the right answer.

3.   D

If Wisteria North gets females, the contrapositive of Rule 5 is triggered, telling us Veblen South also gets females.

$$
\begin{array}{cccccc}
m\,m\,m & f & f & & f \\
f\,f\,\cancel{f}\,\cancel{f} & \boxed{R} & \boxed{T} & \boxed{V} & \boxed{W} \\
& & & f & \\
\rule{1cm}{0.4pt} & \rule{1cm}{0.4pt} & \rule{1cm}{0.4pt} & \rule{1cm}{0.4pt} \\
\end{array}
$$

4.   D

Create a new sketch for this question, placing males into Veblen South. Rule 4 dictates females for Veblen North: enter that fact. Rule 5 explicitly states that if Veblen South gets males, so does Wisteria North, and then Rule 4 demands that we assign females to Wisteria South:

$$
\begin{array}{cccccc}
m\,\cancel{m}\,\cancel{m} & f & f & f & m \\
f\,\cancel{f}\,\cancel{f}\,\cancel{f} & \boxed{R} & \boxed{T} & \boxed{V} & \boxed{W} \\
& & & m & f \\
\rule{1cm}{0.4pt} & \rule{1cm}{0.4pt} & \rule{1cm}{0.4pt} & \rule{1cm}{0.4pt} \\
\end{array}
$$

(D) gives us the list of the wings that CANNOT be assigned males.

5.   D

One last mini-sketch, this including the new fact that Tuscarora South gets females. This is our all-female dorm, so all the others will be male/female, and that mandates males for Richards South, whose North wing is always female. This Allows us to throw out (A) and (B). Since the right answer "could be true," (C) won't do, as making both Veblen North and Wisteria North female would make their South wings male, but that's a clear violation of Rule 5. We can also throw out (E), since it mandates an all-female Veblen, and we already have our one and only all-female dorm in Tuscarora. So (D) is left over and must be correct.

GAME 3: PACING

By this time, you should be pushing yourself to complete every game in under 10 minutes.

Questions 1–5

In a repair facility there are exactly six technicians: Stacy, Urma, Wim, Xena, Yolanda, and Zane. Each technician repairs machines of at least one of the following three types—radios, televisions, and VCRs—and no other types. The following conditions apply:

> Xena and exactly three other technicians repair radios.
>
> Yolanda repairs both televisions and VCRs.
>
> Stacy does not repair any type of machine that Yolanda repairs.
>
> Zane repairs more types of machines than Yolanda repairs.
>
> Wim does not repair any type of machine that Stacy repairs.
>
> Urma repairs exactly two types of machines.

1. For exactly how many of the six technicians is it possible to determine exactly which of the three types of machines each repairs?

    (A) one
    (B) two
    (C) three
    (D) four
    (E) five

2. Which one of the following must be true?

    (A) Of the types of machines repaired by Stacy, there is exactly one type that Urma also repairs.
    (B) Of the types of machines repaired by Yolanda, there is exactly one type that Xena also repairs.
    (C) Of the types of machines repaired by Wim, there is exactly one type that Xena also repairs.
    (D) There is more than one type of machine that both Wim and Yolanda repair.
    (E) There is more than one type of machine that both Urma and Wim repair.

3. Which one of the following must be false?

    (A) Exactly one of the six technicians repairs exactly one type of machine.
    (B) Exactly two of the six technicians repair exactly one type of machine each.
    (C) Exactly three of the six technicians repair exactly one type of machine each.
    (D) Exactly one of the six technicians repairs exactly two types of machines.
    (E) Exactly three of the six technicians repair exactly two types of machines each.

4. Which one of the following pairs of technicians could repair all and only the same types of machines as each other?

    (A) Stacy and Urma
    (B) Urma and Yolanda
    (C) Urma and Xena
    (D) Wim and Xena
    (E) Xena and Yolanda

5. Which one of the following must be true?

    (A) There is exactly one type of machine that both Urma and Wim repair.
    (B) There is exactly one type of machine that both Urma and Xena repair.
    (C) There is exactly one type of machine that both Urma and Yolanda repair.
    (D) There is exactly one type of machine that both Wim and Yolanda repair.
    (E) There is exactly one type of machine that both Xena and Yolanda repair.

Use this space for scratch work

Use this space for scratch work

Game 3 Answers and Explanations

Step 1: Overview

Situation: A repair shop.

Entities: Technicians and types of machines.

Action: Matching types of machines to the technicians who repair them.

Limitations: Six technicians and three types of machines—so we'll see lots of repetition. At least one type of machine per technician; no types of machines other than those listed.

Step 2: Sketch

A table makes it very easy to keep track of who gets what, and is easy to redraw as needed, too (although a scan of the questions shows that none will likely be needed, because none of the five offers a new "if" clause.

r	S	U	W	X	Y	Z
t						
v						

Step 3: Rules

The Rules: We'll build Rule 1 into the sketch right off the bat: The number of TVs and VCRs remains a mystery, but there'll be exactly four "r's," one of which is in Xena's column.

Rules 2 and 3 work in tandem. Yolanda is going to get TVs and VCRs in her column, and radios aren't mentioned…but if Stacy has to repair at least one machine (which she does) and cannot have anything in common with Yolanda (which she can't), then Yolanda must repair TVs and VCRs only, and Stacy, radios only. Note the use of = to indicate "end of the line."

Rule 4 ties into Yolanda, too—Yolanda, we know, repairs two machines. If Zane repairs more than she does, then he must get the full contingent.

Rule 5 offers a useful reminder to turn negative rules into positive facts. If, as we're told, Wim and Stacy have nothing in common, then we shouldn't just note "(no r)" in his column, but the positive fact that Wim must repair either VCRs or TVs—maybe both. Meanwhile, while Rule 6 fails to mention which two types Urma will repair, her column will get exactly two slots filled, and we get this:

no r

r̸̸̸

t v

	S	U	W	X	Y	Z
	r̲̲	—	t/v	r	t	t
		—			v	v
						r̲̲

Step 4: Deductions

We have one radio left, and the only person who can get it is U—so write that in.

t̸t̸t̸t̸

t

v

	S	U	W	X	Y	Z
	r̲̲	r	t/v	r	t	t
		—			v	v
						r̲̲

There's nothing else we know for sure, but we've certainly figured out the lion's share of the game.

Step 5: Questions

1. C

A quick look at the sketch tells us we have completely determined three of the technicians' specialties. Choice (C).

2. A

The only difficult part about Question 2 is that it asks us to compare technicians to each other instead of directly asking what they repair. (A) is the correct answer, as Stacy and Urma necessarily both repair radios.

3. D

Watch out, as Question 3 asks not for what must be true but what must be false. At least two technicians (Urma and Yolanda) repair exactly two types of machines, making (D) impossible.

4. C

Put simply, the question asks for two people whose columns can be exactly alike in number and content. (A) Stacy repairs radios only, and Urma repairs radios plus something else. Eliminate. (B) Both do repair exactly two machines. But with Urma repairing "radios plus something" while Yolanda repairs "TVs plus VCRs," their columns are hardly identical in content. Eliminate. (C) Urma and Xena both repair radios; so far so good. Urma does repair another machine type; Xena could do likewise; and both could repair the second type—TVs or VCRs. Since Urma's and Xena's lists could be identical, (C) is the correct answer. For the record: (D) Wim and Xena's columns will look most unalike since Xena repairs radios and Wim does not. (E) The same is true for Xena and Yolanda, the latter of whom does not repair radios.

5.   C

(A) Wim repairs TVs or VCRs. If he repairs one of them and Urma repairs the other type (along with her usual radios), then the two would have exactly no machine types in common. Eliminate. (B) is true if Xena repairs radios only, but if she takes on another machine type—which she can—and Urma takes on the same type, they'd have exactly two in common. (C) Yolanda repairs TVs and VCRs only. Urma repairs "radios and something else only," and that something is TVs or VCRs. Yes, the two people have exactly that one type in common, and (C) is the correct answer

Unless matching games are a special problem for you, try the three practice sets together in about 30 minutes. If you are having trouble with this game type, though, do each game separately in 10 minutes or less and check your results to learn where you can improve before moving on to the next practice game.

PRACTICE SETS

Directions: Each group of questions is based on a set of conditions. It may be useful to draw a rough diagram to answer some questions. Choose the response that most accurately and completely answers each question.

Game 4

Questions 1–7

To prepare for fieldwork, exactly four different researchers—a geologist, a historian, a linguist, and a paleontologist—will learn at least one and at most three of four languages—Rundi, Swahili, Tigrinya, and Yoruba. They must learn the languages according to the following specifications:

> Exactly one researcher learns Rundi.
>
> Exactly two researchers learn Swahili.
>
> Exactly two researchers learn Tigrinya.
>
> Exactly three researchers learn Yoruba.
>
> Any language learned by the linguist or paleontologist is not learned by the geologist.
>
> Any language learned by the geologist is learned by the historian.

1. Which one of the following could be true?

   (A) The linguist learns three languages—Rundi, Swahili, and Tigrinya.

   (B) The linguist learns three languages—Swahili, Tigrinya, and Yoruba.

   (C) The historian learns three languages—Rundi, Swahili, and Tigrinya.

   (D) The historian learns three languages—Swahili, Tigrinya, and Yoruba.

   (E) The paleontologist learns three languages—Rundi, Swahili, and Tigrinya.

2. If the linguist learns three of the languages, then which one of the following must be true?

   (A) The linguist learns Tigrinya.

   (B) The linguist learns Rundi.

   (C) The linguist learns Swahili.

   (D) The paleontologist learns Rundi.

   (E) The paleontologist learns Swahili.

3. Each of the following could be true of the researcher who learns Rundi EXCEPT:

   (A) The researcher also learns Tigrinya, but not Swahili.

   (B) The researcher learns neither Tigrinya nor Swahili.

   (C) The researcher also learns Tigrinya, but not Yoruba.

   (D) The researcher also learns both Tigrinya and Yoruba.

   (E) The researcher also learns Yoruba, but not Tigrinya.

4. Each of the following could be a complete and accurate list of the researchers who learn both Swahili and Yoruba EXCEPT:

   (A) the historian.

   (B) the paleontologist.

   (C) the historian, the linguist.

   (D) the historian, the paleontologist.

   (E) the linguist, the paleontologist.

5. If the geologist learns exactly two of the languages, then which one of the following could be true?

   (A) The paleontologist learns Rundi.

   (B) The paleontologist learns Swahili.

   (C) The historian learns Rundi.

   (D) The paleontologist learns exactly three of the languages.

   (E) The historian learns exactly two of the languages.

6. Which one of the following must be true?

    (A) Fewer of the languages are learned by the historian than are learned by the paleontologist.

    (B) Fewer of the languages are learned by the geologist than are learned by the historian.

    (C) Fewer of the languages are learned by the geologist than are learned by the linguist.

    (D) Fewer of the languages are learned by the paleontologist than are learned by the linguist.

    (E) Fewer of the languages are learned by the paleontologist than are learned by the historian.

7. If exactly two of the languages are learned by the historian, then which one of the following must be true?

    (A) The paleontologist does not learn Rundi.

    (B) The geologist does not learn Swahili.

    (C) The linguist does not learn Rundi.

    (D) The historian does not learn Rundi.

    (E) The paleontologist does not learn Swahili.

Game 5

Questions 1–5

Six paintings hang next to each other as shown below:

$$1 \quad 2 \quad 3$$
$$4 \quad 5 \quad 6$$

Each of the paintings is an oil or else a watercolor.

Each oil is directly beside, directly above, or directly below another oil.

Each watercolor is directly beside, directly above, or directly below another watercolor.

Each painting is a nineteenth-century painting or else a twentieth-century painting.

Each painting is directly beside, directly above, or directly below another painting painted in the same century.

Painting 2 is a nineteenth-century painting.

Painting 3 is an oil.

Painting 5 is a twentieth-century painting.

1. If all of the nineteenth-century paintings are watercolors, which one of the following must be true?

   (A) Painting 1 is an oil.
   (B) Painting 3 is a nineteenth-century painting.
   (C) Painting 4 is a watercolor.
   (D) Painting 5 is an oil.
   (E) Painting 6 is a twentieth-century painting.

2. It is possible that the only two watercolors among the six paintings are

   (A) paintings 1 and 5.
   (B) paintings 1 and 6.
   (C) paintings 2 and 4.
   (D) paintings 4 and 5.
   (E) paintings 4 and 6.

3. If there are exactly three oils and three watercolors, which one of the following must be true?

   (A) Painting 1 is a watercolor.
   (B) Painting 2 is a watercolor.
   (C) Painting 4 is a watercolor.
   (D) Painting 5 is a watercolor.
   (E) Painting 6 is a watercolor.

4. If exactly two paintings are oils and exactly two paintings are nineteenth-century paintings, which one of the following must be false?

   (A) Painting 1 is a nineteenth-century painting, and painting 6 is an oil.
   (B) Painting 2 is both a nineteenth-century painting and an oil.
   (C) Painting 3 is a nineteenth-century painting.
   (D) Paintings 1 and 2 are both nineteenth-century paintings.
   (E) Painting 2 is an oil, and painting 4 is a nineteenth-century painting.

5. Which one of the following could be true?

   (A) Paintings 1 and 4 are two of exactly three twentieth-century paintings.
   (B) Paintings 1 and 6 are two of exactly three twentieth-century paintings.
   (C) Paintings 1 and 6 are two of exactly three nineteenth-century paintings.
   (D) Paintings 3 and 4 are two of exactly three nineteenth-century paintings.
   (E) Paintings 4 and 6 are two of exactly three nineteenth-century paintings.

Game 6

Questions 1–6

A railway company has exactly three lines: line 1, line 2, and line 3. The company prints three sets of tickets for January and three sets of tickets for February: one set for each of its lines for each of the two months. The company's tickets are printed in a manner consistent with the following conditions: Each of the six sets of tickets is exactly one of the following colors: green, purple, red, yellow.

For each line, the January tickets are a different color than the February tickets.

For each month, tickets for different lines are in different colors.

Exactly one set of January tickets is red.

For line 3, either the January tickets or the February tickets, but not both, are green.

The January tickets for line 2 are purple.

No February tickets are purple.

1. If the line 3 tickets for January are red, then which one of the following statements must be true?

   (A) The line 1 tickets for January are green.
   (B) The line 1 tickets for January are yellow.
   (C) The line 1 tickets for February are red.
   (D) The line 2 tickets for February are yellow.
   (E) The line 3 tickets for February are green.

2. If one set of the line 2 tickets is green, then which one of the following statements must be true?

   (A) The line 1 tickets for January are red.
   (B) The line 3 tickets for January are red.
   (C) The line 1 tickets for February are red.
   (D) The line 3 tickets for February are green.
   (E) The line 3 tickets for February are yellow.

3. Which one of the following statements could be true?

   (A) No January ticket is green.
   (B) No February ticket is green.
   (C) Only line 2 tickets are red.
   (D) One set of January tickets is green and one set of January tickets is yellow.
   (E) The line 2 tickets for January are the same color as the line 1 tickets for February.

4. Which one of the following statements could be true?

   (A) Both the line 1 tickets for January and the line 2 tickets for February are green.
   (B) Both the line 1 tickets for January and the line 2 tickets for February are yellow.
   (C) Both the line 1 tickets for January and the line 3 tickets for February are yellow.
   (D) The line 1 tickets for January are green, and the line 3 tickets for February are red.
   (E) The line 3 tickets for January are yellow, and the line 1 tickets for February are red.

5. If the line 3 tickets for February are yellow, then each of the following statements must be true EXCEPT:

   (A) One set of January tickets is green.
   (B) One set of line 1 tickets is red.
   (C) One set of line 2 tickets is red.
   (D) The tickets in two of the six sets are red.
   (E) The tickets in two of the six sets are yellow.

6. Suppose that none of the ticket sets are purple. If all of the other conditions remain the same, then which one of the following statements could be true?

   (A) None of the January tickets are green.
   (B) None of the February tickets are green.
   (C) None of the line 2 tickets are green.
   (D) No line 1 or line 2 tickets are yellow.
   (E) No line 2 or line 3 tickets are red.

Use this space for scratch work

Game 4 Answers and Explanations

Step 1: Overview

Situation: Fieldwork.

Entities: Researchers and languages.

Action: Match the languages learned to the researcher who learns them.

Limitations: Each researcher learns from 1 to 3 of the languages.

Step 2: Sketch

Simply sketch four columns, one for each researcher, and list the languages spoken (or not spoken) by each researcher. A list of the languages also helps.

Step 3: Rules

The first four rules tell us the number of people that speak each language. Add this to your sketch by indicating it in the number of times you list each language—one "r," two "s," etc. Rule 5 says there's no overlap between either the linguist and the geologist or the paleontologist and the geologist. So if either the linguist or the paleontologist learns a language, then the geologist can't learn that language, and if the geologist learns a language, then neither the linguist nor the paleontologist can learn that language. Rule 6 indicates that if the geologist learns a language, then the historian learns that language. Taking the contrapositive, we know that if the historian doesn't learn a language, then the geologist can't learn that language either. Here's the sketch after the rules:

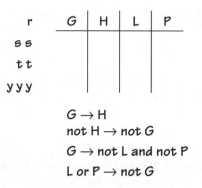

```
G → H
not H → not G
G → not L and not P
L or P → not G
```

Step 4: Deductions

Combine Rules 4 and 5. Three people learn Yoruba, but there's no overlap between the geologist and either the linguist or the paleontologist. So who can learn Yoruba? Not the geologist. If the geologist did learn Yoruba, then the linguist and the paleontologist couldn't, but that's impossible because we need three researchers to learn Yoruba. So the geologist doesn't learn Yoruba, which means everyone else learns Yoruba. We can also make a deduction from Rule 1 and Rule 6. Only one researcher learns Rundi, but who could that be? Not the geologist, since if the geologist learned Rundi, then the historian would have to learn Rundi, too. So what can the geologist learn? Only Swahili and Tigrinya are left. So the geologist (and the historian) learns S or T.

Step 5: Questions

1. D

This one is over quickly if you made the big deduction concerning Yoruba. (A), (C), and (E) have the same problem: since the historian, linguist, and paleontologist all learn Yoruba, they cannot learn the other three languages as well, since the maximum number of languages each researcher can learn is three. You can eliminate (B) since it has the linguist learning both Swahili and Tigrinya. That's impossible, since the geologist must learn at least one of those languages. (D) is the only choice that remains, and in fact, it is possible for the historian to learn every language except Rundi.

2. B

If the linguist learns three languages, which languages could they be? One of them is Yoruba, but what about the other two? You know from your work in the setup (and from eliminating (B) in the previous question) that the linguist cannot learn both Swahili and Tigrinya. So if the linguist learns three languages, one of them will be Yoruba, one of them will be either Swahili or Tigrinya, and the last one must be Rundi, the only other language left. That's (B).

3. C

What do you know about the researcher who learns Rundi? That researcher isn't the geologist, and everybody else learns Yoruba. So whoever learns Rundi also learns Yoruba. Scanning the choices with this deduction you can see that (C) must be false.

4. B

(A) Could the historian be the only researcher learning both Swahili and Yoruba? If so, then the linguist and the paleontologist (who must learn Yoruba) cannot also learn Swahili, and so the geologist must learn Swahili. From here, we can fill in the rest of the languages in a variety of ways as long as we don't violate Rule 5 or Rule 6. (B), however, is impossible. If only the paleontologist learns both Swahili and Yoruba, then neither the historian nor the linguist (who must learn Yoruba) can learn Swahili. But we need two Swahili learners, and so the geologist must learn Swahili. But now Rule 6 comes into play. If the geologist learns Swahili, then the historian has to learn Swahili as well, and then we have two researchers that learn both Swahili and Yoruba. So the paleontologist cannot be the only researcher learning both Swahili and Yoruba, and so (B) is correct.

5. A

If the geologist learns two languages, then what languages could they be? The only options are Swahili and Tigrinya. This means that the historian must learn both Swahili and Tigrinya as well (Rule 6). The only language left to be placed is Rundi, which could be learned by either the linguist or the paleontologist.

r	G	H	L	P
~~s~~ ~~s~~	s	y	y	y
~~t~~ ~~t~~	t	s		
~~y~~ ~~y~~ ~~y~~		t		

↳ r ↱

(A) picks up on this possibility and is correct.

6. B

(A) need not be true. In Question 10, we saw that the historian could learn three languages, and no one can learn more than three. (B) must be true. The geologist doesn't learn Yoruba, and the historian must learn Yoruba. Plus, the historian must learn every language that the geologist learns. So no matter how you slice it, the historian will always learn at least one more language than the geologist, and (B) must be correct.

7. D

If the historian learns exactly two languages, and we know one of them is Yoruba, what is the other one? We know that the geologist will learn either Swahili or Tigrinya, and whichever one the geologist learns, the historian will learn also. So the second language learned by the historian will be either Swahili or Tigrinya, and so it cannot be Rundi, (D) .

Game 5 Answers and Explanations

Step 1: Overview

Situation: Paintings on a wall.

Entities: Paintings, medium, and century.

Action: Match the medium and century to each painting.

Limitation: Each painting comes from exactly one century and is painted in exactly one medium.

Notice that in this game you really get the sense of what's going on from Rules 1 and 4, which are limitations disguised as rules.

Step 2: Sketch

The test maker has given you the sketch here—so use their framework to start. Under each painting, leave two blanks—one for the medium and one for the century.

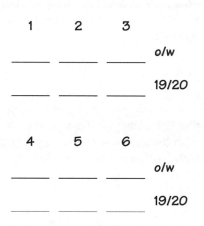

Step 3: Rules

Rules 6, 7, and 8 give concrete information you can draw in the sketch. Rules 2, 3, and 5 don't give you anything concrete on their own, and are difficult to shorthand, so you will do best to just star them and remember that they are in play. At this point your sketch should look like this:

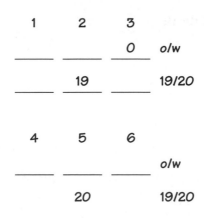

Step 4: Deductions

Think about the rules that each painting must be next to at least one that is of the same medium, and at least one that is from the same century. Painting 3 being an oil means that 2 or 6 must be oils. Because 2 is 19th century, 1 or 3 must also be 19th century. And because 5 is 20th century, 4 or 6 must be 20th century. None of these are definite, so you don't want to draw them in the sketch, but it's good to take note and think through these possibilities now so that you'll quickly recall them as you work the questions.

Step 5: Questions

1.   E

An "if" question requires a new sketch. If all 19th century paintings are watercolors, that means all oils must be 20th century. Thus 2 is a watercolor and 3 is 20th century. The rules about adjacent paintings tell you that 6 must be an oil (and thus 20th century), and 1 must be 19th century (thus a watercolor).

	1	2	3
	W	W	O
	19	19	20

	4	5	6
			O
		20	20

This is enough to see that (E) must be true.

2.   D

The only requirement for a watercolor is that it sit next to (or above or below) another watercolor. So "the only two watercolors" have to be adjacent paintings—and the only choice providing the same is (D). (A), (B), (C) and (E) all leave watercolors surrounded by oils—hence each violates Rule 3.

3.   C

When you re-sketch this "if" question, don't get the centuries involved! Note the stem and choices—their topic is medium only. You already know that 3 is an oil (Rule 7), 3 will have to be one of the three. The other two oils could be at 1 and 2, or 2 and 6, or 5 and 6, but in any of these cases, 4 will have to be a watercolor.

4.   E

There are exactly two oils, and we know one of those oils is 3 (Rule 7). Therefore, in line with Rule 2, either 2 or 6 must be an oil…which means that 1, 4, and 5 are definitely watercolors. The same logic holds for the 19's, of which we're told there are also exactly two. Since one of those 19's is 2, and 5 directly below it is a 20, either 1 or 3 must be a 19, which means that the entire bottom row—4, 5, and 6—must be 20's. This makes (E) false—while 2 might be an oil, 4 can't be 19th century.

5.   A

Just look back at the master sketch and remember the game's requirements—as well as that of the question: the four wrong choices are impossible. (A) works fine. The third 20 that (A) refers to must be 5, and making 1, 4, and 5 20's—leaving 2, 3, and 6 as 19's. (B) is impossible, as it would leave 1, a 20, surrounded by 19's. (C) is impossible, as it would leave 6, a 19, surrounded by 20's. (D) is impossible, as it would leave 4, a 19, surrounded by 20's. (E) is the most blatantly impossible, as it would leave all the 19's surrounded by 20's and vice versa. In other words, if the only 19's are 2, 4, and 6, then all six paintings violate Rule 5.

Game 6 Answers and Explanations

Step 1: Overview

Situation: Rail tickets.

Entities: Lines, months, and colors.

Action: Matching a color to each line for each month.

Limitations: None before looking at the rules, but the rules tell us that the tickets are either green, purple, red, or yellow, and that tickets are different for the same line in different months, and for the same month on different lines.

Step 2: Sketch

A grid works well here, and allows easy comparison across months and lines. What can change from line to line and month to month is the color of the sets of tickets. So when creating our grid, the months and lines will go along the top and side, and we will fill in the grid squares with the color:

Step 3: Rules

Rule 1 just sets the available colors of the game. Rules 2 and 3 state that the same color can't be used across lines or across months. Rule 4 dictates exactly one use of r in the January column. Rule 5 dictates exactly one use of g in the line 3 row. Rule 6 gives a concrete that can be put in the sketch, and Rule 7 eliminates p from the February column.

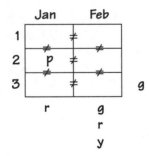

Step 4: Deductions

Rule 6 said that Jan 2 is purple. Rule 3 said that within each month, the sets of tickets for the three lines must be of different colors. So you can deduce that Jan 1 and Jan 3 can't be purple. Rule 7 already said that NO sets of February tickets are purple, so you definitely know that Jan 2 is the only set of tickets that is purple.

You can deduce something else from Rule 7 which says that none of the February tickets are purple. Rule says that each month's set of tickets must be different colors. Since none of the February tickets are purple, that means that all three of the other colors must be used exactly once for the three sets of February tickets, one green, one red, and one yellow. Here's our master sketch:

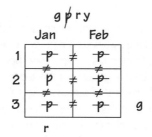

Step 5: Questions

1. E

Rule 5 says that one of the sets of line 3 tickets (either January or February) must be green. The stem says that Jan 3 is red, so Feb 3 must be green, choice (E).

2. A

What must be true if one of the sets of line 2 tickets is green? Jan 2 is purple (Rule 6), so the only 2 line left to be green is Feb 2. Rule 3 says that no two sets of tickets in the same month can be the same color. Since Feb 2 is green, Feb 3 can't be green. Rule 5 (either Jan 3 or Feb 3 must be green) comes into effect again and Jan 3 must be green. Rule 4 says that one of the January tickets is red, and since Jan 2 is purple and Jan 3 is green, Jan 1 must be red. And that's choice (A) and the answer.

3. A

Could none of the January tickets be green? If none are, we're left with purple, red, and yellow as the colors of the three sets of January tickets. Jan 2 is purple (Rule 6). Jan 1 could be red, and as long as Feb 3 is green (to fulfill Rule 5), Jan 3 could be yellow. Answer choice (A) could be true and is the answer. Since none of the sets of February tickets are purple (Rule 7), exactly one set of the February tickets MUST be green, eliminating (B). The Jan 2 tickets are purple (Rule 6) and one set of the January tickets is red (Rule 4), so either Jan 1 or Jan 3 must be red. (C) is wrong. Jan 2 is purple, so if one set of January tickets was green and the other set of January tickets was yellow, there wouldn't be any set of January tickets that was red, which would violate Rule 4. (D) can't be true. Jan 2 is purple, and Rule 7 says that absolutely none of the sets of February tickets can be purple, making (E) incorrect.

4. B

Try out each choice. (A) If Jan 1 and Feb 2 are both green, Rule 3 means that none of the remaining sets of tickets can be green. But Rule 5 insists that either Jan 3 or Feb 3 be green. (A) can't be true and isn't the answer. (B) Can Jan 1 and Feb 2 both be yellow? It could happen this way: Jan 1— Y, Jan 2—P, Jan 3—R; Feb 1—R, Feb 2—Y, Feb 3—G. (B) can be true and is the answer.

5. E

If Feb 3 is yellow, Rule 5 forces Jan 3 to be green. Since Jan 3 is green, Jan 1 is left to be red. Since none of the sets of February tickets are purple, Feb 1 and Feb 2 must be green and red. Since Jan 1 is red, Rule 2 means that Feb 1 can't be red and must be green. Feb 2 is left to be red. The entire setup is fixed: Jan 1—R, Jan 2—P, Jan 3—G; Feb 1—G, Feb 2—R, Feb 3—Y. The only choice that doesn't agree with this setup is (E)—only one of the sets of tickets is yellow.

6.   C

For this question, none of the sets of tickets are purple. This doesn't affect the sets of February tickets since none were purple anyway. But since none of the sets of January tickets are purple, one will be green, one red, and one yellow. These three colors are the only options for both month's tickets. Now check the choices looking for the one that can be true. You can eliminate (A) and (B) immediately. Since none of the sets of tickets are purple, all of the other colors *must* be used exactly once per month. Exactly one set of January tickets and exactly one set of February tickets must be green. (C) Could neither of the sets of line 2 tickets be green? It could work this way: Jan 1—Y, Jan 2—R, Jan 3—G; Feb 1—G, Feb 2—Y, Feb 3—R. (C) could be true and is the answer. (D) If none of the sets of line 1 or line 2 tickets are yellow, then both Jan 3 and Feb 3 must be yellow, which Rule 2 forbids. (E) If none of the sets of line 2 or line 3 tickets are red, then both Jan 1 and Feb 1 must be red, which Rule 2 forbids.

Chapter 9: **Hybrid Games**

Finally, while any single game type may be very difficult, many games are further complicated by combining elements of sequencing, grouping, or matching in a single game.

By now, you've developed strong underlying skills, independent of one another; now see how well you can work with two or more of them at the same time.

GAME 1: THE METHOD

Don't let the fact that this is your first hybrid game, or the fact that the list of rules is fairly long, discourage or daunt you. Plan your own setup and see what you can deduce, and try each question on your own, before reading on.

Questions 1–5

A locally known guitarist's demo CD contains exactly seven different songs—S, T, V, W, X, Y, and Z. Each song occupies exactly one of the CD's seven tracks. Some of the songs are rock classics; the others are new compositions.

The following conditions must hold:

> S occupies the fourth track of the CD.
>
> Both W and Y precede S on the CD.
>
> T precedes W on the CD.
>
> A rock classic occupies the sixth track of the CD.
>
> Each rock classic is immediately preceded on the CD
>
> by a new composition.
>
> Z is a rock classic.

Step 1: Overview

Situation: A guitarist making a demo CD.

Entities: Songs S, T, V, W, X, Y, and Z; types of songs r and n.

Action: Sequence the songs, and match types to songs.

Limitations: Each song occupies exactly one track; only one type per song.

If you need to refresh any of your sequencing or matching skills, look back at those chapters.

Step 2: Sketch

This game is a combination of sequencing and matching, with sequencing being the primary action. As you might expect, you should set up a series of seven blocks for the seven songs. Under each block, you'll want to add a second line for the type.

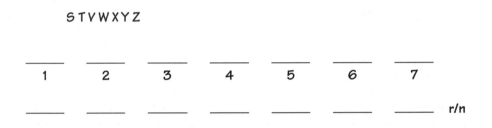

Step 3: Rules

You've seen all the types of issues that can be raised in the different game types, and the form that the rules can take. You'll find nothing new here.

Notice that the first three rules only deal with the sequencing action, and the last three rules deal with the matching action.

The first rule says S must be track 4:

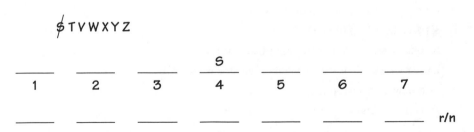

The second rule says that W and Y must come before S. Normally you would shorthand this rule, but knowing S has to be in position 4, W and Y must be in 1–3. Incorporate this into your sketch.

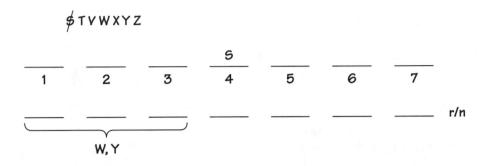

The third rule says T must precede W. You can incorporate this with Rule 2:

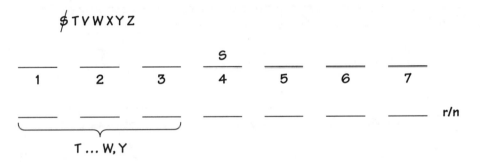

The fourth rule, like the first is concrete and, tells you that the sixth song must be a rock classic. Draw this in:

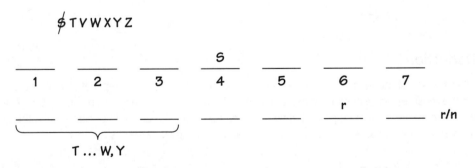

The fifth rule says that each rock classic must have a new composition immediately before it. This indicates two things: there can never be two sequential rock classics, and that the first song must be a new composition (because if the first song were a rock classic, it would be impossible to have a preceding new composition.) Shorthand the first part of this rule, and add the second part to your sketch.

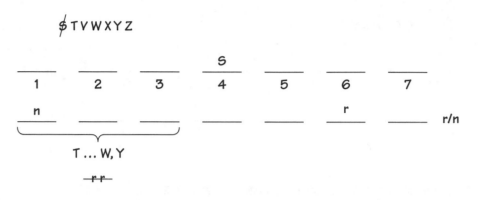

The last rule tells you something definite, but which can't be written in the final sketch quite yet. Z is a rock classic, but Z hasn't been placed. This information is best written in the list of entities.

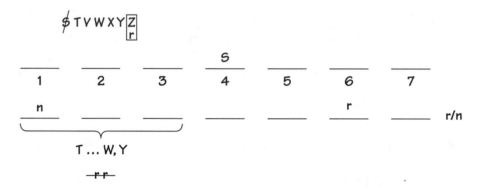

Step 4: Deduction

Look at the sketch you just made. If T, W, and Y are occupying the first three spots, that leaves X, V, and Z to occupy the last three. Z is the most restricted because it must be a rock classic, and thus can't go in positions 5 or 7 because of the rule that each rock classic must be preceded by a new composition. Z must be in position 6. For the same reason, the fifth and seventh songs must be new compositions. X and V must go in positions 5 and 7.

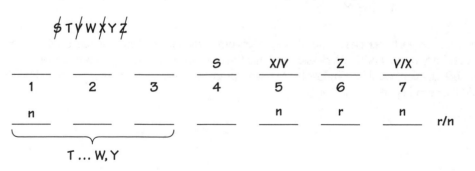

Step 5: Questions

1. Which one of the following could be the order of the songs on the CD, from the first track through the seventh?

   (A) T, W, V, S, Y, X, Z
   (B) V, Y, T, S, W, Z, X
   (C) X, Y, W, S, T, Z, S
   (D) Y, T, W, S, X, Z, V
   (E) Z, T, X, W, V, Y, S

For this acceptability question, eliminate any answer that violates a rule. Rule 1 eliminates (E). Rule 2 eliminates (A) and (B). Rule 3 eliminates (C), leaving (D) as the answer.

2. Which one of the following is a pair of songs that must occupy consecutive tracks on the CD?

   (A) S and V
   (B) S and W
   (C) T and Z
   (D) T and Y
   (E) V and Z

Your master sketch shows that both X and V, whether in position 5 or position 7, will always be adjacent to Z. Answer choice (E) is correct.

3. Which one of the following songs must be a new composition?

   (A) S
   (B) T
   (C) W
   (D) X
   (E) Y

This question, too, can be answered directly off the master sketch if you've made all the possible deductions. The sketch shows that X and V, regardless of position, must be new compositions. This leads to answer choice (D).

4. If W precedes Y on the CD, then which one of the following must be true?

   (A) S is a rock classic.
   (B) V is a rock classic.
   (C) Y is a rock classic.
   (D) T is a new composition.
   (E) W is a new composition.

For this "if," question, draw a new sketch and add that W is before Y. This determines the position of T, W, and Y, but the answer choices all refer to the matching action. Looking at the sketch indicates that (B) is false, (A), (C), and (E) are possible, and (D) is the one which must be true, and which is the correct answer.

$\cancel{\$}\,T\,\cancel{Y}\,W\,\cancel{X}\,Y\,\cancel{Z}$

T	W	Y	S	X/V	Z	V/X	
1	2	3	4	5	6	7	
n				n	r	n	
							r/n

5. If there are exactly two songs on the CD that both precede V and are preceded by Y, then which one of the following could be true?

(A) V occupies the seventh track of the CD.

(B) X occupies the fifth track of the CD.

(C) Y occupies the third track of the CD.

(D) T is a rock classic.

(E) W is a rock classic.

Another new sketch is indicated. The additional information says that there are exactly two songs before V and after Y. If V were to be in position 7, Y would have to be in position 4, which is impossible. V then must be in position 5, putting Y in position 2—so you can eliminate answer choice (C)—and T and W in 1 and 3, respectively. Because T must be first, and it must be a new composition, you can eliminate answer choice (D). Therefore, answer choice (E) is correct.

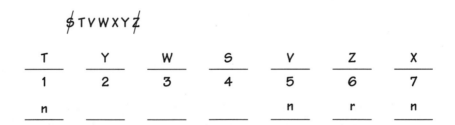

$\cancel{\$}\,T\,V\,W\,X\,Y\,\cancel{Z}$

T	Y	W	S	V	Z	X
1	2	3	4	5	6	7
n				n	r	n

GAME 2: PRACTICE

Once again, work through the example on the following page on your own, focusing on applying Kaplan's Method and strategies, but incorporate some awareness of pacing in all your practice now. Allow yourself no more than 11 minutes for this game.

Questions 1–6

Four boys—Fred, Juan, Marc, and Paul—and three girls—Nita, Rachel, and Trisha—will be assigned to a row of five adjacent lockers, numbered consecutively 1 through 5, arranged along a straight wall. The following conditions govern the assignment of lockers to the seven children:

> Each locker must be assigned to either one or two children, and each child must be assigned to exactly one locker.
>
> Each shared locker must be assigned to one girl and one boy.
>
> Juan must share a locker, but Rachel cannot share a locker.
>
> Nita's locker cannot be adjacent to Trisha's locker.
>
> Fred must be assigned to locker 3.

1. Which one of the following is a complete and accurate list of the children who must be among those assigned to shared lockers?

    (A) Fred, Juan
    (B) Juan, Paul
    (C) Juan, Marc, Paul
    (D) Juan, Marc, Trisha
    (E) Juan, Nita, Trisha

2. If Trisha is assigned to locker 3 and Marc alone is assigned to locker 1, then which one of the following must be true?

    (A) Juan is assigned to locker 4.
    (B) Juan is assigned to locker 5.
    (C) Paul is assigned to locker 2.
    (D) Rachel is assigned to locker 2.
    (E) Rachel is assigned to locker 5.

3. If the four boys are assigned to consecutively numbered lockers and Juan is assigned to locker 5, then which one of the following is a complete and accurate list of lockers each of which CANNOT be a shared locker?

    (A) locker 2
    (B) locker 4
    (C) locker 1, locker 2
    (D) locker 1, locker 4
    (E) locker 2, locker 4

4. Once Rachel has been assigned to a locker, what is the maximum number of different lockers each of which could be the locker to which Juan is assigned?

    (A) one
    (B) two
    (C) three
    (D) four
    (E) five

5. If the first three lockers are assigned to girls, which one of the following must be true?

    (A) Juan is assigned to locker 1.
    (B) Nita is assigned to locker 3.
    (C) Trisha is assigned to locker 1.
    (D) Juan is assigned to the same locker as Trisha.
    (E) Paul is assigned to the same locker as Trisha.

6. If lockers 1 and 2 are each assigned to one boy and are not shared lockers, then locker 4 must be assigned to

    (A) Juan.
    (B) Paul.
    (C) Rachel.
    (D) Juan and Nita.
    (E) Marc and Trisha.

Use this space for scratch work

Use this space for scratch work

Game 2 Answers and Explanations

Step 1: Overview

Situation: Assigning lockers to students.

Entities: Boys F, J, M, and P, and girls n, r, and t.

Action: To distribute students into groups for lockers, and then sequence these groups.

Limitations: Seven students, five lockers, so at least some lockers will have multiple students.

Step 2: Sketch

Without knowing yet who the groups will be composed of, all that's to be done at the beginning is to indicate the lockers, and write down the list of entities.

1	2	3	4	5	F J M P
___	___	___	___	___	n r t

Step 3: Rules

The first rule lays out the numbers for you, which are always key in a distribution game. No lockers are empty, and a locker has at most two children assigned to it. Thus there must be two lockers with two children assigned, and three lockers with one child assigned.

The second rule tells you that a shared locker (of which there are two) will have one girl and one boy assigned to it. This means there will be two lockers with one girl and one boy, two lockers with one boy, and one locker with one girl.

Rule 3 says that Juan is in one of the shared lockers, but Rachel is alone. Indicate this in your sketch.

The fourth rule says Nita can't be adjacent to Trisha; another rule that should be added to the sketch.

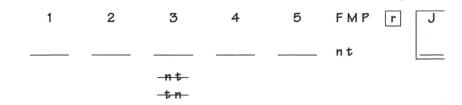

The last rule is the only one with concrete information; Fred must be assigned to locker 3. Indicate this in the sketch.

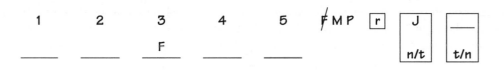

Step 4: Deduction

Juan must share a locker with a girl, and that girl can't be Rachel, so either Nita or Trisha must go with Juan. The other girl, either Nita or Trisha, must be assigned to the other shared locker. And since Nita and Trisha can't be adjacent, the shared lockers thus can't be adjacent.

Step 5: Questions

1. E

One look at your master sketch will tell you that Juan, Nita, and Trisha are the only three who must be assigned to shared lockers. Rachel can't be, and Fred, Marc, and Paul could be, but don't have to be.

2. B

Draw a new sketch and add this information. If Trisha is in locker 3 (with Fred) and Marc is alone at locker 1, the only place Juan (and Nita) can go is at Locker 5.

3. D

Another "if" question and another new sketch. With Juan at 5, the four consecutive lockers assigned to boys must be 2, 3, 4, and 5. Since 5 is a shared locker, the other shared locker can't be locker 4. And because the shared locker must have one boy sharing it, locker 1 (which will have just one girl, Rachel) can't be shared either.

1	2	3	4	5
r	M/P	F	P/M	J
				n/t

4. C

With a maximum question, remember to start with the largest answer and work down. If you assign Rachel to a locker, is it possible that Juan could be assigned to any of the five lockers? No, he certainly can't go to whichever locker Rachel is at, because she's alone. (E) won't work. Could you assign Rachel and then have four possibilities for Juan's location? Again, no, because Juan can't go to the locker Rachel is at, nor can he go in the locker Fred is at (because shared lockers have one boy and one girl). (D) is eliminated. But, if you put Rachel at locker 1, say, Juan could go at locker 2 (as long as the other shared locker is 4 or 5), or locker 4 (as long as the other shared locker is 2) or at locker 5 (as long as the other shared locker is 2 or 3). This gives three possibilities.

5. A

If the first three lockers are assigned to girls, then the shared lockers must be assigned in the first three. In order to keep them separate, the shared lockers must be lockers 1 and 3, and Rachel must be alone at locker 2. Fred is sharing at 3, and Juan is sharing at 1. Marc and Paul are then left alone in lockers 4 and 5.

1	2	3	4	5
J	r	F	M/P	P/M
t/n		n/t		

6. C

If lockers 1 and 2 are not shared, the two shared lockers must be within the last three lockers. To keep them separated, the shared lockers must be at 3 (with Fred) and 5 (Juan). Rachel must be at locker 4 because the single boy lockers are 1 and 2.

1	2	3	4	5
M/P	P/M	F	r	J
		n/t		t/n

GAME 3: PACING

Now it's time to apply all your skills in a timed, test-like practice. Allow yourself no more than 10 minutes to complete this one.

Questions 1–5

A study sponsored by a consumer group tests exactly five of seven cold medications—F, G, H, I, K, L, and M—and ranks the medications tested from first (best) to fifth (worst). There are no ties. The following conditions must apply:

L ranks second.

Either F or G ranks first.

I is tested.

H ranks better than G if both are tested.

K ranks better than F if both are tested.

If M is tested, both F and H are also tested.

1. Which one of the following could be the five cold medications that the study ranks, listed from first to fifth?

(A) F, I, L, H, G

(B) F, L, G, H, M

(C) F, L, I, G, M

(D) F, L, I, H, M

(E) F, L, K, I, G

2. Which one of the following could be true of the study?

(A) G ranks better than M.

(B) H ranks better than F.

(C) I ranks better than F.

(D) K ranks better than G.

(E) M ranks better than G.

3. Which one of the following cold medications must be among those tested in the study?

(A) F

(B) G

(C) H

(D) K

(E) M

4. Which one of the following is a complete and accurate list of the cold medications any one of which could be the cold medication ranked fifth?

(A) F, G, H, M

(B) G, H, I, M

(C) G, H, L, M

(D) F, G, H, I, K

(E) F, G, H, I, M

5. If I ranks third, each of the following could also be true of the study EXCEPT:

(A) M ranks better than H.

(B) K ranks better than G.

(C) I ranks better than F.

(D) H ranks better than M.

(E) G ranks better than K.

Use this space for scratch work

Use this space for scratch work

Game 3 Answers and Explanations

Step 1: Overview

Situation: Testing cold medications.

Entities: Medications F, G, H, I, K, L, and M.

Action: Selection—select five of the seven medications to be tested, and sequencing—sequence the five tested medications.

Limitations: The numbers say that two medications will be rejected, and there are no ties in the sequence.

Step 2: Sketch

A quick glance at the rules tells you that the sequencing will be strict because there are rules about who is tested first and second, and this can be sketched easily with a five-slot strict sequence, and two slots to the side for the two rejected medications. Don't forget to write your list of entities as well.

Step 3: Rules

The first rule places L in position 2. Add this to your sketch.

The second rule says that either F or G goes in the first position. Looking at the rest of the rules indicates that knowing whether F or G is first is likely to allow further deductions, so create two sketches for Limited Options.

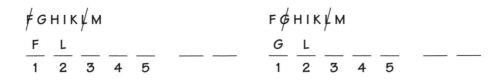

The third rule indicates that I must be tested, so I is in position 3, 4, or 5.

Rule 4 says that if H and G are both tested, H must rank better than, or come before, G. If G is first, though, H can't rank higher, so in the second option H can't be tested. In the first option you can just shorthand this rule.

Rule 5 operates the same way, telling you that in the first option K is not tested, and that in the second option, if K and F are both tested, K is before F.

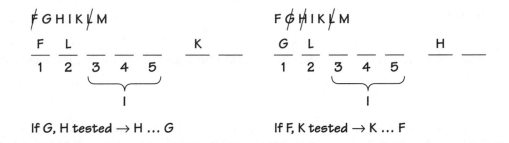

The last rule says that if M is tested, both F and H are also tested. The contrapositive is that if F or H are not tested, then M cannot be tested.

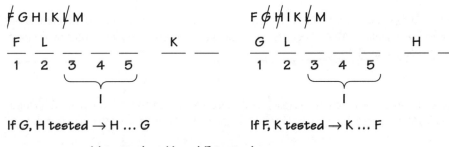

Step 4: Deduction

In the second option, H isn't tested, so M cannot be tested, and M is the second excluded treatment. This leaves I, K, and F to be tested, with K before F.

In the first option, if H is not tested, M cannot be tested, but then there would be three excluded treatments (K, M, and H). So H must be tested. Either G or M could be the second excluded treatment.

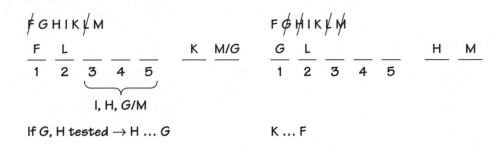

Step 5: Questions

1. D

Apply each rule to eliminate answer choices. Rule 1 eliminates (A). Rule 3 eliminates (B). Rule 5 eliminates (D), and Rule 6 rules out (C).

2. C

Without an "if," the answer to this one should come from your master sketch. G and M won't both be ranked, eliminating (A). If F is ranked, it is ranked first, which eliminates (B). (C) looks possible in the second option; keep checking to make sure (D) and (E) are impossible: neither K nor M could rank better than G, since K is unranked in the first option and M is only ranked in the first option and only if G is unranked.

3. A

In both options, F must be one of the medications tested.

4. E

L definitely cannot be ranked fifth, eliminating (C). F could be fifth in the second option, which eliminates (B). I could go fifth in either option, eliminating (A). And because K, if tested (in the second option), must be better than F, K cannot be fifth, which eliminates (D).

5. B

If I ranks third, you aren't sure which option you're in, so it's necessary to redraw both options. With I third, it's still not possible to place H/G/M in the remaining slots. However, in the second option, placing I third puts K fourth and F fifth.

M could be ranked higher in the first option, if G is not selected. (A) is incorrect. K, however, is only ranked in the second option, and in this option G is ranked higher, which means (B) is impossible and the correct answer.

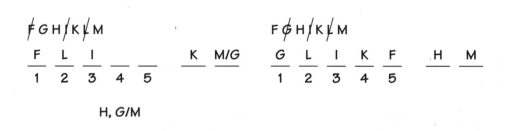

The next practice set is your last chance to try several games without doing a full practice section; try all three in 27 minutes. Then plan on doing the practice Logic Games sections at the back of the book under full, test-like conditions.

Good luck on Test Day!

PRACTICE SETS

<u>Directions:</u> Each group of questions is based on a set of conditions. It may be useful to draw a rough diagram to answer some questions. Choose the response that most accurately and completely answers each question.

Game 4

<u>Questions 1–5</u>

Quentin, Robert, Shiro, Tony, and Umeko are the only members of the Kim family who attend an opera. Each of them sits in a separate seat in either row G or row H, and each sits in a seat numbered 1, 2, or 3. Consecutively numbered seats within each row are adjacent.

Each member of the Kim family sits in a seat adjacent to, and in the same row as, at least one other member of the family.

    Tony and Umeko sit in row H.

    Shiro and Umeko sit in lower numbered seats than does Tony.

    Robert sits in the same row as Quentin or Shiro or both.

    Robert sits in a seat numbered 2.

1. Which one of the following statements could be true?

    (A) Seat G3 is empty.

    (B) Seat H2 is empty.

    (C) Shiro sits in a seat numbered 3.

    (D) Tony sits in a seat numbered 1.

    (E) Umeko sits in a seat numbered 3.

2. Which one of the following statements could be true?

    (A) Robert sits in row H.

    (B) Shiro sits in row H.

    (C) Quentin sits in the same row as, and in a seat adjacent to, Shiro.

    (D) Robert sits in the same row as, and in a seat adjacent to, Tony.

    (E) Robert sits in the same row as, and in a seat adjacent to, Umeko.

3. If Tony sits in a seat numbered 2, then which one of the following statements could be false?

    (A) Quentin sits in a seat numbered 3.

    (B) Umeko sits in a seat numbered 1.

    (C) Quentin sits in the same row as, and in a seat adjacent to, Robert.

    (D) Robert sits in the same row as, and in a seat adjacent to, Shiro.

    (E) Tony sits in the same row as, and in a seat adjacent to, Umeko.

4. Considering only the six seats in which members of the Kim family could sit, which one of the following is a complete and accurate list of those seats any one of which could be empty?

    (A) G1, G3

    (B) G3, H1

    (C) H1, H3

    (D) G1, G3, H1

    (E) G1, G3, H1, H3

5. Which one of the following is a complete and accurate list of those members of the Kim family any one of whom could sit in seat H2?

    (A) Quentin

    (B) Shiro, Umeko

    (C) Robert, Shiro, Umeko

    (D) Tony, Shiro, Umeko

    (E) Quentin, Shiro, Tony, Umeko

Game 5

Questions 1–6

A zoo's reptile house has a straight row of exactly five consecutive habitats—numbered 1 through 5 from left to right—for housing exactly seven reptiles—four snakes and three lizards. Five of the reptiles are female and two are male. The reptiles must be housed as follows:

No habitat houses more than two reptiles.

No habitat houses both a snake and a lizard.

No female snake is housed in a habitat that is immediately next to a habitat housing a male lizard.

1. Which one of the following could be a complete and accurate matching of habitats to reptiles?

   (A) 1: two female snakes; 2: one male snake; 3: one female lizard; 4: one male snake, one female lizard; 5: one female lizard

   (B) 1: empty; 2: two female snakes; 3: two female lizards; 4: two male snakes; 5: one female lizard

   (C) 1: one female snake, one male snake; 2: two female snakes; 3: one male lizard; 4: one female lizard; 5: one female lizard

   (D) 1: two male snakes; 2: empty; 3: one female lizard; 4: one female lizard; 5: two female snakes, one female lizard

   (E) 1: one female snake, one male snake; 2: one female snake, one male snake; 3: one male lizard; 4: one female lizard; 5: one female lizard

2. If habitat 2 contains at least one female snake and habitat 4 contains two male lizards, then which one of the following could be true?

   (A) Habitat 3 contains two reptiles.

   (B) Habitat 5 contains two reptiles.

   (C) Habitat 1 contains a female lizard.

   (D) Habitat 2 contains a female lizard.

   (E) Habitat 5 contains a female lizard.

3. Which one of the following must be true?

   (A) At least one female reptile is alone in a habitat.

   (B) At least one male reptile is alone in a habitat.

   (C) At least one lizard is alone in a habitat.

   (D) At least one lizard is male.

   (E) At least one snake is male.

4. Which one of the following CANNOT be the complete housing arrangement for habitats 1 and 2?

   (A) 1: one female snake, one male snake; 2: one male snake

   (B) 1: one male lizard; 2: one male snake

   (C) 1: two female lizards; 2: one female snake

   (D) 1: one male snake; 2: empty

   (E) 1: empty; 2: one female lizard

5. If habitat 3 is empty, and no snake is housed in a habitat that is immediately next to a habitat containing a snake, then which one of the following could be false?

   (A) All snakes are housed in even-numbered habitats.

   (B) None of the lizards is male.

   (C) No snake is alone in a habitat.

   (D) No lizard is housed in a habitat that is immediately next to a habitat containing a lizard.

   (E) Exactly one habitat contains exactly one reptile.

6. If all snakes are female and each of the lizards has a habitat to itself, then which one of the following habitats CANNOT contain any snakes?

   (A) habitat 1

   (B) habitat 2

   (C) habitat 3

   (D) habitat 4

   (E) habitat 5

Game 6

Questions 1–6

Exactly five cars—Frank's, Marquitta's, Orlando's Taishah's, and Vinquetta's—are washed, each exactly once. The cars are washed one at a time, with each receiving exactly one kind of wash: regular, super, or premium. The following conditions must apply:

The first car washed does not receive a super wash, though at least one car does.

Exactly one car receives a premium wash.

The second and third cars washed receive the same kind of wash as each other.

Neither Orlando's nor Taishah's is washed before Vinquetta's.

Marquitta's is washed before Frank's, but after Orlando's.

Marquitta's and the car washed immediately before Marquitta's receive regular washes.

1. Which one of the following could be an accurate list of the cars in the order in which they are washed, matched with type of wash received?

   (A) Orlando's: premium; Vinquetta's: regular; Taishah's: regular; Marquitta's: regular; Frank's: super

   (B) Vinquetta's: premium; Orlando's: regular; Taishah's: regular; Marquitta's: regular; Frank's: super

   (C) Vinquetta's: regular; Marquitta's: regular; Taishah's: regular; Orlando's: super; Frank's: super

   (D) Vinquetta's: super; Orlando's: regular; Marquitta's: regular; Frank's: regular; Taishah's: super

   (E) Vinquetta's: premium; Orlando's: regular; Marquitta's: regular; Frank's: regular; Taishah's: regular

2. If Vinquetta's car does not receive a premium wash, which one of the following must be true?

   (A) Orlando's and Vinquetta's cars receive the same kind of wash as each other.

   (B) Marquitta's and Taishah's cars receive the same kind of wash as each other.

   (C) The fourth car washed receives a premium wash.

   (D) Orlando's car is washed third.

   (E) Marquitta's car is washed fourth.

3. If the last two cars washed receive the same kind of wash as each other, then which one of the following could be true?

   (A) Orlando's car is washed third.

   (B) Taishah's car is washed fifth.

   (C) Taishah's car is washed before Marquitta's car.

   (D) Vinquetta's car receives a regular wash.

   (E) Exactly one car receives a super wash.

4. Which one of the following must be true?

   (A) Vinquetta's car receives a premium wash.

   (B) Exactly two cars receive a super wash.

   (C) The fifth car washed receives a super wash.

   (D) The fourth car washed receives a super wash.

   (E) The second car washed receives a regular wash.

5. Which one of the following is a complete and accurate list of the cars that must receive a regular wash?

   (A) Frank's, Marquitta's

   (B) Marquitta's, Orlando's

   (C) Marquitta's, Orlando's, Taishah's

   (D) Marquitta's, Taishah's

   (E) Marquitta's, Vinquetta's

6. Suppose that in addition to the original five cars Jabrohn's car is also washed. If all the other conditions hold as given, which one of the following CANNOT be true?

    (A) Orlando's car receives a premium wash.
    (B) Vinquetta's car receives a super wash.
    (C) Four cars receive a regular wash.
    (D) Only the second and third cars washed receive a regular wash.
    (E) Jabrohn's car is washed after Frank's car.

Use this space for scratch work

Use this space for scratch work

Game 4 Answers and Explanations

Step 1: Overview

Situation: The Kim family at the opera.

Entities: The family members—Q, R, S, T, and U.

Action: Distribution—assigning each member to a row; and sequencing—placing each member in seats 1–3.

Limitations: With five family members and six seats, one will be empty.

Step 2: Sketch.

Diagram the seating arrangement with a space next to each row to indicate who is in that row (the Distribution). Add an "x" to the entity list to indicate the empty seat.

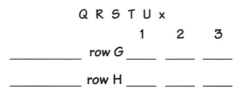

Step 3: Rules

Rule 1 tells you that the empty seat must be an end seat (if the empty seat were in the middle, the family members in seats 1 and 3 of that row wouldn't be adjacent.

The second and fifth rules can be entered into the sketch.

This third rule states that U is before T (in row H) and that S (in either row) precedes T. Shorthand these.

Rule 4, on its face, just says that R sits in the same row as Q, or S, or both. However, thinking through the possibilities reveals that in fact R must be in row G, as R in row H with T and U wouldn't leave room for Q or S.

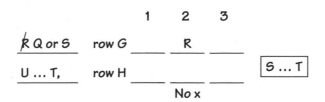

Step 4: Deduction

No more family members can be placed definitely, but it's worth noticing that S, duplicated in the rules, is more restricted in placement than Q; Q is the closest thing to a floater entity in this game.

Step 5: Questions

1. A

Looking quickly at your master sketch shows (B), (C), (D), and (E) cannot be true.

2. B

This is another quick question. (A) can't be true from the master sketch. (C) would violate R being in seat 2. (D) and (E) are both false because you know R is in row G and T and U are in row H.

3. C

Create a new sketch for this "if" question. If Tony is in a seat numbered 2, it must be H2. U must be in H1, and S must be in G1. (C) is the only answer choice that need not be true, or could be false.

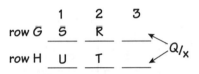

4. E

Complete and accurate list questions are best saved for last because of the ability to use previous work to eliminate answer choices. Question 3 showed that the empty seat could be G3 or H3, and this eliminates every answer choice except E.

5. E

Using the same idea as in Question 4, remember that T must be in your answer choice, which narrows it down to (D) and (E). The only remaining question to ask is whether Q can sit in H2. A quick sketch will show that this is possible and that (E) is correct.

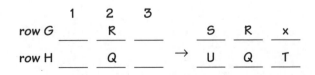

Game 5 Answers and Explanations

Step 1: Overview

Situation: A zoo's reptile house.

Entities: Lizards and snakes, males and females.

Action: Matching—the species and genders; Distributing—the reptiles into groups; Sequencing—the groups into the cages.

Limitations: None before approaching the rules.

Step 2: Sketch

When in doubt, start with the most familiar element. A row of five will help keep track of the five habitats. For each habitat, you need to know the species and genders of all the reptiles that live there. So use one row to keep track of the species, and one to keep track of the genders.

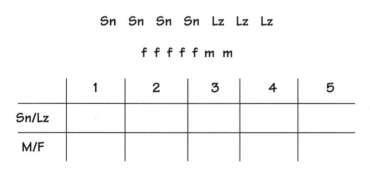

Step 3: Rules

The first rule says that there are at most two reptiles in any habitat. That means at least four habitats must be occupied, and that we could have three doubles and one single, or two doubles and three singles.

Rule 2 says snakes and lizards can't go together—shorthand this one.

Rule 3 involves the sequencing action, and says female snakes can't go next to male lizards.

```
        Sn  Sn  Sn  Sn  Lz  Lz  Lz

          f  f  f  f  f  m  m
```

	1	2	3	4	5
Sn/Lz					
M/F					

2 MAX per habitat
No Sn + Lz together
No fSn next to mLz

Step 4: Deduction

From Rule 1 you know that there are either three Singles and two Doubles, or a Single and three Doubles. But that isn't too helpful since you still don't know the order. You can also make a deduction with the numbers provided in the opening paragraph. There are only two males, but there are four snakes. In other words, there are at most two male snakes, which means that there are at least two female snakes. You don't know whether there will be any male lizards, but there will always be female snakes lurking somewhere. A similar line of reasoning allows a deduction concerning the lizards. Since there are only two males, there can be at most two male lizards. But there are three lizards, so at least one of the lizards is female.

```
        Sn  Sn  Sn  Sn  Lz  Lz  Lz

          f  f  f  f  f  m  m
```

	1	2	3	4	5
Sn/Lz					
M/F					

2 MAX per habitat

No Sn + Lz together

No fSn next to mLz

At least 2 fSn

At least 1 fLz

Step 5: Questions

1. B

Rule 1 eliminates (D). Rule 2 eliminates (A). And Rule 3 eliminates (C) and (E).

2. E

Habitat 4 has two male lizards, and since there are only two males to start with, all the other reptiles must be female. So we have four female snakes (one of which is placed in habitat 2 by the stem) and a female lizard. So who goes where? The female snakes can't go in habitats 3, 4, or 5, since the stem puts male lizards in habitat 4. So the four female snakes must go in habitats 1 and 2, two in each. The female lizard can go in either 3 or 5.

	1	2	3	4	5
Sn/Lz	Sn Sn	Sn Sn		Lz Lz	
M/F	F F	F F		M M	

Lz
F

3. C

The answer choices here are all abstract, indicating there probably wasn't a big deduction to be made, but that you should just think about the numbers. Because there are three lizards, and lizards and snakes can't be mixed in habitats, the lizards either must be alone in three cages, or there must be two lizards in one cage, and one in another cage.

4. D

This is a good question to save for last. Look at each answer choice and if it doesn't quickly seem problematic, move on to the next. If there's one snake and an empty habitat in 1 and 2, there are six reptiles left to put in three cages; but because there are three of each kind of reptile, this requires at least four cages. Choice (D) can't be true.

5. A

There are four snakes, at most two in any habitat, so if habitat 3 is empty and snakes aren't next to each other, where could the snakes go? Two of them will have to go in one of 1 and 2, and two of them will have to go in one of 4 and 5. Do the snakes have to go into the even numbered habitats, as (A) claims? No. They could go in habitat 1, habitat 5, or both. So (A) could be false and is therefore correct.

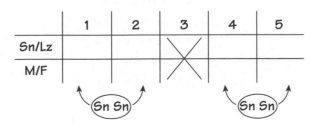

6. C

If each of the lizards has a habitat to itself, then the four snakes must be doubled up in the other two habitats to avoid mixing lizards and snakes. Now we know that those snakes are all female, which in turn tells us that two of the lizards are male (and living alone) and one of the lizards is female (and living alone). Now we have to split up the female snakes and the male lizards. So where can't the snakes go?

(A), (B) We could have female snakes in 1 and 2, the female lizard in 3, and the male lizards in 4 and 5.

(D), (E) These two choices are the flip side of (A) and (B): We could have the female snakes in 4 and 5, the female lizard in 3, and the male lizards in 1 and 2.

(C) Habitat 3, however, cannot contain any snakes. If it did, then habitats 2 and 4 couldn't contain any male lizards, so the male lizards would be forced into both 1 and 5. So far so good, except now the second habitat full of female snakes has to go in either 2 or 4, and no matter which one we choose, it will have to be next to a male lizard in violation of Rule 3.

	1	2	3	4	5
Sn/Lz			Lz		
M/F			F		

```
       ┌─────┐        ┌─────┐
       │Sn Sn│        │Sn Sn│
       │ F  F│        │ F  F│
       └─────┘        └─────┘
              ┌──┬──┐
              │Lz│Lz│
              │M │M │
              └──┴──┘
```

Game 6 Answers and Explanations

Step 1: Overview

Situation: Cars are being washed.

Entities: The cars—F, M, I, T, and V, and the type of wash—r, s, or p.

Action: Sequencing—the cars in the order they are washed; Matching—the type of wash to each car.

Limitations: Each car is washed exactly once and one at a time, and gets exactly one type of wash.

Step 2: Sketch

The sequence is the most concrete, so you should build around that. Under each slot for the car, place another slot for the type of wash.

F M O T V

___ ___ ___ ___ ___
1   2   3   4   5

___ ___ ___ ___ ___
r s p

Step 3: Rules

The first rule says at least one car must have a super wash, but it's not the first car. The first car, then, must have regular or premium.

The second rule says that exactly one car gets a premium wash, but you don't know which one.

The third rule tells you that the second and third cars receive exactly the same kind of wash as each other, which means they can't get premium washes. They must get regular or super.

Rule 4 deals with the sequencing and tells you both O and T must come after V.

Rule 5 indicates that O comes before M, which is before F.

Rule 6 creates a bloc, in which M and the car before M both get regular washes.

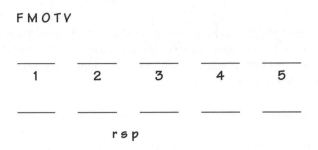

Step 4: Deductions

Merging Rules 4 and 5 gives a loose sequence, with V first. You have the most information about M, who could be third or fourth. In fact, knowing which position M is in gives you a lot of information, which is a clear sign you should use Limited Options and create two sketches. In option 1, M will be third, which means O is second and gets a regular wash. The first car still gets a regular or premium wash; at least one of the last two cars must get a super wash. In option 2, M is fourth, F fifth, and M gets a regular wash, which means the third car (and thus the second car) gets a regular wash, too. With only two washes left, the first car must get a premium wash and the last car the super wash.

V	O	M	T/F	T/F
1	2	3	4	5
r/p	r	r		

$$\searrow s \nearrow$$

V	O/T	T/O	M	F
p	r	r	r	s

Step 5: Questions

1. B

Acceptability. Rule 1 eliminates (D) and (E), Rule 2 eliminates (C), and Rule 4 eliminates (A).

2. A

If V doesn't get a premium wash, the question must be asking about option 1, with V getting a regular wash and 4 and 5 getting super and premium, in some order. With Limited Options, you will often not need to resketch, so try to answer from the picture you already have. (A) must be true, (B), (D), and (E) are false, and (C) is possible, but need not be true.

3. B

This question is asking about option 1 again, here where 4 and 5 must get super washes and V must have a premium wash. T could come fifth; answer choice (B). All of the other choices are false.

4. E

For a "not if" must be true question, look at your master sketch—here, to what is the same in both options. The second car, whatever it is, will always get a regular wash.

5. B

M is in all the answers, so there's no need to consider it. T need not get a regular wash (as you saw in question 3), so (C) and (D) can be eliminated. Whether O is in position 2 or 3, however, it will get a regular wash, making choice (B) correct.

6. A

This question adds a sixth car to the mix, which can go in any position. Examine each choice in turn. Adding a sixth car in any position will still have O in position 2, 3, or 4. Positions 2 and 3 cannot get premium washes, and if O moves to position 4 it must be because J is in position 2, T in 3, O in 4, and M in 5—meaning O will never get a premium wash.

Chapter 10: **Limited Options and Rare Games**

In this chapter, we will examine an additional strategy called Limited Options, as well as strategies for Mapping and Process games—two types of games that rarely appear on the LSAT, but that you should be familiar with nonetheless.

LIMITED OPTIONS

Limited Options should be used whenever a game breaks down into exactly two (or occasionally three) possibilities, and knowing which of the possibilities is in play allows you to make further deductions. To use Limited Options, you should create a separate sketch for each possibility.

In a game that uses Limited Options, "if" questions will frequently direct you to answer based on one of the sketches you've already drawn, instead of requiring that you create a new sketch. In fact, sometimes all that will be needed to answer the question is recognizing which sketch is in play in that particular scenario.

Limited Options will appear in a variety of ways. Some of the most common include having a bloc of entities that can only go in two positions (most often in sequencing games) and making a deduction about the numbers in each group (in a distribution game). Limited Options can also occur when combining rules leads to a major deduction or two Formal Logic rules taken together cover all of the possible scenarios.

When deciding whether Limited Options is appropriate, you should ask yourself two questions—does the game break down into exactly two (or three) possibilities, and would knowing which possibility is in effect allow further deductions? As an example, a game with a rule that, "P is in the first or last position" may be amenable to Limited Options, because there are exactly two possibilities. If no other rules mention P, Limited Options is unlikely to be helpful because placing P will not lead to further deductions. If, however, another rule states that, "M and P must be separated by exactly one position," knowing P would allow the placement of M, and perhaps lead to further deductions. In the latter case, you should create separate Limited Options sketches.

GAME 1: THE METHOD

Attempt to set the game up through the deductions on your own before reading on. As you do so, think about what indicates that you should use Limited Options.

Questions 1–6

On a Tuesday, an accountant has exactly seven bills—numbered 1 through 7—to pay by Thursday of the same week. The accountant will pay each bill only once according to the following rules:

> Either three or four of the seven bills must be paid on Wednesday, the rest on Thursday.
>
> Bill 1 cannot be paid on the same day as bill 5.
>
> Bill 2 must be paid on Thursday.
>
> Bill 4 must be paid on the same day as bill 7.
>
> If bill 6 is paid on Wednesday, bill 7 must be paid on Thursday.

Step 1: Overview

Situation: An accountant paying bills.

Entities: Seven bills, numbered 1 through 7.

Action: To distribute the bills into the days they are paid.

Limitations: Each bill is paid exactly once.

Step 2: Sketch

Create a table with the days at the top of each column.

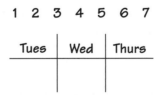

Step 3: Rules

The first rule eliminates Tuesday from your sketch. It also tells you that either three bills are paid on Wednesday and four on Thursday, or four on Wednesday and three on Thursday. This gives you exactly two possibilities for the game. And, because numbers are always key in a distribution game, knowing which option is applicable should lead to further deductions.

```
1  2  3  4  5  6  7          1  2  3  4  5  6  7

   Wed   |   Thurs              Wed   |   Thurs

 __  __  | __  __            __  __  | __  __

     __  | __  __                __  | __  __
```

Rule 2 tells you that 1 and 5 can never be paid on the same day, but since there are only two days, one of them must be paid on each day.

Rule 3 can be added directly to the sketch.

Rule 4 creates a bloc of 4 and 7.

Rule 5 can be shorthanded; don't forget to write the contrapositive as well, and remember that in this game, "not paid on Wednesday" means, "paid on Thursday." Turning negative rules into positives whenever possible will help keep them clear for you.

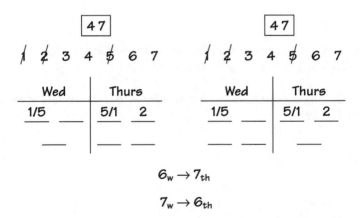

Step 4: Deductions

In the second sketch, 4 and 7 will only fit on Wednesday. Placing 7 on Wednesday triggers the fifth rule, thus 6 must be on Thursday and 3 on Wednesday.

In the first sketch, it's uncertain whether 4 and 7 are paid on Wednesday or Thursday, but, whichever day 4 and 7 are paid, 3 and 6 must be paid on the other day.

1̷ 2̷ 3 4 5̷ 6 7   1̷ 2̷ 3 4 5̷ 6 7

Wed	Thurs		Wed		Thurs	
1/5	5/1 2		1/5	3	5/1	2
			4	7	6	

36/47 $6_w \to 7_{th}$

$7_w \to 6_{th}$

Step 5: Questions

1. If exactly four bills are paid on Wednesday, then those four bills could be

    (A) 1, 3, 4, and 6.
    (B) 1, 3, 5, and 6.
    (C) 2, 4, 5, and 7.
    (D) 3, 4, 5, and 7.
    (E) 3, 4, 6, and 7.

No new sketch is required for this "if" question. Four bills paid on Wednesday is shorthand for, "look at the second sketch." In this option, the bills are 3, 4, 7, and 1 or 5; answer choice (D).

2. Which one of the following is a complete and accurate list of the bills any one of which could be among the bills paid on Wednesday?

    (A) 3, 5, and 6
    (B) 1, 3, 4, 6, and 7
    (C) 1, 3, 4, 5, 6, and 7
    (D) 2, 3, 4, 5, 6, and 7
    (E) 1, 2, 3, 4, 5, 6, and 7

Complete and accurate list questions are usually best left for last, but when the game is almost totally complete, it's easy to answer. A look at the two options shows that 1, 3, 4, 5, 6, or 7 could be paid on Wednesday. Answer choice (C) is correct.

3. If bill 2 and bill 6 are paid on different days from each other, which one of the following must be true?

    (A) Exactly three bills are paid on Wednesday.
    (B) Exactly three bills are paid on Thursday.
    (C) Bill 1 is paid on the same day as bill 4.
    (D) Bill 2 is paid on the same day as bill 3.
    (E) Bill 5 is paid on the same day as bill 7.

This "if" question refers to the first sketch, with the additional information that bill 6 (and thus 3) are paid on Wednesday, and 4 and 7 on Thursday. It's worth making a quick additional sketch to cover this question if you'd like, but all that's needed to answer the question is the realization that the first option is the one in play, with three bills paid on Wednesday—(A).

Wed		Thurs	
1/5	3	5/1	2
	6	4	7

4. If bill 6 is paid on Wednesday, which one of the following bills must also be paid on Wednesday?

    (A) 1

    (B) 3

    (C) 4

    (D) 5

    (E) 7

Question 4 repeats the scenario from the previous question, and it's easiest to refer back to the sketch for Question 3. With 6 being paid on Wednesday, the only other bill that is definitely paid on Wednesday is bill 3. Choice (B) is correct.

5. If bill 4 is paid on Thursday, which one of the following is a pair of bills that could also be paid on Thursday?

    (A) 1 and 5

    (B) 1 and 7

    (C) 3 and 5

    (D) 3 and 6

    (E) 6 and 7

This is yet another question that will reuse the sketch from Question 3. If 4 is paid on Thursday, any combination of 2, 7, and 1 or 5 (but not 1 and 5) could also be paid on Thursday. (A) isn't possible, because 1 or 5, but not both, could be paid on Thursday, but (B) is possible and thus correct.

6. Which one of the following statements must be true?

  (A) If bill 2 is paid on Thursday, bill 3 is paid on Wednesday.
  (B) If bill 4 is paid on Thursday, bill 1 is paid on Wednesday.
  (C) If bill 4 is paid on Thursday, bill 3 is paid on Wednesday.
  (D) If bill 6 is paid on Thursday, bill 3 is also paid on Thursday.
  (E) If bill 6 is paid on Thursday, bill 4 is also paid on Thursday.

For this question, it's necessary to take a look at each answer choice in turn.

If bill 2 is paid on Thursday, either option could be in play. Three might be paid on Wednesday, but need not. (A) is incorrect.

If bill 4 is paid on Thursday, the sketch from Question 3 shows that 1 might be paid on Wednesday, but need not be. (B) can be eliminated.

However, if 4 is paid on Thursday, the same sketch shows that 3 must be paid on Wednesday, and answer choice (C) is correct.

RARE GAMES

There are two game types that have appeared a mere handful of times in total on the LSAT, and primarily on earlier tests. While the chances that one will appear on your LSAT are slim, familiarity with these two game types will put you ahead of other test takers.

Mapping Games

Mapping games require you to create a map, or diagram, and then answer questions about navigating that map. A mapping game will, much like a loose sequencing game, lay out the relationship between the entities in the rules. To solve a matching game, merely sketch out the relationships given and proceed to the questions.

Process Games

Process games will lay out a set of initial conditions, and rules for the possible transitions. The game will then ask about what could or must be true after a certain number of transitions. To solve a process game, sketch out the initial conditions, and look for anything that must be true or can't be true after the first transition; don't try to figure out all of the possible ways multiple transitions might work out.

PRACTICE SETS

<u>Directions:</u> each group of questions is based on a set of conditions. It may be useful to draw a rough diagram to answer some questions. Choose the response that most accurately and completely answers each question.

Game 2

One afternoon, a single thunderstorm passes over exactly five towns—Jackson, Lofton, Nordique, Oceana, and Plattesville—dropping some form of precipitation on each. The storm is the only source of precipitation in the towns that afternoon. On some towns, it drops both hail and rain; on the remaining towns, it drops only rain. It passes over each town exactly once and does not pass over any two towns at the same time. The following must obtain:

The third town the storm passes over is Plattesville.

The storm drops hail and rain on the second town it passes over.

The storm drops only rain on both Lofton and Oceana.

The storm passes over Jackson at some time after it passes over Lofton and at some time after it passes over Nordique.

1. Which one of the following could be the order, from first to fifth, in which the storm passes over the towns?

   (A) Lofton, Nordique, Plattesville, Oceana, Jackson
   (B) Lofton, Oceana, Plattesville, Nordique, Jackson
   (C) Nordique, Jackson, Plattesville, Oceana, Lofton
   (D) Nordique, Lofton, Plattesville, Jackson, Oceana
   (E) Nordique, Plattesville, Lofton, Oceana, Jackson

2. If the storm passes over Oceana at some time before it passes over Jackson, then each of the following could be true EXCEPT:

   (A) The first town the storm passes over is Oceana.
   (B) The fourth town the storm passes over is Lofton.
   (C) The fourth town the storm passes over receives hail and rain.
   (D) The fifth town the storm passes over is Jackson.
   (E) The fifth town the storm passes over receives only rain.

3. If the storm drops only rain on each town it passes over after passing over Lofton, then which one of the following could be false?

   (A) The first town the storm passes over is Oceana.
   (B) The fourth town the storm passes over receives only rain.
   (C) The fifth town the storm passes over is Jackson.
   (D) Jackson receives only rain.
   (E) Plattesville receives only rain.

4. If the storm passes over Jackson at some time before it passes over Oceana, then which one of the following could be false?

   (A) The storm passes over Lofton at some time before it passes over Jackson.
   (B) The storm passes over Lofton at some time before it passes over Oceana.
   (C) The storm passes over Nordique at some time before it passes over Oceana.
   (D) The fourth town the storm passes over receives only rain.
   (E) The fifth town the storm passes over receives only rain.

5. If the storm passes over Oceana at some time before it passes over Lofton, then which one of the following must be true?

   (A) The third town the storm passes over receives only rain.
   (B) The fourth town the storm passes over receives only rain.
   (C) The fourth town the storm passes over receives hail and rain.
   (D) The fifth town the storm passes over receives only rain.
   (E) The fifth town the storm passes over receives hail and rain.

Game 3

Each of exactly six doctors—Juarez, Kudrow, Longtree, Nance, Onawa, and Palermo—is at exactly one of two clinics: Souderton or Randsborough. The following conditions must be satisfied:

Kudrow is at Randsborough if Juarez is at Souderton.

Onawa is at Souderton if Juarez is at Randsborough.

If Longtree is at Souderton, then both Nance and Palermo are at Randsborough.

If Nance is at Randsborough, then so is Onawa.

If Palermo is at Randsborough, then both Kudrow and Onawa are at Souderton.

1. Which one of the following could be a complete and accurate list of the doctors that are at Souderton?

   (A) Juarez, Kudrow, Onawa
   (B) Juarez, Nance, Onawa, Palermo
   (C) Kudrow, Longtree, Onawa
   (D) Nance, Onawa
   (E) Nance, Palermo

2. If Palermo is at Randsborough, then which one of the following must be true?

   (A) Juarez is at Randsborough.
   (B) Kudrow is at Randsborough.
   (C) Longtree is at Souderton.
   (D) Nance is at Randsborough.
   (E) Onawa is at Randsborough.

3. What is the minimum number of doctors that could be at Souderton?

   (A) zero
   (B) one
   (C) two
   (D) three
   (E) four

4. If Nance and Onawa are at different clinics, which one of the following must be true?

   (A) Juarez is at Souderton.
   (B) Kudrow is at Souderton.
   (C) Palermo is at Randsborough.
   (D) Four doctors are at Souderton.
   (E) Four doctors are at Randsborough.

5. Which one of the following CANNOT be a pair of the doctors at Randsborough?

   (A) Juarez and Kudrow
   (B) Juarez and Palermo
   (C) Kudrow and Onawa
   (D) Nance and Onawa
   (E) Nance and Palermo

6. If Kudrow is at Souderton, then which one of the following must be true?

   (A) Juarez is at Souderton.
   (B) Nance is at Souderton.
   (C) Onawa is at Randsborough.
   (D) Palermo is at Souderton.
   (E) Palermo is at Randsborough.

Game 4

Greenburg has exactly five subway lines: L1, L2, L3, L4, and L5. Along each of the lines, trains run in both directions, stopping at every station.

> L1 runs in a loop connecting exactly seven stations, their order being Rincon-Tonka-French-Semplain-Urstine-Quetzal-Park-Rincon in one direction of travel, and the reverse in the other direction.
>
> L2 connects Tonka with Semplain, and with no other station.
>
> L3 connects Rincon with Urstine, and with no other station.
>
> L4 runs from Quetzal through exactly one other station, Greene, to Rincon.
>
> L5 connects Quetzal with Tonka, and with no other station.

1. How many different stations are there that a traveler starting at Rincon could reach by using the subway lines without making any intermediate stops?

    (A) two
    (B) three
    (C) four
    (D) five
    (E) six

2. In order to go from Greene to Semplain taking the fewest possible subway lines and making the fewest possible stops, a traveler must make a stop at

    (A) French.
    (B) Park.
    (C) Quetzal.
    (D) Rincon.
    (E) Tonka.

3. If L3 is not running and a traveler goes by subway from Urstine to Rincon making the fewest possible stops, which one of the following lists all of the intermediate stations in sequence along one of the routes that the traveler could take?

    (A) Quetzal, Tonka
    (B) Semplain, French
    (C) Semplain, Park
    (D) Quetzal, Park, Greene
    (E) Semplain, French, Tonka

4. In order to go by subway from French to Greene, the minimum number of intermediate stops a traveler must make is

    (A) zero.
    (B) one.
    (C) two.
    (D) three.
    (E) four.

5. If the tracks that directly connect Urstine and Quetzal are blocked in both directions, a traveler going from Semplain to Park and making the fewest possible intermediate stops must pass through

    (A) French or Tonka.
    (B) Greene or Urstine.
    (C) Quetzal or Tonka.
    (D) Quetzal or Urstine or both.
    (E) Rincon or Tonka or both.

6. If a sixth subway line is to be constructed so that all of the stations would have two or more lines reaching them, the stations connected by the new subway line must include at least

    (A) French, Greene, and Park.
    (B) French, Greene, and Quetzal.
    (C) French, Greene, and Rincon.
    (D) Park, Tonka, and Urstine.
    (E) Park, Semplain, and Tonka.

KAPLAN

Game 5

In a game, "words" (real or nonsensical) consist of any combination of at least four letters of the English alphabet. Any "sentence" consists of exactly five words and satisfies the following conditions:

> The five words are written from left to right on a single line in alphabetical order.

> The sentence is started by any word, and each successive word is formed by applying exactly one of three operations to the word immediately to its left: delete one letter; add one letter; replace one letter with another letter.

> At most, three of the five words begin with the same letter as one another.

> Except for the leftmost word, each word is formed by a different operation from that which formed the word immediately to its left.

1. Which one of the following could be a sentence in the word game?

   (A) bzeak bleak leak peak pea
   (B) crbek creek reek seek sxeek
   (C) dteam gleam glean lean mean
   (D) feed freed reed seed seeg
   (E) food fool fools fopls opls

2. The last letter of the alphabet that the first word of a sentence in the word game can begin with is

   (A) t.
   (B) w.
   (C) x.
   (D) y.
   (E) z.

3. If the first word in a sentence is "blender" and the third word is "slender," then the second word can be

   (A) bender.
   (B) gender.
   (C) lender.
   (D) sender.
   (E) tender.

4. If the first word in a sentence consists of nine letters, then the minimum number of letters that the fourth word can contain is

   (A) four.
   (B) five.
   (C) six.
   (D) seven.
   (E) eight.

5. If "clean" is the first word in a sentence and "learn" is another word in the sentence, then which one of the following is a complete and accurate list of the positions each of which could be the position in which "learn" occurs in the sentence?

   (A) second
   (B) third
   (C) fourth, fifth
   (D) second, third, fourth
   (E) third, fourth, fifth

6. If the first word in a sentence consists of four letters, then the maximum number of letters that the fifth word in this sentence could contain is

   (A) four.
   (B) five.
   (C) six.
   (D) seven.
   (E) eight.

Game 2 Answers and Explanations

Step 1: Overview

Situation: Afternoon thunderstorms.

Entities: The towns, J, L, N, O, and P, and the types of precipitation (rain or both hail and rain).

Action: Sequencing the towns, and matching the precipitation to each town.

Limitation: The storm goes over each town exactly once; each town gets either rain or both.

Step 2: Sketch

Begin with sketching the sequencing action, and add a line under each slot to fill in the type of precipitation each town receives.

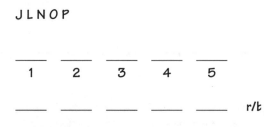

Step 3: Rules

The first rule gives a definite placement that should be added to the sketch, as does the second rule.

The third rule says that L and O are matched with r. Shorthand this rule for now.

The last rule gives two loose blocs; L before J and N before J. Shorthand this rule, as well.

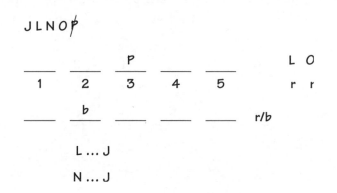

Step 4: Deductions

Since the second town gets both rain and hail, and neither L nor O can get both rain and hail, the only options for the second town are J and N. But, since both L and N must come before J, J can't be second; so the second town must be N. Knowing this, J can only be fourth or fifth. And, knowing J is fourth would place L and, by default, O, thus Limited Options will be helpful. Option I thus places J fourth; notice that knowing the placement of all the towns also allows matching the precipitation to L and O; in Option I the only unknowns are the precipitation types for P and J. In Option II, J is fifth and it's impossible to know whether L or O is first or fourth; but there are only two possibilities, and note that either way, rain will be the precipitation falling on the first and fourth towns.

L	N	P	J	O		L/O	N	P	O/L	J
1	2	3	4	5		1	2	3	4	5
r	b			r		r	b		r	

Step 5: Questions

1. A

In this acceptability question, Rule 1 eliminates (E) and Rule 4 eliminates (C). Using the matching action will be required to eliminate the rest; Rules 2 and 3 combined tell you that neither L nor O can be the second town, eliminating (B) and (D).

2. C

This "if" question directs you squarely to the second option. (C) is impossible; in the second option the fourth town must receive rain only, whether that town is L or O.

3. E

The "if" here directs you again to the second option, and this time adds the deduction that L must be fourth and O first (if L were first, then it would be impossible for every town after L to get only rain). Additionally, J must receive rain only.

Answer choices (A) through (D) must be true; it could, however, be false that P receives rain.

O	N	P	L	J
1	2	3	4	5
r	b		r	r

4. D

Question 4's "if" statement indicates the first option is the relevant one. In Option I, the only statement which could possibly be false is the one in choice (D); all of the rest must be true.

5. B

Once again you are sent to Option II, and the version of Option II that has O before L. A resketch probably isn't necessary; notice that the answer choices only ask what must be true about the precipitation matching. In Option II the fourth town must receive only rain; answer choice (B).

Game 3 Answers and Explanations

Step 1: Overview

Situation: Assigning doctors to clinics.
Entities: The doctors, J, K, L, N, O, and P; the clinics, Souderton and Randsborough.
Action: Distributing the doctors between the two clinics.
Limitation: Each doctor is at exactly one clinic.

Step 2: Sketch

The typical distribution sketch works well here. Create two columns, one for each clinic. It would be ideal to know how many doctors are at each clinic, but that information isn't available yet (though you should certainly keep an eye out for it as you solve the game).

Step 3: Rules

All five of these rules involve formal logic, so write each one down underneath your sketch, along with its contrapositive. Remember that in this game, "not at Souderton" means "at Randsborough," and vice versa; make the negative rules positive!

Sou	Ran
J	K
P	L

J K L N O P

$N_R \rightarrow O_R$

$O_S \rightarrow N_S$

Sou	Ran
O	J
N	L

J K L N O P

$P_R \rightarrow K_S \& O_S$

$K_R \text{ or } O_R \rightarrow P_S$

Step 4: Deductions

Take a look at the first two rules together. One says "if J is at Souderton. . . " and the other says "if J is at Randsborough. . ." These two rules encompass all the possibilities of the game. A quick vertical scan of the rules reveals that placing J will certainly lead to further placements.

Create two sketches. In the first sketch, J will be at Souderton. If J is at Souderton, K is at Randsborough. If K is at Randsborough, Rule 5's contrapositive says P is at Souderton. If P is at S, Rule 3's contrapositive says L is at Randsborough. Only O and N remain unplaced, and you need only worry about Rule 4 in this sketch.

The second sketch will begin with J at Randsborough. If J is at Randsborough, O is at Souderton. Rule 4's contrapositive places N at Souderton. The contrapositive of Rule 3 then tells you that L must be at Randsborough. Only K and P are left, and you need only worry about Rule 5 in this sketch.

Step 5: Questions

1. B

Choice (A) is impossible, as if J is at Souderton (sketch 1) K is at Randsborough. (B), however, could occur in sketch 1, which already places J and P at Souderton and says if O is at Souderton, N is at Souderton.

2. A

The "if" in Question 2 specifies the second sketch, and adds information, but you needn't recopy the sketch to determine the answer. If P is at Randsborough, this must occur in the second sketch, so J must also be at Randsborough—answer choice (A).

3. C

Remember with a minimum question to start with the smallest number and work up. Each sketch has at least two doctors at Souderton, eliminating choices (A) and (B). To have only two doctors at Souderton, look for a sketch in which the two unplaced doctors could go to Randsborough. This is the case in the first sketch, so (C) is the correct answer choice as there could be just two doctors at Souderton.

4. A

If N and O are at different clinics, you can't be concerned with the second sketch. And, just by knowing the focus is on the first sketch, answer choice (A) must be true; J must be at Souderton. (B) and (C) are false in the first sketch; (D) and (E) are merely possible.

5. E

Check each pair against your sketches. K and O, or N and O, could be two of the doctors at Randsborough in the first sketch, eliminating (C) and (D). J and K could be two of the doctors at Randsborough in the second sketch, as could J and P, eliminating (A) and (B). Only (E) is left, and the sketch confirms at least one of N and P will always be at Souderton.

6. B

If K is at Souderton, the second sketch must be applicable. Just knowing you are looking at sketch 2 leads to answer choice (B).

Game 4 Answers and Explanations

Step 1: Overview

Situation: Subway lines.

Entities: The five subway lines; the stations along the lines (which appear in the rules).

Action: To map out the lines and the stations they connect.

Limitation: Lines run in both directions, and the lines never "skip" a station.

Step 2: Sketch

Your sketch will come entirely from drawing out the rules. Be careful to indicate the different lines and to work neatly; you'll need to be able to read your sketch to answer the questions.

Step 3: Rules

The first rule creates the main loop, R–T–F–S–U–Q–P and back to R. The second rule adds a line between T and S, and the third rule adds a line connecting R and U. Rule 4 adds a new line, G, which goes between Q and R, and the fifth rule adds a line that links Q and T.

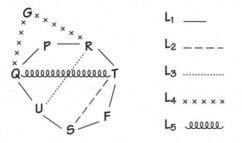

Step 4: Deductions

There's not much to deduce here, since the game isn't about figuring out which entities go where (that was given to you) but about getting from one place to another. However, it's worth noting the stops that are "well-connected" (T, R, and Q) and the stops that are not so well-connected (G, P, and F).

Step 5: Questions

1. **C**

The question merely asks how many stations are directly accessible from R. That would be G, P, U, and T; four stops in all.

2. C

A traveler leaving G must use line 4 and must go to either R or Q. From Q, it's two stops along Line 1 to get to S; from R, a traveler must take both Lines 3 and 1, or take three stops along Line 1, which means the question is asking you to take the G to Q to U to S route. The traveler must go through Q to minimize lines and stops; answer choice (C) is correct.

3. A

No need to create a new sketch for the "if" questions (particularly since the sketch is complex for this game); just cover up L3 with your hand or pretend it doesn't exist.

If L3 is not running, the shortest path from U to R would be U to Q to P to R, or U to Q to T to R, or U to Q to G to R, or U to S to T to R (all three stops). The second of these possible routes leads to answer choice (A).

4. C

To get from F to G, a traveler must get from F to Q or F to R, then take L4. The shortest way to get to Q or R from F will be take L1 from F to T, then R, making the whole route F–T–R–G. This takes two intermediate stops; answer choice (C).

5. E

Question 5 removes a segment of track. As in Question 3, there's no need to recopy the sketch; merely cover over this part of track.

To go from S to P, without going along the section between Q and U, in the least number of stops, a traveler could go from S to T to R to P, or S to T to Q to P, or S to U to R to P (S to U to Q to P is no longer an option). Each trip will take three stops. The route need not pass through F or T (choice (A)), nor G or U (choice (B)). The third route passes through neither Q nor T (choice (C)). The first route bypasses both Q and U (choice (D)). However, each possible route does go through R or T or both. Answer choice (E) is correct.

6. A

Your initial instinct might be to draw a new sketch for this question, but read carefully. Question 6 is asking which stations would need to be on the new line in order to have two or more lines reaching them; this is really a disguised way of asking for the stations that are only on one line in the original master sketch. You looked at this in your deductions; Q, P, and F are the stations that are only on one line, and answer choice (A) is correct.

Game 5 Answers and Explanations

Step 1: Overview

Situation: Creating "words" and "sentences."

Entities: English letters.

Action: Making a sentence out of words.

Limitation: Each sentence has five words; each word has at least four letters, and there is an elaborate set of rules that govern the relationship of sequential words. The rules governing the change from word to word indicate this is a process game.

Step 2: Sketch

In this game there's no "starting" word to sketch up front.

Step 3: Rules

The rules are difficult to shorthand, since they operate so differently from the rules in most games you've seen. Best to merely be sure that you understand each one, and then apply them as written as you work through the questions.

Rule 1 is merely part of the layout, telling you the word on the left is "first" and the word on the right is "last."

The second rule indicates how each word is formed from the previous word. One may add a letter, delete a letter, or replace one letter with another. Rule 4 says that any two successive words must be formed by performing different operations (so if word 2 is created by deleting a letter, word 3 may only be formed by adding or substituting a letter).

The third rule adds the restriction that no more than three words in a sentence may begin with the same letter.

Step 4: Deductions

Without a universal starting point, there's nothing to deduce in this game. Notice the high number of "if" questions, one acceptability question, and a "could be true," which reinforces that there's nothing to have worked out ahead of time.

Step 5: Questions

1.   B

Even in an unusual game, the acceptability question still just requires an application of the rules. Rule 1 is more of a limitation, so skip using that one.

Making sure that each word is formed by a permissible operation (defined by Rule 2) eliminates (C)—"dteam" to "gleam" requires two substitutions.

Rule 3 eliminates (E).

Rule 4 knocks out (D), which uses replacement to form the fourth and fifth words.

With (A) and (B) still acceptable answer choices, look for other limitations that might have been overlooked. Each word must be at least four letters, which means (A) is not acceptable, and (B) is the correct answer.

2.   E

This is akin to a minimum/maximum question, asking what's the latest letter of the alphabet that the first word can begin with. Start with the latest letter and work backwards.

If the first word starts with "z," say, "zaaa," the second word could be "zaaab." Third could be "aaab," fourth "yaaab," and last "yaaa." There's no reason "z" can't start the first word, and (E) is the answer.

3. C

To get from "slender" to "blender," with one word in the middle, you could delete the "s" then add the "b." No other path is possible; if word 2 is formed by replacing "s" with another letter, blender can't be formed by replacing that letter with "b" because of rule 4; and adding a letter to "slender" won't lead to a word that can go through any of the acceptable changes to become "blender." Thus, the intermediate word must be "lender."

4. D

If the first word has nine letters, performing three deletions to reach the fourth word would still leave six letters. Eliminate choices (A) and (B). Rule 4 says that three deletions in a row is impermissible, eliminating (C). The fourth word could be formed by deletion (to a word of 8 letters), then replacement (still 8 letters), then another deletion (to a word of 7 letters), making seven the smallest possible number of letters and answer choice (D) correct.

5. E

Remember to use your answer choices to direct your work on a complete and accurate list question. If a list starts with "clean," "learn" couldn't be second; there's no possible single transition from "clean" to "learn." Eliminate choices (A) and (D).

"Learn" could come third, if the transitions were to delete "c," leaving "lean," and then to add "r". Answer choice (C) is eliminated since "learn" could be third.

Choosing between (B) and (E) depends on whether "learn" could come fourth. The transitions could be a replacement from "clean" to "alean," then a deletion to "lean," then an addition to "learn." Since "learn" could be fourth, answer choice (E) is correct.

6. C

Going from a word with four letters to one with eight in four transitions would require four additions, which is prohibited by Rule 4. Since no two successive transitions can be additions, the maximum number of letters for the fifth word comes from performing two additions and two substitutions, giving the fifth word six letters.

Chapter 11: **Logic Games Sketching Practice**

Directions: For each scenario, create a Master Sketch and integrate the rules, and answer any questions given.

SKETCHING DRILL 1

1. Each of five students—Hubert, Lori, Paul, Regina, and Sharon—will visit exactly one of three cities—Montreal, Toronto, or Vancouver—for the month of March, according to the following conditions:

   Sharon visits a different city than Paul.

   Hubert visits the same city as Regina.

   Lori visits Montreal or else Toronto.

2. A radio talk show host airs five telephone calls sequentially. The calls, one from each of Felicia, Gwen, Henry, Isaac, and Mel, are each either live or taped (but not both). Two calls are from Vancouver, two are from Seattle, and one is from Kelowna. The following conditions must apply:

Isaac's and Mel's calls are the first two calls aired, but not necessarily in that order.

The third call aired, from Kelowna, is taped.

Both Gwen's and Felicia's calls air after Henry's.

3. Morrisville's town council has exactly three members: Fu, Gianola, and Herstein. During one week, the council members vote on exactly three bills: a recreation bill, a school bill, and a tax bill. Each council member votes either for or against each bill. The following is known:

Each member of the council votes for at least one of the bills and against at least one of the bills.

Exactly two members of the council vote for the recreation bill.

Exactly one member of the council votes for the school bill.

Exactly one member of the council votes for the tax bill.

Fu votes for the recreation bill and against the school bill.

Gianola votes against the recreation bill.

Herstein votes against the tax bill.

If Gianola votes for exactly two of the three bills, which one of the following statements must be true?

(A) Fu votes for the tax bill.

(B) Gianola votes for the recreation bill.

(C) Gianola votes for the school bill.

(D) Gianola votes against the tax bill.

(E) Herstein votes for the school bill.

4. There are exactly six groups in this year's Civic Parade: firefighters, gymnast, jugglers, musicians, puppeteers, and veterans. Each group marches as a unit; the groups are ordered from first, at the front of the parade, to sixth, at the back. The following conditions apply:

At least two groups march behind the puppeteers but ahead of the musicians.

Exactly one group marches behind the firefighters but ahead of the veterans.

5. The members of two committees, a planting committee and a trails committee, are to be selected from among seven volunteers—F, G, H, J, K, L, and M. The following conditions govern the composition of the committees:

Each committee must have at least three members.

F cannot be on the same committee as K.

If K is on a committee, J must also be on that committee.

The two committees must have at least one member in common.

6. Six cars are to be arranged in a straight line, and will be numbered 1 through 6, in order, from the front of the line to the back of the line. Each car is exactly one color: two are green, two are orange, and two are purple. The arrangement of cars is restricted as follows:

No car can be the same color as any car next to it in line.

Either car 5 or car 6 must be purple.

Car 1 cannot be orange.

Car 4 cannot be green.

If car 2 is the same color as car 4, then which one of the following statements must be true?

(A) Car 1 is purple.

(B) Car 2 is orange.

(C) Car 3 is green.

(D) Car 5 is purple.

(E) Car 6 is green.

If car 4 is purple, which one of the following must be true?

(A) Car 1 is orange.

(B) Car 2 is green.

(C) Car 3 is orange.

(D) Car 5 is green.

(E) Car 6 is purple.

7. During each of the fall, winter, spring, and summer seasons of one year, Nikki and Otto each participate in exactly one of the following five sports: hockey, kayaking, mountaineering, running, and volleyball.

Each child participates in exactly four different sports during the year.

In the fall, each child participates in mountaineering, running, or volleyball.

In the winter, each child participates in hockey or volleyball.

In the spring, each child participates in kayaking, mountaineering, running, or volleyball.

In the summer, each child participates in kayaking, mountaineering, or volleyball.

Nikki and Otto do not participate in the same sport during the same season.

Otto's summer sport is volleyball.

8. Exactly six employees—officers F, G, and H, and supervisors K, L, and M—must be assigned to exactly three committees—Policy, Quality, and Sales—with exactly three employees per committee. Committee assignments must conform to the following conditions:

    Each committee must have at least one officer assigned to it.

    Each employee must be assigned to at least one committee.

    All three officers must be assigned to the Policy Committee.

    G cannot be assigned to the same committee as L.

    K must be assigned to the Sales Committee.

9. The Mammoth Corporation has just completed hiring nine new workers: Brandt, Calva, Duvall, Eberle, Fu, Garcia, Haga, Irving, and Jessup.

    Fu and Irving were hired on the same day as each other, and no one else was hired that day.

    Calva and Garcia were hired on the same day as each other, and no one else was hired that day.

    On each of the other days of hiring, exactly one worker was hired.

    Eberle was hired before Brandt.

    Haga was hired before Duvall.

    Duvall was hired after Irving but before Eberle.

    Garcia was hired after both Jessup and Brandt.

    Brandt was hired before Jessup.

10. Exactly six tourists—Harry, Irene, Klaus, Laura, Michael, Norma—are to be assigned to four guides: Valois, Xerxes, Yossarian, Zalamea. Each tourist is assigned to exactly one guide, with at least one tourist assigned to each guide. Valois speaks only French. Xerxes speaks only Turkish and Spanish. Yossarian speaks only French and Turkish. Zalamea speaks only Spanish and Russian. Each tourist speaks exactly one of the languages spoken by his or her guide and speaks no other language.

The following rules govern the assignment of the tourists to the guides:

At least Harry and Irene are assigned to Yossarian.

At least Laura is assigned to Zalamea.

Answers and Explanations

Game 1

In this Distribution game, your task is to distribute the five children among the three cities. There is no indication as to how many children will visit each city, so it's not possible to indicate that in the sketch; just draw a table with the names of the groups (the cities) at the top of each column.

Rule 1 says Sharon and Paul are never together.

Rule 2 says Hubert and Regina must always be together.

Rule 3 says Lori must go to Montreal or Toronto (she can't go to Vancouver).

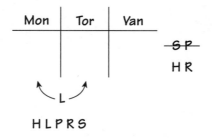

Game 2

This game is a hybrid, asking you to sequence the five calls to the talk show, and then to match the location and whether the call was live or taped to each call. Build your sketch around the most concrete action (the sequence) and then add lines to fill in the matching information; don't forget to indicate that you've been told exactly how many calls are from each location.

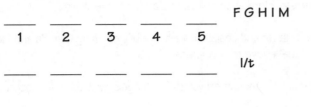

Rule 1 says Isaac and Mel are first and second, but maybe not in that order; it could be Mel first and Isaac second.

Rule 2 says the third call is both from Kelowna and taped.

Rule 3 says that Gwen and Felicia are after Henry, which means Henry must be third, and Felicia and Gwen must be, in some order, fourth and fifth.

I/M	M/I	H	G/F	F/G	F G H I M
1	2	3	4	5	
___	___	t	___	___	I/t
___	___	Ke	___	___	Se Se K̶e Va Va

Game 3

This game is a matching game, asking for you to match a vote to each member for each bill. Because there are three types of entities, and a small number of each, the game is best suited to a grid; write the councilmember's along one edge and the bills along another, and fill in the votes in the squares.

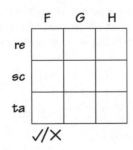

Rules 5, 6, and 7 indicate concrete information that can be added to the sketch.

Rule 1 says each person must vote for and against at least one bill, meaning Gianola and Herstein still need to vote for something. Remind yourself of that above their columns.

Rules 2, 3, and 4 tell you how many for and against votes each bill gets; write this information at the end of each bill's row.

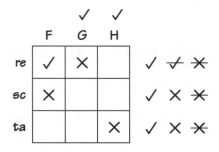

If Gianola votes for exactly two of the three bills, she must vote for both school and tax. Adding this information to a new sketch reveals that Herstein votes no for schools and yes to recreation, and that Fu votes no to tax. Answer choice (C) must be true.

	F	G	H
re	✓	✗	✓
sc	✗	✓	✗
ta	✗	✓	✗

Game 4

This game requires you to sequence six groups in a parade. A quick look at the rules shows that information is given about specific positions, so a strict sequencing sketch is in order. And, if you notice that the setup indicates that first is the "front" and sixth is the "back," adding a note to this effect to your sketch will help prevent confusion later.

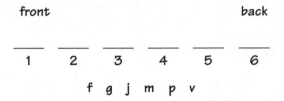

Rule 1 says that there must be at least two (but possibly more) groups behind the puppeteers but ahead of the musicians. So puppeteers come before musicians, and there are definitely two positions between them, and maybe more.

Rule 2 is more concrete; exactly one group is between firefighters and veterans, and firefighters must come before veterans.

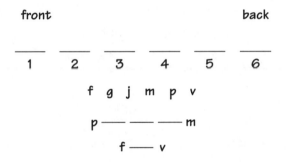

Game 5

This game is a matching game, requiring you to match members to each committee. It might look like a distribution game on first glance, but notice the usual limitation (each person will serve on exactly one committee) isn't here, so it's entirely possible a person could be on both until you're told otherwise. It's best to proceed only with what you know; that you'll match up some of the members to each committee. A table with the committee names across the top works best.

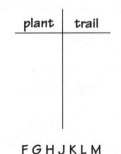

Rule 1 helps out somewhat with the numbers. Draw three slots in each column, but don't assume that this is all you can have (a question mark can help remind you that the column isn't quite finished).

Rule 2 says F and K are never together.

Rule 3 says if a committee has K, it must have J; if it does not have J it can't have K. Remember that a committee can have J without K—be careful about the contrapositive!

Rule 4 says that there's one member the committees share (it's a good thing you didn't assume this was a distribution game), and a good way to remind yourself of that is to save the first position in each column for that member that's shared, indicated by an equals sign.

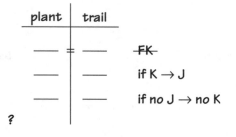

Game 6

This sequencing game calls for placing six cars in six positions, but instead of having six different cars, there are two cars each of three colors—green, orange, and purple. This can be most easily done by writing each color twice in the entity list.

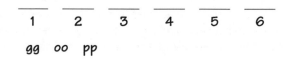

Rule 1 can be shorthanded by writing what would not be acceptable—two oranges, two greens, or two purples in a row.

Rule 2 says that either car 5 or 6 (or both) must be purple.

The third and fourth rules give negatives, which should be turned into positives—if car 1 can't be orange, what can it be? Green or purple. If car 4 isn't green? It can be orange or purple.

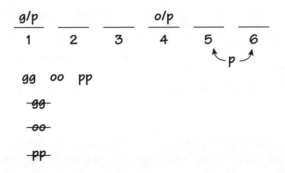

If car 2 is the same color as car 4, you should ask yourself, "which color?" The only possibilities are orange and purple. Since purple must go fifth or sixth, it can't also be the colors of the second and fourth cars, or there would be three purple cars. So car 2 and car 4 must be orange. Create a new sketch with this deduction. This means that cars 1, 3, 5, and 6 must be green or purple since there are no orange cars left, but answer choice (B) is the only one that must be true.

g/p	o	g/p	o	g/p	
1	2	3	4	5	6

If car 4 is purple, car 3 and car 5 can't be purple (thus must be orange or green), making car 6 purple, and car 1 green (because all the purples have been placed). Car 2 must then be orange (Rule 1), car 3 green, and car 5 orange. Answer choice (E) must be true.

g	o	g	p	o	p
1	2	3	4	5	6

Game 7

This game requires you to match the sport each child plays in each season. This is another game where a grid is appropriate; there are three types of entities (children, seasons, and sports) and a small number of each. Since each rule will indicate which sports are available entities in each season, leave the grid blank to start with.

	fall	winter	spring	summer
Nikki				
Otto				

Rules 2, 3, 4, and 5 should be written into the sketch, as they allow you to fill in the possibilities for each section of the grid. Rule 7 then allows you to establish that Otto participates in volleyball in the summer, and Rules 6 and 1 eliminate volleyball from being Nikki's summer sport, or a sport Otto can play in any other season. Thus Otto must play hockey in the winter, so Nikki can't play hockey in the winter and must play volleyball in the winter (and can't play volleyball any other time). Rules 1 and 6 are perhaps easiest to work with by simply circling them in your test booklet and keeping an eye on them; expect that "if" questions will give you one of the sports and require you to apply these two rules to make deductions.

	fall	winter	spring	summer
Nikki	m r ~~v~~	~~h~~ Ⓥ	k m r ~~v~~	k m ~~v~~
Otto	m r ~~v~~	Ⓗ ~~v~~	k m r ~~v~~	~~k~~ ~~m~~ Ⓥ

Game 8

Game 8 presents a slight twist on the typical distribution game; there are six entities (further divided into officers and supervisors) distributed into three groups of three members each. A quick check of the numbers reveals that this amounts to nine slots; some employees will have to be members of more than one group. The basic sketch, however, is still the same as for any Distribution game; the group names head the columns and the number of slots for the number of members of each group go below. Additionally, using capital letters for officers and lower case letters for supervisors will help keep the types of entities straight.

Rule 1, indicating that each committee must have at least one officer, is best incorporated by designating the top row as "officer's row," and only placing F, G, or H in these slots.

Rule 2 is more of a limitation and just reminds you that each person must be used at least once.

Rules 3 and 5 give established entities; Rule 3 telling you that F, G, and H are on Policy, and Rule 5 placing K on Sales.

Rule 4 creates a negative bloc; G and L can never be on the same committee. Notice who has not been used yet; L and M still must be placed at least once. And since L and M are both supervisors, they won't both fit on the Sales committee, so at least one (and maybe both) must go on Quality.

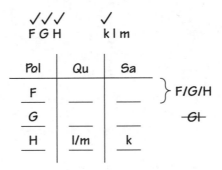

Game 9

A quick look at the rules to this game reveals that the sequencing action will be loose, with all of the rules being about relative positioning; thus the sketch will be built from the rules.

Rules 1 and 2 create blocs of two entities—Fu and Irving, and Calva and Garcia. Rule 3 is more of a limitation; stating that everyone left will be the solo hire for the day (so once the two blocs are made, there are no more "ties.") Rules 4 through 8 give pieces of the sketch—Eberle before Brandt, Haga before Duvall, Irving then Duvall then Eberle, Jessup and Brandt in some order before Garcia, and Brandt before Jessup.

Simple enough to combine these individual pieces into one master sketch. By looking for pieces of overlap between the individual rules, one chain is created that has two possibilities for the first element (FI and H) but determines everyone else's position exactly.

Game 10

This game asks you to match tourists to tour guides and languages, making sure that each guide gets at least one tourist (but some guides will have multiple tourists) and adding the information about which language(s) each guide speaks, which should be expected to be relevant in the rules and questions. Start off with the typical matching game table, and add the information about the languages above each guide.

The Rules give you three definite placements of Harry, Irene, and Laura; you should add these to your master sketch and feel confident in having half of the game worked out.

Fr	Tur/Sp	Fr/Tur	Sp/Rus
Val	Xer	Yos	Zal
		H	L
		I	

H̶ / K / L̶ M N

SKETCHING DRILL 2

1. Five children—F, G, H, J, and K—and four adults—Q, R, S, and T—are planning a canoeing trip. The canoeists will be divided into three groups—groups 1, 2, and 3—of three canoeists each, according to the following conditions:

   There must be at least one adult in each group.

   F must be in the same group as J.

   G cannot be in the same group as T.

   H cannot be in the same group as R.

   Neither H nor T can be in group 2.

2. At an automobile exhibition, cars are displayed on each floor of a three-floor building. On each floor the cars are either all family cars or all sports cars, either all new or all used, and either all production models or all research models. The following conditions apply to this exhibition:

   The exhibition includes no used research models.

   The exhibition includes no research models that are sports cars.

   There are new cars on floor 1.

   There are used cars on floor 3.

3. Seven singers—Jamie, Ken, Lalitha, Maya, Norton, Olive, and Patrick—will be scheduled to perform in the finals of a singing competition. During the evening of the competition, each singer, performing alone, will give exactly one performance. The schedule for the evening must conform to the following requirements:

Jamie performs immediately after Ken.

Patrick performs at some time after Maya.

Lalitha performs third only if Norton performs fifth.

If Patrick does not perform second, he performs fifth.

If Norton is scheduled for the fifth performance, which one of the following could be true?

(A) Jamie is scheduled for the sixth performance.

(B) Ken is scheduled for the second performance.

(C) Lalitha is scheduled for the fourth performance.

(D) Maya is scheduled for the third performance.

(E) Olive is scheduled for the first performance.

4. A university library budget committee must reduce exactly five of eight areas of expenditure—G, L, M, N, P, R, S, and W—in accordance with the following conditions:

If both G and S are reduced, W is also reduced.

If N is reduced, neither R nor S is reduced.

If P is reduced, L is not reduced.

Of the three areas L, M, and R, exactly two are reduced.

If P is reduced, which one of the following is a pair of areas of expenditure both of which must be reduced?

(A) G, M

(B) M, R

(C) N, R

(D) R, S

(E) S, W

5. Lara, Mendel, and Nastassia each buy at least one kind of food from a street vendor who sells only fruit cups, hot dogs, pretzels, and shish kebabs. They make their selections in accordance with the following restrictions:

   If any of the three buys a hot dog, that person does not also buy a shish kebab.

   At least one of the three buys a hot dog, and at least one buys a pretzel.

   Neither Lara nor Nastassia buys a pretzel.

   Mendel does not buy any kind of food that Nastassia buys.

6. In a theater company, four two-day workshops—Lighting, Production, Rehearsals, and Staging—are conducted over the course of five days, Monday through Friday. The workshops are conducted in a manner consistent with the following constraints:

   The two days on which a given workshop is in session are consecutive.

   The workshops on Production and Rehearsals begin no earlier than the day immediately following the second day of the workshop on Lighting.

KAPLAN

7. An airline has four flights from New York to Sarasota—flights 1, 2, 3, and 4. On each flight there is exactly one pilot and exactly one copilot. The pilots are Fazio, Germond, Kyle, and Lopez; the copilots are Reich, Simon, Taylor, and Umlas. Each pilot and copilot is assigned to one flight.

Fazio's flight takes off before Germond's, and at least one other flight takes off between their flights.

Kyle is assigned to flight 2.

Lopez is assigned to the same flight as Umlas.

Which one of the following pilot and copilot teams could be assigned to flight 1?

(A) Fazio and Reich

(B) Fazio and Umlas

(C) Germond and Reich

(D) Germond and Umlas

(E) Lopez and Taylor

8. A car drives into the center ring of a circus and exactly eight clowns—Q, R, S, T, V, W, Y, and Z—get out of the car, one clown at a time. The order in which the clowns get out of the car is consistent with the following conditions:

    V gets out at some time before both Y and Q.

    Q gets out at some time after Z.

    T gets out at some time before V but at some time after R.

    S gets out at some time after V.

    R gets out at some time before W.

9. A showroom contains exactly six new cars—T, V, W, X, Y, and Z—each equipped with at least one of the following three options: power windows, leather interior, and sunroof. No car has any other options. The following conditions must apply:

    V has power windows and a sunroof.

    W has power windows and a leather interior.

    W and Y have no options in common.

    X has more options than W.

10. Of the five Pohl children—Sara, Theo, Uma, Will, and Zoe—three are left-handed and two are right-handed. Each of the five children was born in a different one of seven calendar years, 1990 through 1996. The following conditions apply:

No two left-handed children were born in consecutive years.

No two right-handed children were born in consecutive years.

Sara, who is left-handed, was born before Uma.

Zoe was born before both Theo and Will.

A left-handed child was born in 1991.

Uma, who is right-handed, was born in 1993.

Answers and Explanations

Game 1

This game requires that you distribute nine boaters (five children and four adults) across three boats; thankfully you know that each boat has three people in it. Create a table with three slots in each of the three columns, and use lower case letters to represent the children and capitals to represent the adults.

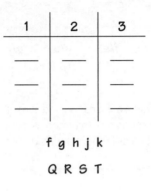

Rule 1 requires an adult in each group; this is most easily represented by designating the first row "adults only." Rule 2 creates a bloc, and Rules 3 and 4 create negative blocs, which should be shorthanded for now. Turn Rule 5 into a positive rule; if h and T cannot be in group 2, then they can only be in groups 1 or 2.

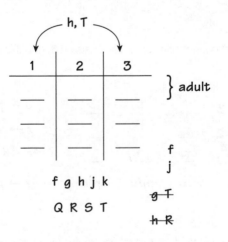

Game 2

This matching game necessitates figuring out the attributes of the cars on each floor of a showroom. You'll match three attributes to each floor—new or used, family or sports, and research or production. Create your sketch to reflect the actual floors of a building, with three slots next to each floor number for the matching element.

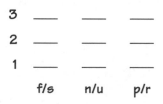

Rule 1 says there are no used research models—so if a car is used, it must be production and if it is research it must be new. Rule 2 similarly states that there are no sports research models, so sports cars must be production, and research cars must be family. Both of these rules can be easily shorthanded using formal logic.

$$
\begin{array}{c}
3 \quad \underline{} \quad \underline{u} \quad \underline{} \qquad u \rightarrow p \\[4pt]
2 \quad \underline{} \quad \underline{} \quad \underline{} \qquad r \rightarrow n \\[4pt]
1 \quad \underline{} \quad \underline{n} \quad \underline{} \qquad r \rightarrow f \\[4pt]
\quad\;\; f/s \quad\; n/u \quad\; p/r \qquad\quad s \rightarrow p
\end{array}
$$

Rules 3 and 4 give concrete information; new cars on 1, used cars on 3. Add this directly to the sketch.

$$
\begin{array}{c}
3 \quad \underline{} \quad \underline{u} \quad \underline{p} \qquad u \rightarrow p \\[4pt]
2 \quad \underline{} \quad \underline{} \quad \underline{} \qquad r \rightarrow n \\[4pt]
1 \quad \underline{} \quad \underline{n} \quad \underline{} \qquad r \rightarrow f \\[4pt]
\quad\;\; f/s \quad\; n/u \quad\; p/r \qquad\quad s \rightarrow p
\end{array}
$$

Written this way it should be easy to see that floor 3 must be production; giving new information in the form of an "if" question should lead to easy deductions along the formal logic rules you've jotted down.

Game 3

Game 3 is a strict sequencing game, fitting seven singers into seven position. This game should be familiar; seven dashes with the entities written underneath.

Rule 1 creates the bloc "KJ." Rule 2 says P is some time, but you don't know how long, after M.

Be careful translating the formal logic in Rule 3; "only if" becomes "then" and you have "if Lalitha is third Norton is fifth." Don't forget the contrapositive.

While Rule 4 may sound like another formal logic rule, think before you write. If Patrick isn't second, he's fifth; if he isn't fifth he's second...so he must be in one of these two positions. More straightforward to just show he must be second or fifth than to write out an if/then statement to the side.

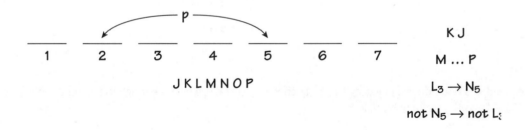

If Norton is scheduled fifth, be careful not to use Rule 3. You don't know that Lalitha is third! Norton fifth does mean Patrick is second, and Patrick influences Maya, who must be first. The Ken and Jamie block could go third and fourth, or sixth and seventh; leaving Lalitha and Olive to fill the other two positions. Choice (C) is the only choice that is possible.

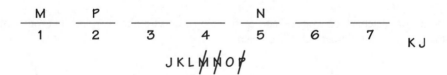

Game 4

Game 4 is a straightforward selection game that asks you to select five of the eight areas; that means three will be rejected. Unsurprisingly, there are several formal logic rules. Remember that the base Master Sketch for Selection is a simple list of the entities. Jot up top that you'll select 5.

Rules 1 through 3 are all straightforward formal logic; write each one and its contrapositive. The last rule indicates that exactly 2 of L, M, and R will be reduced; this is easiest to mark on the list of entities. Thus either L and M, M and R, or R and L will be reduced, and the third member of the trio rejected.

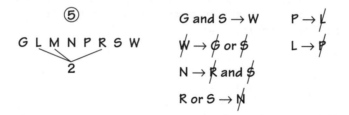

If P is reduced, L is not reduced. Rejecting L leads to choosing M and R, which is enough to answer the question with choice (B)—M and R must both be reduced.

Game 5

In this game, you will be Matching the types of food each person orders from the vendor. Start with a table with the names across the top and a list of the foods underneath.

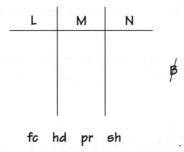

Rule 1 says nobody will ever buy both a hot dog and a shish kebab. Rule 3 says Lara and Nastassia don't get a pretzel, but Rule 2 says as least one person does, so Mendel must get the pretzel, and must be the only one. Rule 2 also tells you at least one person buys a hot dog. Rule 4 says Mendel and Nastassia don't buy any of the same types of food; this can be indicated across the top of the sketch as a reminder.

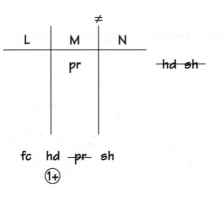

Game 6

This sequencing game places four two day workshops across one Monday–Friday week. You might notice right off the bat that there are eight days of workshops; some day will necessarily have multiple workshops (notice that the usual "one entity per position" limitation is missing here). A good sketch starts with listing the days of the week and writing the entities underneath.

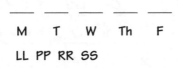

Rule 1 says that the each workshop will run on consecutive days; best to add this information by creating blocs in the list of entities.

Rule 2 gives a loose sequence, placing the days of Lighting ahead of both the days of Production and the days of Rehearsal. Jot this down underneath your sketch.

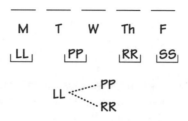

Game 7

Game 7 creates two sequences; one of pilots and one of co-pilots. The typical sequencing sketch is in order, but with two rows of slots. To keep the entities straight, lower case letters will represent the co-pilots.

```
___  ___  ___  ___     F G K L

___  ___  ___  ___     r s t u

 1    2    3    4
```

Rule 2 gives an established entity and a good place to start; Kyle is on flight 2.

Rule 1 places Fazio before Germond, and since there must be at least one flight between them, they can't be the third and fourth flights—so Fazio must be the first flight, and G and L must be the third and fourth flights.

Rule 3 places Umlas with Lopez; and adding Umlas to the sketch with Lopez keeps this information handy.

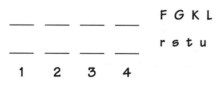

Fazio must be the pilot on flight 1, and Umlas can only be on flights 3 or 4 (with Lopez), so only choice (A) gives a possible team for flight 1.

Game 8

This game requires you to order (i.e. sequence) the clowns getting out of the car, but notice that the rules are all relative, indicating a loose sequence which will be built from the rules.

Rule 1 places V before Y and Q. Rule 2 places Q after Z. Rule 3 creates a chain of R then T then V. Rule 4 places V before S, and Rule 5 says R is before W.

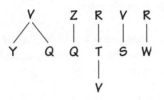

Look for the common elements to create one large sketch. Use V to join R, T, Y and Q. Z can be attached to Q, S to V, and W to R.

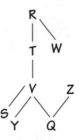

Game 9

This game uses a common matching scenario of choosing some combination of three entities. It is easily sketched in a table, with the cars heading the columns and the options used written in each column as they are determined. Indicate the options with lower case letters to distinguish from the cars (capital letters) and remember that each car gets at least one—but no more than three—option.

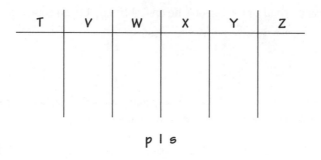

T	V	W	X	Y	Z

p l s

Rules 1 and 2 indicate two options that cars V and W have. Be careful; this doesn't mean these are the only options for V and W, just that they must have at least these two options.

Rule 3 seems abstract, but working with it will help make it solid. If W and Y have no options in common, then if W had all three options, Y couldn't have any. Thus W must have only power and leather, and that's all (good to indicate), and Y can have a sunroof, but that's the only possibility, and Y has nothing else.

Rule 4, that X has more options than W, is also less abstract than it appears; more options than W means all three. Just from these four rules, you've made tremendous progress on making the game definite.

T	V	W	X	Y	Z
	p	p	p	s	
	s	l	l		
			s		

Game 10

Game 10 is a hybrid sequencing/matching with an interesting deviation. You're asked so sequence the children by the year they were born, 1990–1996, and each was born in a different year, but there were seven years, and only five children, so two of the years will not have a child assigned. A good way to indicate this is with an X in the entity list. You'll then match the left or right-handedness to each child with the limitation that there are three lefties and two righties, and, again, the two blank years will have an X for the matching action.

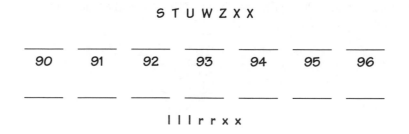

S T U W Z X X

90	91	92	93	94	95	96

l l l r r x x

Rules 1 and 2 indicate there will never be two lefties or righties in a row (but two consecutive children could be lefties or righties, as long as there's a blank year in the middle).

Rule 3 creates a loose bloc—Sara a leftie before Uma.

Rule 4 creates another loose sequence—Zoe before Theo and Will.

Rule 5 allows the placement of a leftie in 1991.

Rule 6, perhaps the most concrete, places Uma and right in 1993.

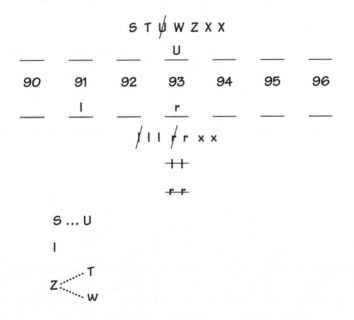

Because of Rule 1, Sara, coming before Uma, can't be left handed in 90 or 92, so she must be the leftie in 1991 and can be placed definitely. Then neither a leftie nor a rightie can be in 92, so 92 must be a year no child was born.

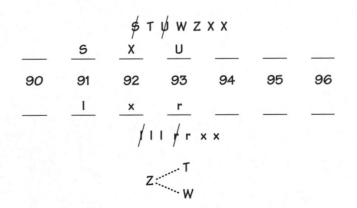

SKETCHING DRILL 3

1. A worker will insert colored light bulbs into a billboard equipped with exactly three light sockets, which are labeled lights 1, 2, and 3. The worker has three green bulbs, three purple bulbs, and three yellow bulbs. The selection of bulbs for the sockets is governed by the following conditions:

    Whenever light 1 is purple, light 2 must be yellow.

    Whenever light 2 is green, light 1 must be green.

    Whenever light 3 is either purple or yellow, light 2 must be purple.

2. Musicians perform each of exactly five pieces—Nexus, Onyx, Synchrony, Tailwind, and Virtual—once, and one at a time; the pieces are performed successively (though not necessarily in that order). Each piece is performed with exactly two instruments: Nexus with fiddle and lute, Onyx with harp and mandolin, Synchrony with guitar and harp, Tailwind with fiddle and guitar, and Virtual with lute and mandolin. The following conditions must apply:

    Each piece shares one instrument with the piece performed immediately before it or after it (or both).

    Either Nexus or Tailwind is performed second.

3. Exactly eight consumers—F, G, H, J, K, L, M, and N—will be interviewed by market researchers. The eight will be divided into exactly two four-person groups—group 1 and group 2—before interviews begin. Each person is assigned to exactly one of the two groups according to the following conditions:

F must be in the same group as J.

G must be in a different group from M.

If H is in group 1, then L must be in group 1.

If N is in group 2, then G must be in group 1.

4. Eight physics students—four majors: Frank, Gwen, Henry, and Joan; and four nonmajors: Victor, Wanda, Xavier, and Yvette—are being assigned to four laboratory benches, numbered 1 through 4. Each student is assigned to exactly one bench, and exactly two students are assigned to each bench. Assignments of students to benches must conform to the following conditions:

Exactly one major is assigned to each bench.

Frank and Joan are assigned to consecutively numbered benches, with Frank assigned to the lower-numbered bench.

Frank is assigned to the same bench as Victor.

Gwen is not assigned to the same bench as Wanda.

If Victor is assigned to bench 2 and Wanda is assigned to bench 4, which one of the following must be true?

(A) Frank is assigned to bench 1.

(B) Gwen is assigned to bench 1.

(C) Henry is assigned to bench 3.

(D) Xavier is assigned to bench 1.

(E) Yvette is assigned to bench 3.

5. A rowing team uses a boat with exactly six seats arranged in single file and numbered sequentially 1 through 6, from the front of the boat to the back. Six athletes—Lee, Miller, Ovitz, Singh, Valerio, and Zita—each row at exactly one of the seats. The following restrictions must apply:

Miller rows closer to the front than Singh.

Singh rows closer to the front than both Lee and Valerio.

Valerio and Zita each row closer to the front than Ovitz.

If Valerio rows at seat 5, then which one of the following must be true?

(A) Miller rows at seat 1.

(B) Singh rows at seat 2.

(C) Zita rows at seat 3.

(D) Lee rows at seat 4.

(E) Ovitz rows at seat 6.

6. From among eight candidates, four astronauts will be selected for a space flight. Four of the candidates—F, J, K, and L—are experienced astronauts and four—M, N, P, and T—are inexperienced astronauts. F, M, P, and T are geologists whereas J, K, L, and N are radiobiologists. The astronauts must be selected according to the following conditions:

Exactly two experienced astronauts and two inexperienced astronauts are selected.

Exactly two geologists and two radiobiologists are selected.

Either P or L or both are selected.

7. Each of nine students—Faith, Gregory, Harlan, Jennifer, Kenji, Lisa, Marcus, Nari, and Paul—will be assigned to exactly one of three panels: Oceans, Recycling, and Wetlands. Exactly three of the students will be assigned to each panel. The assignment of students to panels must meet the following conditions:

    Faith is assigned to the same panel as Gregory.

    Kenji is assigned to the same panel as Marcus.

    Faith is not assigned to the same panel as Paul.

    Gregory is not assigned to the same panel as Harlan.

    Jennifer is not assigned to the same panel as Kenji.

    Harlan is not assigned to the Oceans panel if Paul is not assigned to the Oceans panel.

8. At an evening concert, a total of six songs—O, P, T, X, Y, and Z—will be performed by three vocalists—George, Helen, and Leslie. The songs will be sung consecutively as solos, and each will be performed exactly once. The following constraints govern the composition of the concert program:

    Y must be performed earlier than T and earlier than O.

    P must be performed earlier than Z and later than O.

    George can perform only X, Y, and Z.

    Helen can perform only T, P, and X.

    Leslie can perform only O, P, and X.

9. During a period of six consecutive days—day 1 through day 6—each of exactly six factories—F, G, H, J, Q, and R—will be inspected. During this period, each of the factories will be inspected exactly once, one factory per day. The schedule for the inspections must conform to the following conditions:

F is inspected on either day 1 or day 6.

J is inspected on an earlier day than Q is inspected.

Q is inspected on the day immediately before R is inspected.

If G is inspected on day 3, Q is inspected on day 5.

10. Bird-watchers explore a forest to see which of the following six kinds of birds—grosbeak, harrier, jay, martin, shrike, wren—it contains. The findings are consistent with the following conditions:

If harriers are in the forest, then grosbeaks are not.

If jays, martins, or both are in the forest, then so are harriers.

If wrens are in the forest, then so are grosbeaks.

If jays are not in the forest, then shrikes are.

Which one of the following is the maximum number of the six kinds of birds the forest could contain?

(A)   two

(B)   three

(C)   four

(D)   five

(E)   six

Answers and Explanations

Game 1

Here you're asked to match a color to each of three light bulb sockets. It's Matching, not Sequencing, because there are multiple bulbs of each color. If you put the yellow bulb in 1, there's another yellow bulb available to go in 2. The sketch here is simple (and the game small); three slots for the sockets, and a list of the colors to be used.

1	2	3
g	p	y

All three rules are formal logic based. If light 1 is purple, 2 is yellow. When forming the contrapositive, turn negatives into positives (which will make it easy to check the rules when working the game)—"if 2 is not yellow" is the same as "if 2 is green or purple". Then 1 is not purple, or "is green or yellow."

Similarly, Rule 2 can be contraposed as "if 1 is yellow or purple, 2 is yellow or purple." And Rule 3, "if 3 is purple or yellow, 2 is purple" can be controposed as "if 2 is green or yellow, 3 is green."

1	2	3	
g	p	y	1p → 2y
			2p or 2g → 1y or 1g
			2g → 1g
			1p or 1y → 2p or 2y
			3p or 3y → 2p
			2g or 2y → 3g

Game 2

Don't be thrown by the information about the instruments; this is really just a sequencing game that provides rules in a slightly unusual manner (via the instruments). At the end of the day, you're being asked to order the five musical pieces, one piece per position, and that's the same familiar Sequencing game. When writing the list of entities, add the instrument information below each entity.

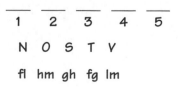

Rule 2 is easier to understand, which makes it a good starting point; Nexus or Tailwind is second. This might later lead to limited options; for now you can just write this in the sketch.

Rule 1 takes a bit more analysis. If each piece must "share" with the piece before or after it or both, what does that mean for the first piece? The first piece must share with the second piece because there's nothing before it to share with. Likewise, the fifth piece can only share with the fourth piece. The third piece must share with the second or fourth, or both, but there's no way to know which one it will share with. This rule is worth marking in the places you know there must be sharing, and remembering that 3 must share with 2 or 4.

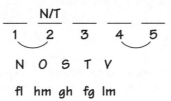

Game 3

Game 3 is a distribution game which gives concrete numbers; four in each group. To sketch, just create a table with two groups of four members each, and the list of entities off to the side.

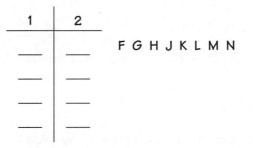

Rule 1 creates a bloc, FJ.

Rule 2 says G and M must be in different groups. This could be written as "never GM," but this actually tells you that one of them must be in each group. Best to account for these slots already by setting aside one slot in each group for G or M.

Rule 3 tells you that if H is in 1, L is in 1; be positive when forming the contrapositive, that if L is in 2, H is in 2. Be careful; this doesn't say H and L have to go together! H could go in 2 and L in 1 and this rule would never be triggered.

Rule 4, similarly, says that if N is in 2, G is in 1; the contrapositive is that if G is in 2, N is in 1. This doesn't mean they are in different groups! G and N could both be in group 1 without triggering the rule.

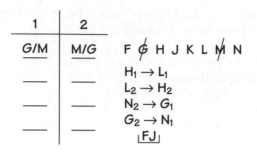

Game 4

This game is a hybrid combining distribution (groups of two students) and sequencing (assigning the pairs to one of the four benches). The ultimate sketch should reflect this, and consist of a sequence of four pairs of students. Indicate majors with capital letters and nonmajors in lower case.

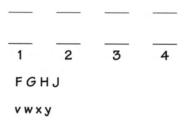

Rule 1 puts one major (and thus one nonmajor) in each group; this is best done by making the top row for majors and the bottom row for nonmajors.

Rule 2 creates a bloc of Frank and Joan.

Rule 3 creates a bloc of Frank and Victor. Combine this with the bloc from Rule 2.

Rule 4 separates Gwen and Wanda.

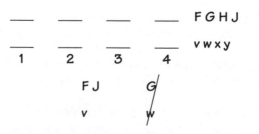

If Victor is at bench 2, Frank must be at bench 2, and Joan at bench 3. If Wanda is on bench 4, Gwen cannot be at bench 4 and must be at bench 1; leaving Henry on bench 4. Answer choice (B) must be true and is thus correct.

$\underline{G}$	$\underline{F}$	$\underline{J}$	$\underline{H}$
	v		w
$\underline{}$	$\underline{}$	$\underline{}$	$\underline{}$
1	**2**	**3**	**4**

Game 5

Game 5 creates a sequence of six athletes, and the rules tell you that the sequence will be loose; all the rules are relative. Save the sketch for one you create as you step through the rules, and remember to keep track of the front (1) and back (6) of the boat.

Rule 1 says Miller comes before Singh.

Rule 2 says Singh comes before Lee and Valerio.

Rule 3 says Valerio and Zita are before Ovitz.

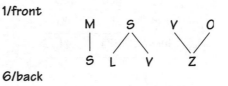

Combine pieces to make one large master sketch; use Singh and Valerio as the common entities.

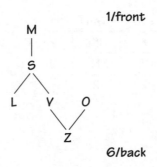

If Valerio is in seat 5, Zita must be in seat 6. Miller must be first and Singh must be second. L and O are in seats 3 and 4, in some order. Choice (A) is correct.

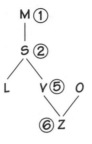

Game 6

The twist isn't in the game type here (just selection), but in the entities. Four of eight will be selected, but the entities are listed twice, and characterized in two different ways—experienced or inexperienced, and geologists or radiobiologists. Really F is an experienced geologist, M, P, and T are inexperienced geologists; J, K, and L are experienced radiobiologists and N is an inexperienced radiobiologist. Instead of just listing the entities, put them in a grid based on classification. Four will be selected; four will be rejected.

④	geo	rad
exp	F	JKL
inex	MPT	N

Rules 1 and 2 give the numbers of each type selected, which can easily be written next to the rows and columns; two each of experienced, inexperienced, radiobiologist and geologist. Additionally, Rule 3 says that at least P or L is selected.

④	geo	rad		
exp	F	JKL	2	P or L or both
inex	MPT	N	2	
	2	2		

Game 7

Game 7 is a straightforward, concrete distribution game; split nine students into three groups of three. Your sketch, unsurprisingly, will thus be three columns with three slots in each column, and the list of students.

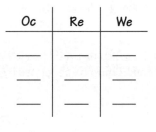

Rules 1 and 2 create blocs. Faith with Gregory, Kenji with Marcus.

Rules 3, 4, and 5 create negative blocs. Never Faith and Paul, never Gregory and Harlan, never Jennifer and Kenji.

Rule 6 is formal logic, but perhaps easier to examine as its contrapositive. If Harlan is on Oceans, Paul must be as well. And if Paul is not on Oceans (thus on Wetlands or Recycling), Harlan cannot be (and thus must be on Wetlands or Recycling).

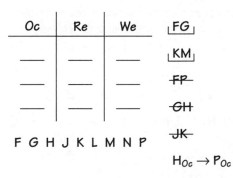

Game 8

Game 8 combines sequencing and matching; you must sequence the six songs and match the vocalist to each song. Your sketch should build around the most concrete action (the Sequence) and add the Matching beneath.

The first two rules give much of the sequence, though only loosely; Y is before T and O, and O then comes before P, which is before Z.

The next three rules give the possibilities for the match-ups. A side sketch will reveal that O must be performed by Leslie, T must be performed by Helen, and Y and Z must be performed by George.

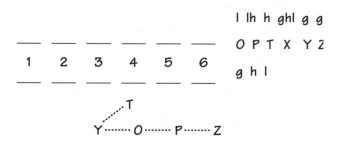

Game 9

Here is a straightforward strict sequencing game; six positions, six entities, one entity per position, with rules that deal with definite placement. Your sketch should contain six slots and a list of the entities.

Rule 1 places F on day 1 or 6. Indicate this with arrows.

Rule 2 gives a loose rule, J some time before Q.

Rule 3 creates a bloc, QR.

Rule 4 gives formal logic; if G on 3, Q on 5; if Q not on 5, G not on 3.

Notice how Q is mentioned in three rules—expect that it will play a large role in the questions.

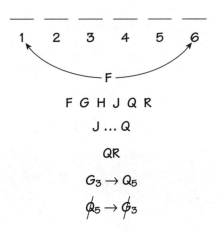

Game 10

The final game asks you to select some of a group of six birds that are found in the forest. There are no numbers given, so initially anywhere from none to all six might be chosen. Start the game by sketching, consisting of a list of the entities.

G H J M S W

Rule 1 says it's impossible to select both harriers and grosbeaks.

Rule 2 indicates if both jays and martins are selected, then harriers must be. The contrapositive is that if harriers are not selected, the forest must not contain jays or not contain martins.

Rule 3 is another formal logic rule; if wrens then grosbeaks; if no grosbeaks, no wrens.

So is Rule 4; if no jays, then shrikes, if no shrikes then jays. In fact, Rule 4 says there must be at least one of jays or shrikes, and this rule can be added to the list of entities.

$$G \; H \; \underbrace{J \; M}_{1+} \; S \; W$$

~~H G~~

J and M → H

H̸ → J̸ or M̸

W → G

G̸ → W̸

To answer a maximum question, start with the largest number and work down. Could the forest have all six types of birds? Definitely not; it can't have both harriers and grosbeaks. What about five? To have five would necessitate having harriers (because if there are no harriers, there can't be jays or wrens), which eliminates grosbeaks. But no grosbeaks means no wrens. Working this possibility out, however, shows that there could be four types of birds in the forest—harriers, jays, martins, and shrikes—without violating any rules. (C) is the correct answer.

G̸ Ⓗ Ⓙ Ⓜ Ⓢ W̸

PART THREE

Practice Logic Games Sections

Practice Logic Games Section 1

ANSWER SHEET

Remove (or photocopy) the answer sheet and use it to complete the practice test section.

<u>Directions:</u> Before taking each practice test section, find a quiet place where you can work uninterrupted for 35 minutes. Make sure you have a comfortable desk and several No. 2 pencils. Once you start a practice section, don't stop until you're done.

Good luck!

Start with number 1 for each section. If a section has fewer questions than answer spaces, leave the extra spaces blank.

1. Ⓐ Ⓑ Ⓒ Ⓓ Ⓔ   9. Ⓐ Ⓑ Ⓒ Ⓓ Ⓔ   17. Ⓐ Ⓑ Ⓒ Ⓓ Ⓔ   25. Ⓐ Ⓑ Ⓒ Ⓓ Ⓔ
2. Ⓐ Ⓑ Ⓒ Ⓓ Ⓔ   10. Ⓐ Ⓑ Ⓒ Ⓓ Ⓔ   18. Ⓐ Ⓑ Ⓒ Ⓓ Ⓔ   26. Ⓐ Ⓑ Ⓒ Ⓓ Ⓔ
3. Ⓐ Ⓑ Ⓒ Ⓓ Ⓔ   11. Ⓐ Ⓑ Ⓒ Ⓓ Ⓔ   19. Ⓐ Ⓑ Ⓒ Ⓓ Ⓔ   27. Ⓐ Ⓑ Ⓒ Ⓓ Ⓔ
4. Ⓐ Ⓑ Ⓒ Ⓓ Ⓔ   12. Ⓐ Ⓑ Ⓒ Ⓓ Ⓔ   20. Ⓐ Ⓑ Ⓒ Ⓓ Ⓔ   28. Ⓐ Ⓑ Ⓒ Ⓓ Ⓔ
5. Ⓐ Ⓑ Ⓒ Ⓓ Ⓔ   13. Ⓐ Ⓑ Ⓒ Ⓓ Ⓔ   21. Ⓐ Ⓑ Ⓒ Ⓓ Ⓔ   29. Ⓐ Ⓑ Ⓒ Ⓓ Ⓔ
6. Ⓐ Ⓑ Ⓒ Ⓓ Ⓔ   14. Ⓐ Ⓑ Ⓒ Ⓓ Ⓔ   22. Ⓐ Ⓑ Ⓒ Ⓓ Ⓔ   30. Ⓐ Ⓑ Ⓒ Ⓓ Ⓔ
7. Ⓐ Ⓑ Ⓒ Ⓓ Ⓔ   15. Ⓐ Ⓑ Ⓒ Ⓓ Ⓔ   23. Ⓐ Ⓑ Ⓒ Ⓓ Ⓔ
8. Ⓐ Ⓑ Ⓒ Ⓓ Ⓔ   16. Ⓐ Ⓑ Ⓒ Ⓓ Ⓔ   24. Ⓐ Ⓑ Ⓒ Ⓓ Ⓔ

KAPLAN

Questions 1–6

In the course of one month Garibaldi has exactly seven different meetings. Each of her meetings is with exactly one of five foreign dignitaries: Fuentes, Matsuba, Rhee, Soleimani, or Tbahi. The following constraints govern Garibaldi's meetings:

> She has exactly three meetings with Fuentes, and exactly one with each of the other dignitaries.
>
> She does not have any meetings in a row with Fuentes.
>
> Her meeting with Soleimani is the very next one after her meeting with Tbahi.
>
> Neither the first nor last of her meetings is with Matsuba.

1. Which one of the following could be the sequence of the meetings Garibaldi has with the dignitaries?

   (A) Fuentes, Rhee, Tbahi, Soleimani, Fuentes, Matsuba, Rhee

   (B) Fuentes, Tbahi, Soleimani, Matsuba, Fuentes, Fuentes, Rhee

   (C) Fuentes, Rhee, Fuentes, Matsuba, Fuentes, Tbahi, Soleimani

   (D) Fuentes, Tbahi, Matsuba, Fuentes, Soleimani, Rhee, Fuentes

   (E) Fuentes, Tbahi, Soleimani, Fuentes, Rhee, Fuentes, Matsuba

2. If Garibaldi's last meeting is with Rhee, then which one of the following could be true?

   (A) Garibaldi's second meeting is with Soleimani.

   (B) Garibaldi's third meeting is with Matsuba.

   (C) Garibaldi's fourth meeting is with Soleimani.

   (D) Garibaldi's fifth meeting is with Matsuba.

   (E) Garibaldi's sixth meeting is with Soleimani.

3. If Garibaldi's second meeting is with Fuentes, then which one of the following is a complete and accurate list of the dignitaries with any one of whom Garibaldi's fourth meeting could be?

   (A) Fuentes, Soleimani, Rhee

   (B) Matsuba, Rhee, Tbahi

   (C) Matsuba, Soleimani

   (D) Rhee, Tbahi

   (E) Fuentes, Soleimani

4. If Garibaldi's meeting with Rhee is the very next one after Garibaldi's meeting with Soleimani, then which one of the following must be true?

   (A) Garibaldi's third meeting is with Fuentes.

   (B) Garibaldi's fourth meeting is with Rhee.

   (C) Garibaldi's fifth meeting is with Fuentes.

   (D) Garibaldi's sixth meeting is with Rhee.

   (E) Garibaldi's seventh meeting is with Fuentes.

5. If Garibaldi's first meeting is with Tbahi, then Garibaldi's meeting with Rhee could be the

   (A) second meeting

   (B) third meeting

   (C) fifth meeting

   (D) sixth meeting

   (E) seventh meeting

6. If Garibaldi's meeting with Matsuba is the very next meeting after Garibaldi's meeting with Rhee, then with which one of the following dignitaries must Garibaldi's fourth meeting be?

   (A) Fuentes

   (B) Matsuba

   (C) Rhee

   (D) Soleimani

   (E) Tbahi

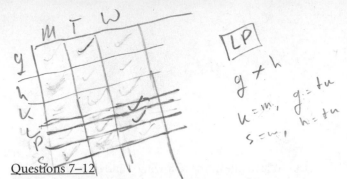

Questions 7–12

During a certain week, an animal shelter places exactly six dogs—a greyhound, a husky, a keeshond, a Labrador retriever, a poodle, and a schnauzer—with new owners.

Two are placed on Monday, two on Tuesday, and the remaining two on Wednesday, consistent with the following conditions:

The Labrador retriever is placed on the same day as the poodle.

The greyhound is not placed on the same day as the husky.

If the keeshond is placed on Monday, the greyhound is placed on Tuesday.

If the schnauzer is placed on Wednesday, the husky is placed on Tuesday.

7. Which one of the following could be a complete and accurate matching of dogs to the days on which they are placed?

(A) Monday: greyhound, Labrador retriever; Tuesday: husky, poodle; Wednesday: keeshond, schnauzer

(B) Monday: greyhound, keeshond; Tuesday: Labrador retriever, poodle; Wednesday: husky, schnauzer

(C) Monday: keeshond, schnauzer; Tuesday: greyhound, husky; Wednesday: Labrador retriever, poodle

(D) Monday: Labrador retriever, poodle; Tuesday: greyhound, keeshond; Wednesday: husky, schnauzer

(E) Monday: Labrador retriever, poodle; Tuesday: husky, keeshond; Wednesday: greyhound, schnauzer

8. Which one of the following must be true?

(A) The keeshond is not placed on the same day as the greyhound.

(B) The keeshond is not placed on the same day as the schnauzer.

(C) The schnauzer is not placed on the same day as the husky.

(D) The greyhound is placed on the same day as the schnauzer.

(E) The husky is placed on the same day as the keeshond.

9. If the poodle is placed on Tuesday, then which one of the following could be true?

(A) The greyhound is placed on Monday.

(B) The keeshond is placed on Monday.

(C) The Labrador retriever is placed on Monday.

(D) The husky is placed on Tuesday.

(E) The schnauzer is placed on Wednesday.

10. If the greyhound is placed on the same day as the keeshond, then which one of the following must be true?

(A) The husky is placed on Monday.

(B) The Labrador retriever is placed on Monday.

(C) The keeshond is placed on Tuesday.

(D) The poodle is not placed on Wednesday.

(E) The schnauzer is not placed on Wednesday.

11. If the husky is placed the day before the schnauzer, then which one of the following CANNOT be true?

(A) The husky is placed on Monday.

(B) The keeshond is placed on Monday.

(C) The greyhound is placed on Tuesday.

(D) The poodle is placed on Tuesday.

(E) The poodle is placed on Wednesday.

12. If the greyhound is placed the day before the poodle, then which one of the following CANNOT be placed on Tuesday?

(A) the husky

(B) the keeshond

(C) the Labrador retriever

(D) the poodle

(E) the schnauzer

GO ON TO THE NEXT PAGE

KAPLAN

Questions 13–17

A tour group plans to visit exactly five archaeological sites. Each site was discovered by exactly one of the following archaeologists—Ferrara, Gallagher, Oliphant—and each dates from the eighth, ninth, or tenth century (A.D.). The tour must satisfy the following conditions:

The site visited second dates from the ninth century.

Neither the site visited fourth nor the site visited fifth was discovered by Oliphant.

Exactly one of the sites was discovered by Gallagher, and it dates from the tenth century.

If a site dates from the eighth century, it was discovered by Oliphant.

The site visited third dates from a more recent century than does either the site visited first or that visited fourth.

13. Which one of the following could be an accurate list of the discoverers of the five sites, listed in the order in which the sites are visited?

   (A) Oliphant, Oliphant, Gallagher, Oliphant, Ferrara

   (B) Gallagher, Oliphant, Ferrara, Ferrara, Ferrara

   (C) Oliphant, Gallagher, Oliphant, Ferrara, Ferrara

   (D) Oliphant, Oliphant, Gallagher, Ferrara, Gallagher

   (E) Ferrara, Oliphant, Gallagher, Ferrara, Ferrara

14. If exactly one of the five sites the tour group visits dates from the tenth century, then which one of the following CANNOT be a site that was discovered by Ferrara?

   (A) the site visited first

   (B) the site visited second

   (C) the site visited third

   (D) the site visited fourth

   (E) the site visited fifth

15. Which one of the following could be a site that dates from the eighth century?

   (A) the site visited first

   (B) the site visited second

   (C) the site visited third

   (D) the site visited fourth

   (E) the site visited fifth

16. Which one of the following is a complete and accurate list of the sites each of which CANNOT be the site discovered by Gallagher?

   (A) third, fourth, fifth

   (B) second, third, fourth

   (C) first, fourth, fifth

   (D) first, second, fifth

   (E) first, second, fourth

17. The tour group could visit at most how many sites that were discovered by Ferrara?

   (A) one

   (B) two

   (C) three

   (D) four

   (E) five

<u>Questions 18–22</u>

Each day of a five-day workweek (Monday through Friday), Anastasia parks for the entire day in exactly one of three downtown parking lots—X, Y, and Z. One of the lots costs $10 for the day, another costs $12, and the other costs $15. Anastasia parks in each of the three lots at least once during her work week. The following conditions must apply:

> On Thursday, Anastasia parks in the $15 lot.
>
> Lot X costs more than lot Z.
>
> The lot Anastasia parks in on Wednesday costs more than the one she parks in on Friday.
>
> Anastasia parks in lot Z on more days of the workweek than she parks in lot X.

18. Which one of the following could be a complete and accurate list of which lot Anastasia parks in each day, listed in order from Monday through Friday?

    (A) Y, Z, X, Y, Z
    (B) Y, Z, Z, Y, X
    (C) Z, Z, X, X, Y
    (D) Z, Z, X, X, Z
    (E) Z, Z, X, Z, Y

19. Anastasia CANNOT park in the $15 lot on which one of the following days?

    (A) Monday
    (B) Tuesday
    (C) Wednesday
    (D) Thursday
    (E) Friday

20. If lot Z is the $12 lot, then on which one of the following days must Anastasia park in lot Y?

    (A) Monday
    (B) Tuesday
    (C) Wednesday
    (D) Thursday
    (E) Friday

21. Anastasia CANNOT park in lot Z on which one of the following days?

    (A) Monday
    (B) Tuesday
    (C) Wednesday
    (D) Thursday
    (E) Friday

22. Which one of the following could be a complete and accurate list of the days on which Anastasia parks in the $10 lot?

    (A) Monday
    (B) Tuesday
    (C) Monday, Tuesday
    (D) Monday, Wednesday
    (E) Monday, Thursday

ANSWERS AND EXPLANATIONS

Game 1 (Questions 1–6)

Step 1: Overview

Situation: A schedule of meetings.

Entities: The dignitaries; F M R S and T.

Action: To sequence the meetings.

Limitations: Seven meetings with five people leaves some ambiguity as to who is repeated.

Step 2: Sketch

The Master Sketch is a simple strict sequencing sketch:

```
___   ___   ___   ___   ___   ___   ___
 1     2     3     4     5     6     7

F M R S T
```

Step 3: Rules

The first rule reveals which entity will be reused in the sequence; F will be used three times and all other entities will be used once. This can be added to the list of entities in the Master Sketch.

Rule 2 tells you that there can never be two F's adjacent to each other, "NEVER FF" is a good reminder of the rule to jot down.

Rule 3 offers a bloc of entities: "T S" will have to appear somewhere in the sequence.

Meanwhile, Rule 4 tells you where not to place M—at either end—which doesn't reveal much about where M is placed, or who is first or seventh. Jot down "not M" at slots 1 and 7 in your Master Sketch.

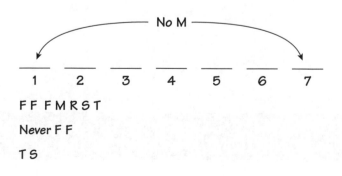

```
              ┌─────── No M ───────┐
              ↓                     ↓
___   ___   ___   ___   ___   ___   ___
 1     2     3     4     5     6     7

F F  F M R S T

Never F F

T S
```

Step 4: Deductions

Beyond the individual rules, there's little to be added to the sketch—no reason to set up Limited Options, no additional deductions to be made. Sometimes there's nothing to be done but to plow through the questions.

Step 5: Questions

1.   C

Rule 4 knocks out (E); Rule 2 eliminates (B), and Rule 3 gets rid of (D). (A) violates Rule 1, leaving (C).

2.   D

This "if" clause directs you to create a sketch with R in the seventh, or last, slot. Placing R leaves three F's, M, and the TS bloc, and since the F's must be separated, the sketch must place M and TS between the F's. There are two possible ways to do this; checking the two possible sketches shows that (D) is possible.

F	M	F	T	S	F	R
1	2	3	4	5	6	7

F	T	S	F	M	F	R
1	2	3	4	5	6	7

3.   E

If the second meeting is with F, the first meeting can only be with M or R (F's can't be adjacent and TS is a bloc). The last meeting must also be with F, because slots 3–7 will have to contain R or M, TS, and two F's, and an F can't be in position 3.

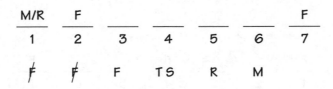

The fourth meeting could be with F, if the third meeting is with R or M, and TS is in the fifth and six slots. This eliminates choices (B), (C), and (D). R, however, cannot go in position 4; to do so would leave nobody to go in position 3 (F would be adjacent to the F in 2, and TS is a bloc). This eliminates (A) and leaves (E).

4. E

If R is immediately after S, which is immediately after T, there is now a bloc "TSR," and this leaves only this bloc and the single meeting with M to separate the three meetings with F. Thus F must be the first and last meetings, with the third F either the third or fifth meeting. (E) must be true.

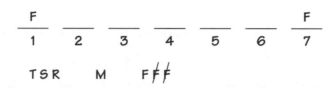

5. D

If T is the first meeting, S must be the second. Remaining are three meetings with F, and only M and R to separate them; the pattern must be F third, fifth, and seventh, with M and R in fourth and sixth; answer choice (D) covers the possibility that R is sixth.

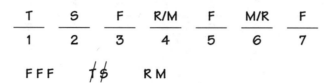

6. A

If M is immediately after R, there are now two blocs of two meetings—TS and RM. These blocs must separate the three F's, so the patterns must be F, then a bloc, then F, then another bloc, then the last F. Thus the fourth meeting must be with F.

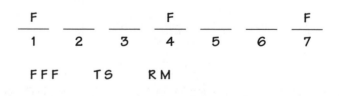

Game 2 (Questions 7–12)

Step 1: Overview

Situation: Placements at an animal shelter.

Entitities: The dogs to be placed: G, H, K, R, P, S.

Action: To distribute the dogs by the day on which they are placed.

Limitation: Exactly two dogs are placed on each day.

Step 2: Sketch

A straightforward distribution sketch does the trick nicely here; create a column for each day with two blanks underneath.

Mon	Tues	Wed
—	—	—
—	—	—

G H K   R P S

Step 3: Rules

Rule 1 creates a bloc of the retriever and the poodle.

The second rule gives you a negative bloc—never GH.

Rules 3 and 4 are formal logic. Write out each rule and its contrapositive, and remember when you negate each rule that "not Tuesday" in this game means "on Monday or Wednesday." Always try to turn a negative statement into a positive one.

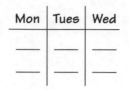

Step 4: Deductions

Think about the possible pairings in this game. If R and P are together, and G can't go with H, then G could only go with K or S, and H must go with S or K. It's worth writing these groups out. Beyond that, though, the rules are conditional and there's little to work out ahead of time.

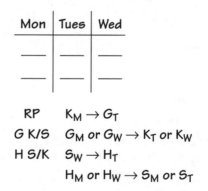

Step 5: Questions

7.   E

Rule 1 eliminates (A). Rule 2 eliminates (C). Rule 3 eliminates (B), and Rule 4 eliminates (D).

8. B

Notice that though this question asks for what must be true, there weren't any concrete deductions about which dogs were adopted on which days, and the answer choices just ask about the pairings. This should be answerable from the Master Sketch. K and G could be placed on the same day, so (A) is incorrect. However, your sketch indicates that K and S will always be placed on different days, so (B) must be true and is the correct answer.

9. A

If the poodle is placed on Tuesday, so is the retriever. This also fills up Tuesday, which means the contrapositive of Rule 3 is triggered; the greyhound cannot be placed on Tuesday, so the keeshond must not be placed on Monday, and must be on Wednesday. If K is on Wednesday, S must be on Monday (because K and S are always placed on different days). Only G and H are let, and one of each of them will go on Monday and Tuesday. Choices (B), (C), (D) and (E) are all impossible; only (A) could be true.

Mon	Tues	Wed
S	R	K
G/H	P	H/G

10. E

If G and K are placed on the same day, H and S are the other pair. Each of these pairs triggers one of the conditional rules; if G and K are on the same day that day can't be Monday; if H and S are paid on the same day that day can't be Wednesday. Choice (E) must be true.

11. D

The "if" here once again gives you the pairings; H with K and S with G. H placed the day before S indicates H and K cannot be on Monday. If HK is on Monday, SG is on Tuesday and RP is on Wednesday; if HK is on Tuesday then SG is on Wednesday and RP is on Monday. Either way, RP cannot be on Tuesday, and choice (D) cannot be true.

12. A

With G before P, G must be on Monday (with RP on Tuesday) or on Tuesday (with RP on Wednesday). Draw out both options. If G's on Monday, Rule 3 says K can't be on Monday, so K must be Tuesday, placing H and S on Monday. If G is on Tuesday, H cannot be, so H must be on Monday. In either option, H cannot be paid on Tuesday; answer choice (A).

Mon	Tues	Wed
H	G	R
S	K	P

Mon	Tues	Wed
H	G	R
		P

Game 3 (Questions 13–17)

Step 1: Overview

Situation: Archaeologists discovering and dating sites.

Entities: The archaeologists F, G, and O, and the centuries 8, 9, and 10.

Action: To match up each site with its discoverer and its century.

Limitations: Archaeologists and centuries will be reused, but each site is matched to exactly one of each.

Step 2: Sketch

Represent each site with two dashes; one for the archaeologist and one for the century.

$$\begin{array}{ccccc} — & — & — & — & — \\ \hline \rule{0pt}{2.2ex}— & — & — & — & — \\ 1 & 2 & 3 & 4 & 5 \end{array} \quad \begin{array}{l} F\,G\,O \\ 8\,9\,10 \end{array}$$

Step 3: Rules

Rule 1 can be written in the sketch.

Turn the second rule from a negative into a positive rule; if the site isn't discovered by O, it must have been discovered by F or G.

Rule 3 indicates that G discovers one site, and that site is from the tenth century. Be careful to remember this does NOT say that all tenth century sites were discovered by G.

The fourth rule indicates that any site (and maybe there are none) discovered in the eighth century is discovered by O.

Rule 5 knocks out eighth century for site 3, and tenth century for site 1 or 4. Also shorthand this rule to preserve the relationship.

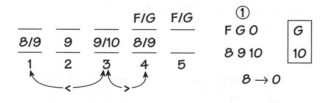

Step 4: Deductions

Since site 2 is ninth century, it can't be discovered by G. And since site 2 isn't tenth century, G couldn't have discovered it either, so F or O must have discovered site 2. Similarly, site 4 must have been discovered by F since 4 is not a tenth century site. Knowing 4 was discovered by F eliminates eighth century as a possibility, and site 4 must be ninth century, which means site 3 must be tenth century (but not necessarily discovered by G!). Site 5 can't be eighth century because it wasn't discovered by O.

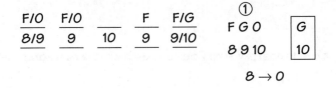

Step 5: Questions

13. E

Rule 2 eliminates (A) and Rule 3 eliminates (D), but a check of your sketch will be necessary to make the other eliminations. Sites 1 and 2 must be F or O, which eliminates (B) and (C), leaving choice (E).

14. C

The new "if" indicates that only site 3 is tenth century, thus G must have discovered site 3 and only site 3, and F thus must have discovered site 5. No sketch required here to see that (C) is correct; site 3 must have been discovered by G and thus could not have been discovered by G.

15. A

One quick look at your Master Sketch reveals that the only possible eighth century site is site 1.

16. E

Again, the Master Sketch reveals the answer with no additional drawing; G cannot discover sites 1, 2, or 4.

17. D

Since G must discover exactly one site, F could discover at most four. There's nothing that prevents him from discovering sites 1, 2, 4, and 5 while G discovers site 3, and (D) is the correct answer.

Game 4 (Questions 18–22)

Step 1: Overview

Situation: Anastasia's parking during a week.

Entities: Parking lots X, Y, and Z; costs $10, $12, and $15.

Action: Matching parking lots to days of the week, and costs to parking lots.

Limitations: Anastasia must park in each lot at least once.

Step 2: Sketch

To match a parking lot and a cost to each day, simply create a sketch with the days across the top and a space for both lot and cost under each day.

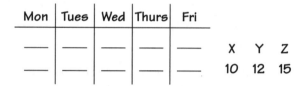

Step 3: Rules

Rule 1 is concrete and can be added to the sketch.

Rule 2 should be shorthanded; "X > Z." Notice that this means X must be $12 or $15, and Z must be $10 or $12.

Rule 3, similarly, limits Wednesday to $12 or $15 and Friday to $10 or $12, and should also be added to the sketch.

The fourth rule is abstract, and warrants careful attention. If Anastasia parks in Z on more days than X, she must park in Z on at least two days (as she must park in X on at least one day). If Anastasia parks in Z on more than three days, she won't be able to spend at least one day in each parking lot; so she must park in Z on two or three days. And she can't park in lot X on two days, because then she would need to park in Z on three days and would never park in Y. Thus she must park in X exactly once, in Z twice or three times, and in Y once or twice.

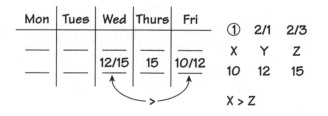

Step 4: Deductions

Since Z must be cheaper than X, Z can't be the $15 lot, which means Anastasia must park in X or Y on Thursday. This is worth adding to the sketch.

Mon	Tues	Wed	Thurs	Fri
—	—	—	X/Y	—
—	—	12/15	15	10/12

① 2/1 2/3

X Y Z

10 12 15

X > Z

Step 5: Questions

18. A

Rule 4 quickly eliminates (C) and (D), but this is the only elimination you can quickly make based on the rules. Your deduction that Z cannot be the lot on Thursday eliminates choice (E), and putting Rules 2 and 3 together eliminates (B) (which has X, the more expensive lot by Rule 2, on Friday, and Z, the less expensive lot by Rule 2, on Wednesday—though Wednesday's lot must be more expensive than Friday's!)

19. E

A glance at your Master Sketch shows Anastasia cannot park in the $15 lot on Friday (to do so would necessarily violate Rule 3).

20. E

If Z is the $12 lot, X must be the $15 lot and Y must be the $10 lot. Thus X must be the lot used on Thursday. Because Anastasia only parks in lot X once, she must park in the $12 lot, lot Z, on Wednesday, and in the $10 lot, lot Y, on Friday (because the Friday lot is less expensive than the Wednesday lot). Answer choice (E).

Mon	Tues	Wed	Thurs	Fri
—	—	Z	X	Y
—	—	12	15	15

21. D

With no additional work, your Master Sketch shows it's impossible for Anastasia to park in lot Y on Thursday; choice (D).

KAPLAN

22. C

Your Master Sketch already shows that Anastasia can't park in the $10 lot on Wednesday or Thursday, eliminating answer choices (D) and (E).

If Anastasia parks in the $10 lot on Monday only, she must park in the $12 lot on Friday and the $15 lot on Wednesday. Thursday then cannot be lot X (or X would be used twice), so Y must be the $15 lot, and be the lot she parks in on Wednesday and Thursday. Since X is more expensive than Z, X must be the $12 lot and Z the $10 lot. However, for Z to be used more than X, Anastasia would have to park in lot Z twice, which would contradict her parking in the $10 lot on Monday only. This eliminates (A), and the exact same analysis will eliminate (B). However, if she parks in the $10 lot, lot Z, on both Monday and Tuesday, all rules are satisfied.

Mon	Tues	Wed	Thurs	Fri
		Y	Y	X
		15	15	12

Practice Logic Games Section 2

ANSWER SHEET

Remove (or photocopy) the answer sheet and use it to complete the practice test section.

Directions: Before taking each practice test section, find a quiet place where you can work uninterrupted for 35 minutes. Make sure you have a comfortable desk and several No. 2 pencils. Once you start a practice section, don't stop until you're done.

Good luck!

Start with number 1 for each section. If a section has fewer questions than answer spaces, leave the extra spaces blank.

1. Ⓐ Ⓑ Ⓒ Ⓓ Ⓔ   9. Ⓐ Ⓑ Ⓒ Ⓓ Ⓔ   17. Ⓐ Ⓑ Ⓒ Ⓓ Ⓔ   25. Ⓐ Ⓑ Ⓒ Ⓓ Ⓔ
2. Ⓐ Ⓑ Ⓒ Ⓓ Ⓔ   10. Ⓐ Ⓑ Ⓒ Ⓓ Ⓔ   18. Ⓐ Ⓑ Ⓒ Ⓓ Ⓔ   26. Ⓐ Ⓑ Ⓒ Ⓓ Ⓔ
3. Ⓐ Ⓑ Ⓒ Ⓓ Ⓔ   11. Ⓐ Ⓑ Ⓒ Ⓓ Ⓔ   19. Ⓐ Ⓑ Ⓒ Ⓓ Ⓔ   27. Ⓐ Ⓑ Ⓒ Ⓓ Ⓔ
4. Ⓐ Ⓑ Ⓒ Ⓓ Ⓔ   12. Ⓐ Ⓑ Ⓒ Ⓓ Ⓔ   20. Ⓐ Ⓑ Ⓒ Ⓓ Ⓔ   28. Ⓐ Ⓑ Ⓒ Ⓓ Ⓔ
5. Ⓐ Ⓑ Ⓒ Ⓓ Ⓔ   13. Ⓐ Ⓑ Ⓒ Ⓓ Ⓔ   21. Ⓐ Ⓑ Ⓒ Ⓓ Ⓔ   29. Ⓐ Ⓑ Ⓒ Ⓓ Ⓔ
6. Ⓐ Ⓑ Ⓒ Ⓓ Ⓔ   14. Ⓐ Ⓑ Ⓒ Ⓓ Ⓔ   22. Ⓐ Ⓑ Ⓒ Ⓓ Ⓔ   30. Ⓐ Ⓑ Ⓒ Ⓓ Ⓔ
7. Ⓐ Ⓑ Ⓒ Ⓓ Ⓔ   15. Ⓐ Ⓑ Ⓒ Ⓓ Ⓔ   23. Ⓐ Ⓑ Ⓒ Ⓓ Ⓔ
8. Ⓐ Ⓑ Ⓒ Ⓓ Ⓔ   16. Ⓐ Ⓑ Ⓒ Ⓓ Ⓔ   24. Ⓐ Ⓑ Ⓒ Ⓓ Ⓔ

KAPLAN

Questions 1–7

A closet contains exactly six hangers—1, 2, 3, 4, 5, and 6—hanging, in that order, from left to right. It also contains exactly six dresses—one gauze, one linen, one polyester, one rayon, one silk, and one wool—a different dress on each of the hangers, in an order satisfying the following conditions:

> The gauze dress is on a lower-numbered hanger than the polyester dress.
>
> The rayon dress is on hanger 1 or hanger 6.
>
> Either the wool dress or the silk dress is on hanger 3.
>
> The linen dress hangs immediately to the right of the silk dress.

1. Which one of the following could be an accurate matching of the hangers to the fabrics of the dresses that hang on them?

   (A) 1: wool; 2: gauze; 3: silk; 4: linen; 5: polyester; 6: rayon

   (B) 1: rayon; 2: wool; 3: gauze; 4: silk; 5: linen; 6: polyester

   (C) 1: polyester; 2: gauze; 3: wool; 4: silk; 5: linen; 6: rayon

   (D) 1: linen; 2: silk; 3: wool; 4: gauze; 5: polyester; 6: rayon

   (E) 1: gauze; 2: rayon; 3: silk; 4: linen; 5: wool; 6: polyester

2. If both the silk dress and the gauze dress are on odd-numbered hangers, then which one of the following could be true?

   (A) The polyester dress is on hanger 1.

   (B) The wool dress is on hanger 2.

   (C) The polyester dress is on hanger 4.

   (D) The linen dress is on hanger 5.

   (E) The wool dress is on hanger 6.

3. If the silk dress is on an even-numbered hanger, which one of the following could be on the hanger immediately to its left?

   (A) the gauze dress

   (B) the linen dress

   (C) the polyester dress

   (D) the rayon dress

   (E) the wool dress

4. If the polyester dress is on hanger 2, then which one of the following must be true?

   (A) The silk dress is on hanger 1.

   (B) The wool dress is on hanger 3.

   (C) The linen dress is on hanger 4.

   (D) The linen dress is on hanger 5.

   (E) The rayon dress is on hanger 6.

5. Which one of the following CANNOT be true?

   (A) The linen dress hangs immediately next to the gauze dress.

   (B) The polyester dress hangs immediately to the right of the rayon dress.

   (C) The rayon dress hangs immediately to the left of the wool dress.

   (D) The silk dress is on a lower-numbered hanger than the gauze dress.

   (E) The wool dress is on a higher-numbered hanger than the rayon dress.

6. Which one of the following CANNOT hang immediately next to the rayon dress?

    (A) the gauze dress
    (B) the linen dress
    (C) the polyester dress
    (D) the silk dress
    (E) the wool dress

7. Assume that the original condition that the linen dress hangs immediately to the right of the silk dress is replaced by the condition that the wool dress hangs immediately to the right of the silk dress. If all the other initial conditions remain in effect, which one of the following must be false?

    (A) The linen dress is on hanger 1.
    (B) The gauze dress is on hanger 2.
    (C) The wool dress is on hanger 4.
    (D) The silk dress is on hanger 5.
    (E) The polyester dress is on hanger 6.

GO ON TO THE NEXT PAGE

QRSTVZ

S — Z   T—Q
(P) (m) (m)

V = 2nd

1	m / z	P
2	z	v	3v
3	T	Q	

Questions 8–12

Exactly six of an artist's paintings, entitled *Quarterion, Redemption, Sipapu, Tesseract, Vale,* and *Zelkova,* are sold at auction. Three of the paintings are sold to a museum, and three are sold to a private collector. Two of the paintings are from the artist's first (earliest) period, two are from her second period, and two are from her third (most recent) period. The private collector and the museum each buy one painting from each period. The following conditions hold:

  Sipapu, which is sold to the private collector, is from an earlier period than *Zelkova,* which is sold to the museum.

  Quarterion is not from an earlier period than *Tesseract.*

  Vale is from the artist's second period.

8. Which one of the following could be an accurate list of the paintings bought by the museum and the private collector, listed in order of the paintings' periods, from first to third?

   (A) museum: *Quarterion, Vale, Zelkova*; private collector: *Redemption, Sipapu, Tesseract*

   (B) museum: *Redemption, Zelkova, Quarterion*; private collector: *Sipapu, Vale, Tesseract*

   (C) museum: *Sipapu, Zelkova, Quarterion*; private collector: *Tesseract, Vale, Redemption*

   (D) museum: *Tesseract, Quarterion, Zelkova*; private collector: *Sipapu, Redemption, Vale*

   (E) museum: *Zelkova, Tesseract, Redemption*; private collector: *Sipapu, Vale, Quarterion*

9. If Sipapu is from the artist's second period, which one of the following could be two of the three paintings bought by the private collector?

   (A) *Quarterion* and *Zelkova*

   (B) *Redemption* and *Tesseract*

   (C) *Redemption* and *Vale*

   (D) *Redemption* and *Zelkova*

   (E) *Tesseract* and *Zelkova*

10. Which one of the following is a complete and accurate list of the paintings, any one of which could be the painting from the artist's first period that is sold to the private collector?

   (A) *Quarterion, Redemption*

   (B) *Redemption, Sipapu*

   (C) *Quarterion, Sipapu, Tesseract*

   (D) *Quarterion, Redemption, Sipapu, Tesseract*

   (E) *Redemption, Sipapu, Tesseract, Zelkova*

11. If *Sipapu* is from the artist's second period, then which one of the following paintings could be from the period immediately preceding *Quarterion's* period and be sold to the same buyer as *Quarterion*?

   (A) *Redemption*

   (B) *Sipapu*

   (C) *Tesseract*

   (D) *Vale*

   (E) *Zelkova*

12. If *Zelkova* is sold to the same buyer as *Tesseract* and is from the period immediately preceding *Tesseract's* period, then which one of the following must be true?

   (A) *Quarterion* is sold to the museum.

   (B) *Quarterion* is from the artist's third period.

   (C) *Redemption* is sold to the private collector.

   (D) *Redemption* is from the artist's third period.

   (E) *Redemption* is sold to the same buyer as *Vale.*

(handwritten annotations at top of page)

```
        1  2  3  4  5  6  7
on      _  _  _  _  _  _  _
off     x  _  _  x  _  _  _

1 on, 3+5 = off
4 on, 2+5 = off
```

Questions 13–18

A lighting control panel has exactly seven switches, numbered from 1 to 7. Each switch is either in the on position or in the off position. The circuit load of the panel is the total number of its switches that are on. The control panel must be configured in accordance with the following conditions:

> If switch 1 is on, then switch 3 and switch 5 are off.
>
> If switch 4 is on, then switch 2 and switch 5 are off.
>
> The switch whose number corresponds to the circuit load of the panel is itself on.

13. Which one of the following could be a complete and accurate list of the switches that are on?

    (A) switch 2, switch 3, switch 4, switch 7
    (B) switch 3, switch 6, switch 7
    (C) switch 2, switch 5, switch 6
    (D) switch 1, switch 3, switch 4
    (E) switch 1, switch 5

14. If switch 1 and switch 3 are both off, which one of the following could be two switches that are both on?

    (A) switch 2 and switch 7
    (B) switch 4 and switch 6
    (C) switch 4 and switch 7
    (D) switch 5 and switch 6
    (E) switch 6 and switch 7

15. If exactly two of the switches are on, then which one of the following switches must be off?

    (A) switch 3
    (B) switch 4
    (C) switch 5
    (D) switch 6
    (E) switch 7

16. If switch 6 and switch 7 are both off, then what is the maximum circuit load of the panel?

    (A) one
    (B) two
    (C) three
    (D) four
    (E) five

17. If switch 5 and switch 6 are both on, then which one of the following switches must be on?

    (A) switch 1
    (B) switch 2
    (C) switch 3
    (D) switch 4
    (E) switch 7

18. What is the maximum circuit load of the panel?

    (A) three
    (B) four
    (C) five
    (D) six
    (E) seven

(handwritten annotations)

F J O R

2:J

	S	T	V	X	Z
F	✓	✗	✓	✓	✗
J	✓	✗	✗	✓	✗
O	✓	✓		✓	
R	✗	✓		✓	

(handwritten top right)

S = 3
X ... most
✓ ≠ 7

Questions 19–24

In Crescentville there are exactly five record stores, whose names are abbreviated S, T, V, X, and Z. Each of the five stores carries at least one of four distinct types of music: folk, jazz, opera, and rock. None of the stores carries any other type of music. The following conditions must hold:

> Exactly two of the five stores carry jazz.
>
> T carries rock and opera but no other type of music.
>
> S carries more types of music than T carries.
>
> X carries more types of music than any other store in Crescentville carries.
>
> Jazz is among the types of music S carries.
>
> V does not carry any type of music that Z carries.

19. Which one of the following could be true?

    (A) S carries folk and rock but neither jazz nor opera.
    (B) T carries jazz but neither opera nor rock.
    (C) V carries folk, rock, and opera, but not jazz.
    (D) X carries folk, rock, and jazz, but not opera.
    (E) Z carries folk and opera but neither rock nor jazz.

20. Which one of the following could be true?

    (A) S, V, and Z all carry folk.
    (B) S, X, and Z all carry jazz.
    (C) Of the five stores, only S and V carry jazz.
    (D) Of the five stores, only T and X carry rock.
    (E) Of the five stores, only S, T, and V carry opera.

21. If exactly one of the stores carries folk, then which one of the following could be true?

    (A) S and V carry exactly two types of music in common.
    (B) T and S carry exactly two types of music in common.
    (C) T and V carry exactly two types of music in common.
    (D) V and X carry exactly two types of music in common.
    (E) X and Z carry exactly two types of music in common.

22. Which one of the following must be true?

    (A) T carries exactly the same number of types of music as V carries.
    (B) V carries exactly the same number of types of music as Z carries.
    (C) S carries at least one more type of music than Z carries.
    (D) Z carries at least one more type of music than T carries.
    (E) X carries exactly two more types of music than S carries.

23. If V is one of exactly three stores that carry rock, then which one of the following must be true?

    (A)   S and Z carry no types of music in common.

    (B)   S and V carry at least one type of music in common.

    (C)   S and Z carry at least one type of music in common.

    (D)   T and Z carry at least one type of music in common.

    (E)   T and V carry at least two types of music in common.

24. If S and V both carry folk, then which one of the following could be true?

    (A)   S and T carry no types of music in common.

    (B)   S and Z carry no types of music in common.

    (C)   T and Z carry no types of music in common.

    (D)   S and Z carry two types of music in common.

    (E)   T and V carry two types of music in common.

IF YOU FINISH BEFORE TIME IS CALLED, YOU MAY CHECK YOUR WORK ON THIS SECTION ONLY. DO NOT TURN TO ANY OTHER SECTION IN THE TEST.   STOP

ANSWERS AND EXPLANATIONS

Game 1 (Questions 1–7)

Step 1: Overview

Situation: A closet.

Entities: Six dresses and six hangers.

Action: To sequence the dresses on the hangers from left to right.

Limitations: One dress per hanger.

Step 2: Sketch

This is a relatively straightforward Sequencing game that can be sketched in the standard way, with six numbered slots for the six dresses and a roster of entities above.

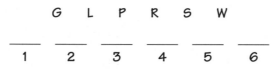

Step 3: Rules

Rule 1 gives you a relationship between two of the dresses. Gauze must be on a lower numbered (that is, closer to #1) hanger than polyester. You should note this rule nearby in shorthand, "G…P".

Rule 2 offers two possible positions for the rayon dress. This kind of rule—an "either/or" option for a single entity—suggests that you will want to create two sketches for this game: one with rayon on hanger 1, one with rayon on hanger 6. Those will be Options I and II, respectively.

Rule 3 gives you another either/or situation. In this case, you can build wool or silk right into our two sketches on hanger 3. Indeed, you can set them up like this:

	1	2	3	4	5	6
Ia.	R		W			
Ib.	R		S			
IIa.			W			R
IIb.			S			R

Four concrete possibilities—that's a lot to work out! But doing so doesn't take very long, and this is really just two options slightly extended. And working out the possibilities is right in line with classic Kaplan practice: drive the data to the definite. Turn the ambiguous into the concrete.

Rule 4 gives you a bloc of entities that may lead you to some more deductions in our two options. For the moment, you can jot a note down that shows that somewhere in the sequence you need "SL."

Step 4: Deduction

To carry out Step 4 of the Kaplan Method, you need to work with concrete rules first, and SL is the most concrete. In Options Ib and IIb, silk is already definitely set on hanger 3, so L for linen will of course be assigned to hanger 4. In both "b" options, you have gauze and polyester left over (and they must go in that order, "G . . . P") as well as wool, which is a floater here. The "a" options are more interesting. In Option Ia, the only way to hang the two consecutive dresses, "SL," is at the far right, among the last three hangers. And because gauze has to be placed to the left of polyester, G must hang on 2. Make that insertion and jot down the rest of what you know.

In Option IIa, we have two pairs of consecutive slots open: hangers 2 and 3, and hangers 4 and 5. "SL" will take one of those pairs, leaving for the other pair "G . . . P," which here has to be "GP." It all looks like this, as you proceed into the questions:

	1	2	3	4	5	6	
Ia.	R	G	W	___	___	___	P, S L
Ib.	R	___	S	L	___	___	W, G...P
IIa.	___	___	W	___	___	R	S L / G P
IIb.	___	___	S	L	___	R	W, G...P

Step 5: Questions

1. A

You don't need to refer to your limited options, because the rules themselves do all the dirty work. (C) violates Rule 1 by hanging gauze and polyester in the exact wrong order. (E) violates Rule 2 by hanging rayon somewhere other than hanger 1 or 6. Rule 3 is violated when (B) puts the gauze dress onto hanger 3. And just as (C) got the G/P relationship backwards, (D) gets the S/L relationship (Rule 4) ditto. (A) is the possible sequence; note that it corresponds to a completed Option IIb as we've set things up.

2. B

Because the odd hangers are #1, 3, and 5, Options Ib and IIb are the only ones we can refer to in this question. (In Option Ia, gauze is placed on an even-numbered hanger, #2; in Option IIa, either silk or gauze would have to hang on even-numbered hanger 4. So both of those sub-options can be disregarded here.) In Ib and IIb, silk is already on

KAPLAN

odd-numbered hanger 3, so your attention turns to gauze, which has only one odd-numbered hanger available to it, #5. So gauze hangs there for the purposes of this question. And with polyester to gauze's right, the completed sequence becomes "R W S L G P." That's one possibility—and indeed the only one you end up needing, because wool on hanger 2 is listed as choice (B), and you've proved that that can be true. You need not go on to see that in Option IIb gauze would be on hanger 1, creating two more possible sequences ("G P S L W R" and "G W S L P R") and one more confirmation that the wool dress can in fact be on hanger 2, as (B) states.

3. E

This hypothetical question asks you what could be true. In addition to creating a new sketch, you're going to need to make that redrawing as concrete as possible. The immediate question is, "If the silk dress is on an even-numbered hanger, which hanger is it on?" Well, you know it's not on hanger 3, which means that wool must be on hanger 3, which in turn means Options Ia and IIa only. In the former, the only way to hang "SL" such that they're consecutive and S gets an even-numbered hanger is to assign them hangers 4 and 5. And there, wool is to silk's immediate left, making (E) correct. [Note that in Option IIa it would work out the same way—S on hanger 4 and W on hanger 3—meaning that this question could've been written as a must be true and the right answer would still have been (E).]

4. E

As you work through the setup for a question, check the choices each time you make a deduction, so that you do no more work than you need to. The polyester dress can hang on #2 in either Option IIa or IIb (but not in Ia or Ib).

	1	2	3	4	5	6
IIa.	G	P	W	S	L	R
IIb.	G	P	S	L	W	R

Either way, the rayon dress is indeed on hanger 6, choice (E), and the sooner you notice that, the better.

Of the wrong choices, (A) is downright false (gauze, not silk, occupies hanger 1), whereas (B), (C), and (D) are possible only. None of them must be true.

5. B

In a "Not-if" question, first use your Master Sketch to evaluate choices, then see whether past questions' scratch work can help. Because the right answer "CANNOT be true," it follows that the wrong choices are all possible, which means that all of the sketches we've previously set up—that is, all of the possibilities you've already worked out—are potentially of use to you. None of question 5's choices appears in the right answer—(A)—to question 1, but notice what happens when you look at question 2: fully three of the choices here—(C), (D), and (E)—can all be found in the sequences you worked out during question 2.

That leaves (A) and (B), and some trial and error is in order. Choice (A)—gauze and linen consecutive, in either order—is readily doable, as for instance if Option Ib is filled out as "R W S L G P." But (B) is impossible, because R is always on hanger 1 or 6, and P cannot be assigned to the slot immediately to R's right because of its relationship with G (Rule 1).

6.   D

Use previous scratch work on later questions whenever possible. Because rayon hangs on #1 or #6, the question is really asking, "Which entity cannot hang on hanger 2 or 5"? You've seen polyester (C) hang next to rayon in question 1's right answer; wool (E) next to rayon in question 2; gauze (A) next to rayon in question 3; and linen (B) next to rayon in question 4. What you've never seen—and never can see—is silk (D) next to rayon. Hanging silk and rayon that way would require a rule violation.

7.   D

Consider skipping a question in which a rule is changed or replaced; your time may be better spent elsewhere. You need to notice that the only rule that changes is Rule 4. All the other rules remain the same. "SL" is to be replaced by "SW," and consider that fact in light of Rule 3. Because one of those two dresses—silk or wool—always hangs on #3, then either "SW" hangs on #2 and #3, or #3 and #4. It is thus impossible for silk to hang on #5, so (D) must be false and is thus the correct answer. All of the other choices are possible under this new condition and the remaining rules.

Game 2 (Questions 8–12)

Step 1: Overview

Situation: An art auction.

Entities: Six paintings to be sold.

Action: To distribute the paintings (half to the museum and half to the private collector), and also sequence them in terms of the artist's periods (a classic Hybrid game).

Limitations: The paintings are distributed 3/3, and there's one each from the first, second, and third periods; each source—museum and collector—gets exactly one painting from each period.

Step 2: Sketch

Your Master Sketch must allow you to keep track of the sequencing and distribution, and Kaplan suggests this:

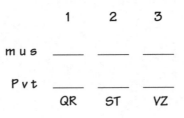

Notice that you can track the distribution off to the side if you need to, listing the museum works on top and the private collector's works below. But with luck, you'll be able to enter the letters right into the sequence, and fairly quickly, too.

Step 3: Rules

Rule 1, like any complex rule, needs to be handled with care. We know that S's period is earlier than Z's, although we don't know how much earlier; certainly S is from the first or second, Z from the second or third. What we do know is that S goes to the private collector—at the bottom of our sketch—with Z on top. How about jotting it down like so:

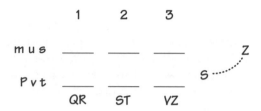

Notice how we carefully position the S and Z such that the sketch can readily, and accurately, remind us of where each goes.

Rule 2 wants you to remember never to have Q precede T. You can jot down "NEVER Q...T" as a potent reminder, and ought to think through the implications: Either T will precede Q in the sequence, or one of your columns—one of the artist's periods—will be represented by "T and Q."

Finally, there is Rule 3. If V is one of the second-period paintings, then of course V will occupy the second slot in one of the two sequences, museum or private collector. Why not build that right in? Doing so is always more effective than jotting it down off to the side. You can note for yourself that R is not mentioned by the rules (you can therefore call this entity a "floater"), dropping in as needed, and you're left with this:

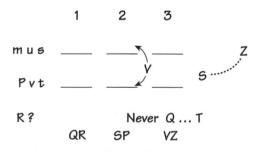

Four concrete possibilities—that's a lot to work out! But doing so doesn't take very long, and this is really just two options slightly extended. And working out the possibilities is right in line with classic Kaplan practice: drive the data to the definite. Turn the ambiguous into the concrete.

Rule 4 gives you a bloc of entities that may lead you to some more deductions in our two options. For the moment, you can jot a note down that shows that somewhere in the sequence you need "SL."

Step 4: Deduction

There aren't many rules here, and none of the entities is in more than one rule, so deductions will be scarce here. From the first rule, you can conclusively deduce that S must be from the artist's first or second period, and Z must be from the artist's second or third period. Be careful not to misinterpret Rule 2. Knowing that Q is not earlier than T is not the same as knowing that Q is from a later period than T. You know that if T is from the second period, then Q must be from the third period (since there would be no more room for Q to be placed in the second period), but this isn't worth putting into the sketch because it's highly conditional.

Step 5: Questions

8. B

It's perhaps easiest to check the assignment of V, Rule 3, and (D) can be eliminated: V is from the second period, not the third. Next, there's Rule 1, which you can check in two parts. First, let's confirm that S always goes to the private collector...and you can toss out (C), with its assignment of S to the museum. Next, how about checking whether S comes from an earlier period than the museum's Z? (E) is out, because it puts both S and Z into the 1st period. All that's left is to check the Q/T relationship against the remaining choices, and you can quickly see that (A) violates Rule 2. That leaves (B), the correct answer.

9. B

Insert new "if" clause information into a new sketch. Combine the new information about S (it's from the second period) with what we already know (that S goes to the private collector, preceding Z), to yield:

```
              1      2      3
MUS         ____   ____    Z
                          ___

PVT         ____    S    ____
                   ___
```

You should hasten to insert V into the remaining slot 2, at the museum, and then sort things out. R (the floater), and Q and T (the former of which cannot precede the latter), are left for the remaining spaces. Note, too, this question: What can be the remaining two private collector paintings? The answer is both Q and T (with R going to the museum), or R and either Q or T. Correct choice (B) gives you the latter, and indeed, as long as R is the private collector's third period painting, Q and T can represent the first period for the museum and the private collector, respectively.

10. D

Unless you plan to skip it altogether, a lengthy and complex question stem needs to be read carefully and understood correctly the first time out. Our focus is the first slot in the private-collector row. Essentially, what you're being asked for is the list of paintings—entities—that can go into that slot. Clearly V, as a second period painting, cannot; but then V isn't listed in any choices. You should also see that Z is ineligible for that slot because Z, besides being a museum painting, must fall to the right of S on the sketch. Otherwise, any of the paintings is eligible for that slot, making (D) the credited choice.

KAPLAN

11. B

Because S is a private collector painting, the question stem directs you to put it into his #2 slot, leaving V for #2 at the museum and Z as the museum's #3. Left open are the #1 slots for both museum and collector, and the latter's #3.

```
              1    2    3

    MUS      ___   V    Z

    PVT      ___   S   ___
```

What are you being asked? There must be a painting that can be sold just before Q, and to the same buyer as Q. Well, that means that Q has to be a third period painting, and the only third period slot open is the private collector's, and his painting just before that is…S, choice (B).

12. B

Because Z, a museum painting, must follow S (Rule 1), the only way that Z's period can precede T's, for the same buyer, is for the museum's second and third period works to be Z and T, respectively. S must be the private collector's first period painting, of course, and V (Rule 2) takes the second period slot for the private collector.

```
              1    2    3

    mus      ___   Z    T

    Pvt       S    V   ___
```

To avoid violating Rule 3, you cannot have Q precede T, so Q will be the private collector's third period painting…and (B) is confirmed as correct. Note that although you must make R the museum's first period painting, that doesn't impact the correct answer choice.

Game 3 (Questions 13–18)

Step 1: Overview

Situation: A lighting panel.

Entities: Seven light switches.

Action: To determine which switches are on or off. This may have been confusing at first, but it's actually exactly like the in/out action of a Selection game. Switches are on ("selected") or off ("rejected").

Limitations: The on/off is simple enough to remember, since switches usually are one or the other in everyday life. There's no set number of on vs. off, which adds a layer of complexity. And the "circuit load" business—which by rights really ought to have been an indented rule—doesn't make a lot of sense until we get into the rules, though even at the outset we can infer that it'll be important to note the total number of "on switches."

Step 2: Sketch

The "circuit load" limitation will no doubt be useful, but we haven't learned how yet. We'll make a note of it off to the side. For now, we can start with our basic Selection sketch, a roster of entities:

$$1 \quad 2 \quad 3 \quad 4 \quad 5 \quad 6 \quad 7$$

"CL" = # on

Step 3: Rules

Rule 1 is a pretty simple Formal Logic rule: if switch 1 is on, switches 3 and 5 are off. Remember to formulate the contrapositive! In negating this result, you have to be careful to turn negatives into positives. Remember that if a switch is not on, it is off, and vice versa. You also have to change "and" to "or." The sketch for the rule comes out to:

If 1 on → 3 off and 5 off

If 3 on or 5 on → 1 off

Rule 2 is another Formal Logic rule, with the same structure:

4 on → 2 off and 5 off

2 on or 5 on → 4 off

Rule 3 adds more than just another fact; it's the key to the game. Don't just read and annotate the abstract idea that, "The switch whose number corresponds to the circuit load of the panel is itself on." Think it through. Apply it to concrete behavior.

KAPLAN

If the circuit load is one (which it could be), then only one switch is on, and it must be switch #1. See how that works? If the circuit load is two, only two switches are on, one of which must be switch #2. And so forth down the line. A circuit load of seven means that everything's on (a possibility that you may already realize is denied by the rules—that's a hint for later on). In the same vein, we can be sure that if a switch is off, the circuit load of the panel cannot be that number. Don't waste time working out all of the possibilities. You'll see the ones you need to work with in the questions. For now, you must remember to circle (select) the switch with the same number as the circuit load—and that might be done with a notation, or simply by circling the rule on the page.

Step 4: Deduction

Switches 6 and 7 are floaters—that is, unmentioned by the rules—so we can select or reject them as we need to.

You do have one potent duplication—i.e., switch #5 is mentioned in two rules—and it allows us to draw an interesting conclusion, namely that if switch 5 is on, then switches 1 and 4 must be off. (Ordinarily we don't advise your combining if/then rules, but in this case the deduction is so useful, and for many so clear, that it's worth spelling out.) If we write this deduction out with its contrapositive, we find that it looks just like Rules 1 and 2:

$$5 \text{ on} \rightarrow 1 \text{ off and } 4 \text{ off}$$

$$1 \text{ on or } 4 \text{ on} \rightarrow 5 \text{ off}$$

This combination is true irrespective of the other switches mentioned in the first two rules; it's simply an additional fact that we can affirm before going forward. The Final Visualization includes just our roster and our if/then rules, stacked up so that all of the arrows line up:

$$1 \quad 2 \quad 3 \quad 4 \quad 5 \quad 6 \quad 7 \quad \text{``CL''} = \# \text{ on}$$

$$1 \text{ on} \rightarrow 3 \text{ off and } 5 \text{ off}$$

$$3 \text{ on or } 5 \text{ on} \rightarrow 1 \text{ off}$$

$$4 \text{ on} \rightarrow 2 \text{ off and } 5 \text{ off}$$

$$2 \text{ on or } 5 \text{ on} \rightarrow 4 \text{ off}$$

$$5 \text{ on} \rightarrow 1 \text{ off and } 4 \text{ off}$$

$$1 \text{ on or } 4 \text{ on} \rightarrow 5 \text{ off}$$

Step 5: Questions

13. B

A "complete and accurate list of the entities selected" is really an Acceptability question. The correct answer to this question will be a group of switches that can be on without violating any rules. Remember, you'll probably have to check the switches that are off, too. But you can still start eliminating choices based on the rules. Rule 1 tells us that if switch 1 is on, switches 3 and 5 must be off, which (D) and (E) violate. Rule 2 eliminates (A): if switch 4 is on, switch 2 cannot be. Finally, Rule 3 eliminates (C). This choice has three switches turned on, which means that the circuit load of the panel would be three; but in a circuit load of three, switch 3 must be on, and here it isn't. Only (B) remains, and indeed "3, 6, 7" violates no rules.

14. A

If a question stem mentions numbers, use those numbers to find the answer. Your new sketch for this question starts by simply crossing out switches 1 and 3. Rules 1 and 2 aren't immediately triggered, but you may have seen that the circuit load of the panel can't be one or three.

$$\cancel{1} \quad 2 \quad \cancel{3} \quad 4 \quad 5 \quad 6 \quad 7$$

Stick with the circuit load, and use the question stem to guide you: you're asked to find two switches that could both be on. So what would happen if the circuit load was two? Switch 2 would be on, along with one other switch (which couldn't be switch 4, thanks to Rule 2). Choice (A) matches this perfectly: switch 2 and a floater could be on.

The rest of the choices get the numbers wrong. With switches 1 and 3 off, the circuit load must be 2, 4, or 5. But it can't be five because all of the remaining switches can't be on at the same time (Rule 2). And the circuit load can't be four: if you select switch 4, you must reject switches 2 and 5, which would leave you with a maximum circuit load of three.

15. B

Always look for ways in which your previous work can help you. While you were looking at the very last question, you noted that if the circuit load of the panel is two (that's what "exactly two on switches" means), then switch 2 must be on, which in turn means that switch 4 must be off (Rule 2). This leads you straight to (B).

16. C

In a minimum/maximum question with an "if" clause, check the numbers before you jump to conclusions. If switches 6 and 7 are both off, there are five switches left. But don't leap to the conclusion that the maximum circuit load will be five! Check things out first.

$$1 \quad 2 \quad 3 \quad 4 \quad 5 \quad \cancel{6} \quad \cancel{7}$$

KAPLAN

If the circuit load is five, all of the remaining switches must be on. Yet Rule 2 tells you that switches 4 and 5 can't be on at the same time. You have the same problem with a circuit load of four: switch 4 would have to be on, which means that switches 2 and 5 would be off, leaving a maximum of only three switches. So you try three, which finally succeeds. If switch 3 is on, then switch 1 must be off:

But of the remaining three switches, we could still select 2 and 5 (not switch 4, because of Rule 2). A maximum circuit load of three is (C).

17. C

In a grouping game, even questions that don't seem to involve the numbers usually do. If switches 5 and 6 are on, then switches 1 and 4 must be off:

This finishes off Rules 1 and 2, but what about the circuit load of the panel? It can't be two, since two switches are already on and switch 2 is not. It can't be one or four, since those switches are off; and it cannot be six or seven, since two switches are already off. That leaves three or five as possibilities for the circuit load, and in either case, switch 3 must be on, choice (C).

18. C

Use previous work to save time on minimum/maximum questions. You saw a circuit load of three in questions 16 and 17, and a circuit load of five in question 17. Could the circuit load of the panel be any higher? No. If six of the switches are on, only one of them can be off. This means you couldn't avoid selecting switch 1 or switch 4, either of which would force you to turn off two other switches for a maximum circuit load of five. Five is the highest possible circuit load—choice (C).

Game 4 (Questions 19–24)

Step 1: Overview

Situation: Record stores in Crescentville.

Entities: Specific stores in Crescentville, and the types of music they carry.

Action: When there are two types of entities, invariably the Action is to match them. Here, you have to match the types of music to the stores that carry them.

Limitations: At least one type of music per store; no types of music other than those listed.

Step 2: Sketch

Remember, a table can work for matching games. The record stores are the more concrete set of entities (exactly five, each one with at least one type of music), while the types of music are fluid: You don't know how many stores carry each type of music, or even that each type of music is definitely carried. That means you should put the stores across the top of our table:

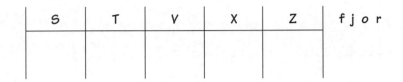

Step 3: Rules

Rule 1 gives you a number rule for one of the types of music: exactly two stores carry jazz. Whenever a rule tells you how many of an entity are used, write the entity that many times: in this instance, "j j" will remind you that we need to use jazz twice.

Rule 2 begins to tell you which stores carry which types of music. Store T gets an r and an o in its column, and nothing else.

Rule 3 ties right into what you just learned. Since T gets exactly two types of music, then S gets…exactly three, or all four. Noting three slots in the S column—without a "=" notation to indicate "end of the road"—is much more useful than simply writing "S > T" (which isn't wrong, but isn't helpful either).

Rule 4 solidifies the numbers even further. Again, think through the implications of this rule. If store X carries more types of music than any other store, how many does it carry? You already knew from the previous rule that store S has to carry at least three types, so store X must carry all four types of music. This limits store S to three types, so you can add "=" at the bottom of S's column after all. Moreover, filling all four music types in X's column gets rid of one of your two j's.

Rule 5 finishes off the jazz: S and X both carry jazz, which means that no other stores can do so. That's a big deduction, right there.

Rule 6 creates a relationship between the last two stores: V and Z cannot carry the same types of music. This means that whatever V carries, Z won't and vice versa, which distinctly limits the number as well as the types of music available to each. "V ≠ Z" expresses this relationship nicely, as does a noted "V AND Z ALWAYS DIFFERENT."

Step 4: Deduction

Hopefully you already began deducing during Rules 3, 4, and 5, where duplications of entities in the rules allowed you to determine the exact numbers in stores S, T, and X. Moreover, you've allocated jazz to S and X only, so all other slots will contain f, o, or r. There are no floaters (unmentioned entities) among the stores, but you still don't know how many stores will carry folk, opera, or rock. In general, you should follow the Kaplan Method for Logic Games pretty strictly, but if you happen to notice a deduction while you're thinking through the rules (and in this game, Rules 3 and 4 almost seemed structured to lead to an immediate Numbers deduction), don't hold back.

What about V and Z? Back in Rule 6 you might have noted that with jazz gone, V and Z must split up folk, opera, and rock without duplicating each other. That means each will have one, or one will have two while the other takes the third. It all looks like this:

S	T	V	X	Z	
j	r		f		f j̶ o r
—	o		j		
—	—		o		V ≠ Z (1 : 1 or 2 : 1)
=			r		

Step 5: Questions

19. E

A quick scan of the choices can tell you how long it will take to answer a question. Each of the choices in this question mentions a different store, and conveniently enough, they are in alphabetical order. You can just read across your table to answer this question.

(A) Rule 5 tells us that S carries jazz—Eliminate.

(B) According to Rule 1, only two stores carry jazz, and you've already noted that those two stores must be S and X. Rule 2 also tells you that T does carry rock and opera. This choice is wrong on every count.

(C) is a bit tougher, but remember that V and Z cannot carry any of the same types of music. If V carries folk, rock, and opera, the only thing left for Z is jazz, and you already know that all of the jazz is taken. Eliminate.

(D) violates Rule 4: X must carry all four types of music.

(E) must be correct, because you've eliminated all of the other choices. A quick test proves it to be a possibility: if Z carries folk and opera, V could carry rock, and all of the other record stores are unaffected.

20. D

If you're able to get lots of information into your Master Sketch, you should be able to answer "could be true" questions quickly and easily. Your Master Sketch for this game has quite a lot of information; in fact, there's very little you don't know. This means that testing possibilities in a "could be" question should be a pretty quick process. Let's look at the choices:

(A) may look good at first glance, but Rule 6 eliminates it: V and Z cannot both carry folk. Eliminate.

(B) violates Rule 1 in that only two stores can carry jazz, not three. Eliminate.

(C) is very close, but remember that we deduced that X (which sells all four types) must carry jazz. Eliminate.

(D) You know from Rules 2 and 4, respectively, that T and X both carry rock. Could they be the only stores to do so? That would mean that S, V, and Z would be limited to folk, jazz, and opera. S could carry all three, while V and Z could split folk and opera. This choice works, and is correct.

For the record (no pun intended): (E) is wrong because X must carry every type of music, so it cannot be omitted from the list of stores that carry opera.

21. B

When the question involves numbers, doing the math will speed up your evaluation of the answer choices. Your question stem tells us that only one store carries folk, and a quick glance at your Master Sketch tells you that that store must be X, since it has all four types of music. You can cross "f" off our list of entities, and fill in the remainder of our sketch: S's three types of music must be jazz, opera, and rock, and V and Z must split opera and rock. Your sketch for this question should look something like this:

S	T	V	X	Z	f j̶ j̶ o r
j	r	o/r	f	o/r	
o	o		j		
r	‗		o		
‗			r		

The only pairs that share exactly two types are T and X, and T and S. The latter is choice (B). All of the remaining choices include either V or Z. Without folk, V and Z can only carry one type of music, which means that they cannot have two types of music in common with any other store.

22. C

Use your Master Sketch to quickly evaluate the choices in a "must be true" question. Up to this point, all the questions for this game have been "could be" questions. This "must be" changes your characterization of the choices. Before, you were looking for a possibility. Now, you're looking for a statement that is always the case. The wrong answers will be anything that could be (or must be) false.

(A) could be false. Store T carries two types of music, but store V could only carry one, in which case they wouldn't match. Eliminate.

(B) is tricky: many test-takers assume that V and Z can only carry one type of music. V and Z could carry one type of music each, but remember your deduction that V could carry two types of music when Z carries one, or vice versa. Eliminate.

(C) must be true, and is correct. Don't let the "at least" throw you off: (C) is true whether Z carries one type of music or two, as S will always carry three types. For the record:

(D) must be false. Z can only carry one or two types of music, and T carries two types. A careful characterization of the choices can keep you from falling for a choice like this—one that's the exact opposite of what you are looking for.

(E) also must be false. S carries three types of music, and X carries four.

23. C

Nail down ambiguous "if" clauses before you try to answer the accompanying question. Treat an ambiguous "if" just like an ambiguous rule: think it through and try to make it concrete. If, as question 16 says, V is one of exactly three stores that carry rock, what are the other two? Your Master Sketch tells us the answer: T and X already carry rock, so they must be the last two out of three. This in turn means that S and Z cannot carry rock, so S carries jazz, folk, and opera, and Z carries either folk or opera (maybe both). Your sketch for this question should look like this:

S	T	V	X	Z	
j	r	r	f	f/o	f j̶ j̶ o r̶ r̶ r̶
f	o		j		
o	——		o		
——			r		

(A) is impossible: whether Z carries folk or opera or both, S must carry one of the same types of music.

(B) could be false. If V carries rock only, which it can, then S and V would have nothing in common.

(C) must be true, and is correct for the same reason that (A) is wrong. Whether Z carries folk or opera, S will always have at least one of those two types in common with Z. For the record:

(D) could be true, but as such could also be false. If Z carries folk instead of opera, T and Z won't have any types of music in common.

(E) likewise is only possibly true. If V carried both rock and opera (leaving folk for Z), then V and T would have two types of music in common. But if V carried rock and folk, or rock only, then V and T would only have one type of music in common.

24. B

Be wary of confusing possibilities with certainties in your sketches. The correct answer could be true, so the four wrong answers must be false. Then fill in your sketch according to the Kaplan Method: recopy the Master Sketch, plug in the new rule, then make deductions. Here, if V carries folk, then Z cannot (Z must carry either rock or opera or both). One of the open slots in S's column must be taken by folk, but the last one will be either rock or opera. Your final sketch:

S	T	V	X	Z	f j̶ o r
j	r	f	f	o/r	
f	o		j		
o/r	—		o		
—			r		

(A) must be false: T carries rock and opera, and S must carry one of those types of music.

(B) could be true, and is correct. If S carries opera and Z carries rock, or vice versa, then two stores will have nothing in common. This is rendered tough in that the sketch seems to suggest S/Z commonality, but as always, your sketch is an aid to thought, not a substitute for it. When you think through (B), you need to see that it's possible and hence correct. To mop up the others:

(C) must be false. Whether Z carries rock, or opera, or both, it will have something in common with T.

(D) must be false. Even if Z carries two types of music, they would have to be rock and opera, and S can only carry one or the other of those two types.

(E) must be false. Even if V carries two types of music, one of them must be folk, which T cannot carry.

The Key to 1L Success

You made it to law school! The success you have had as an undergrad will translate into law school. Right? Not so fast. No matter what your background and success habits were as an undergrad, law school is different. It is as different as college was from high school. The faster you embrace the differences the better your chances are of success in law school. You may be smart, but so is everyone else.

Don't let this unnerve you. You've got Kaplan PMBR on your side to help you succeed. We provide invaluable guidance for all three years of law school, and *then* we help you pass the Bar Exam. Kaplan PMBR offers the most realistic, complete, up-to-date, and effective bar review prep through live courses, home study material, and small group tutorials. The following pages provide just a small preview of the insights and advice, tools and tactics that you'll receive in Kaplan PMBR's 1L Success Program. Visit our website at kaplanpmbr.com to learn more!

Your law school experience is likely to be the most challenging academic process of your life. Just remember, it can be done. Kaplan PMBR will help you do it. Good luck and we will see you on campus!

WHAT IS A "1L"? WHAT IS YOUR "SOL" ON YOUR "COA"?
WHO IS THE "π"? WHO IS THE "Δ"?

If you answered these questions with a "Huh?" that is perfectly normal. Law school has its own language. A 1L is simply what first year law school students are called. "SOL" stands for statute of limitations. "COA" is your cause of action. π is shorthand for "Plaintiff", and Δ is shorthand for "Defendant". At first, it is a lot like learning Klingon, but you will learn quickly, and it is a language that will last you a lifetime. With a large legal dictionary in hand, you can create your own shorthand for note-taking and start using words like negate, moot, or sua sponte!

BE PROFESSIONAL

At first glance, law school seems to be very much like college. There are social events, a lot of studying, and new friends. However, keep in mind you are building a professional reputation that will follow you through the rest of your legal career. Your professors and classmates are learning who you are and those impressions last. Make sure they are good ones, and enjoy the process of becoming an attorney along the way.

NIGHT OWLS VS. EARLY BIRDS

Just because you've made it to law school doesn't mean you have to reinvent the wheel. In fact, don't. What and how you studied worked for you. If you study best at night, keep up that practice. If you study best first thing in the morning, continue to do so. Your study patterns have long been established and law school doesn't necessarily require you to change them. Stick with what works!

STUDY GROUPS AND STUDY MATERIALS

Two important issues you will face are whether you should join a study group, and when and how to use study aids.

Study Groups

Early in law school people usually scramble to get together to form study groups with other students. They are completely optional. Some groups will go fast, others slow. Others will study more of the social conditions in law school rather than anything substantive. To get the most from a study group, you must position yourself in the best group *for you*—should you choose to join one.

Study Materials

There are as many opinions about study aids. Used correctly, study aids can help you understand your class notes, let you see how things relate to each other, provide focus on the rationale of cases, and in the end, help you better understand the topic of law covered in class. Commercial outlines are prepackaged outlines in skeletal form of the law you need to know for a particular course. Hornbooks are the comprehensive and expansive overview of the particular course. They are also referred to as *treatises*.

Finally, there are the bar review programs. Don't let the term "bar review" fool you. True, Kaplan PMBR is a bar review company, but we also are a *law student* company. We have materials for first years, second years, third years, and *then* we help you pass the Bar Exam. For example, Kaplan PMBR offers substantive black letter law course outlines and audio CDs to help you prepare for classes. These are resources you will turn to again and again—throughout law school and beyond. Visit our website at kaplanpmbr.com to learn more or to enroll.

OUTLINES

What goes into an outline? Essentially, it contains the rules of law, exceptions, and defenses to it. As a brief example, a Battery is a harmful or offensive touching of another with Intent. Consent is a defense to battery.

You might choose to incorporate some of your professor's pet topics or the like to keep them in the front of your mind. They very well could show up on the exam. Sometimes students split up different sections of the course with each creating an outline for her or his portion. However, if you focus on only one portion of the course, you will likely have a good understanding of only that one area and must rely on someone else's perception of their section of the course. Make your own outlines for each course. This allows you to understand the material and how it relates together.

THE EXAM PROCESS

Your exam can include multiple choice questions, short answer, and most popular, essay questions. Your grade depends on how you perform on the exam. However, it is what you do prior to xam day that will have the most impact on your success. Developing a good outline, learning to spot issues, honing your exam skills by practicing on old exams, and designing your test strategy are all solid ways to get ahead of the game and likely many of your classmates as well.

Issue spotting

The first step is knowing the law. The next—issue spotting—is a real time test of your ability to identify legal issues or causes of action. Your professor will test you on material you covered in class and material you were assigned but didn't cover in class. Every law school exam is invented using complex situations that may involve multiple lawsuits or defendants, and usually the professor will ask multiple questions. Truly, some facts are trash while some are treasure. You'll have to decide which is which.

Practice Exams

Practice exams are an essential tool to building your law school success. Sample exams are an underappreciated and underutilized tool. Too often, in the heat of preparing for exams, they are overlooked or ignored due to time constraints. Not only are they are a great barometer of the issues the professor likes, the style of the exam, but you could luck out and one those questions could end up on your actual final exam. Remember to allocate the time to use them!